CHILD-CUSTODY JURISDICTION

THE UCCJEA & PKPA

MARIE FAHNERT
MÉLYSE MPIRANYA

The materials contained herein represent the opinions of the authors and/or the editors, and should not be construed to be the views or opinions of the law firms or companies with whom such persons are in partnership with, associated with, or employed by, nor of the American Bar Association or the Family Law Section unless adopted pursuant to the bylaws of the Association.

Nothing contained in this book is to be considered as the rendering of legal advice for specific cases, and readers are responsible for obtaining such advice from their own legal counsel. This book is intended for educational and informational purposes only.

Printed in the United States of America.

18 17 16 15 14 5 4 3 2 1

ISBN: 978-1-62722-870-1

e-ISBN: 978-1-62722-871-8

Library of Congress Cataloging-in-Publication Data

Fahnert, Marie, author.
Child custody jurisdiction : the UCCJEA and PKPA / Marie Fahnert, American Bar Association.
pages cm
Includes index.
ISBN 978-1-62722-870-1 (softcover : alk. paper)—ISBN 978-1-62722-871-8 (e-book)
1. Conflict of laws—Custody of children—United States. 2. Custody of children—United States. 3. Guardians ad litem—United States. 4. Uniform Child Custody Jurisdiction and Enforcement Act. 5. United States. Parental Kidnapping Prevention Act of 1980. I. Title.
KF418.C78F34 2014
346.7301'73--dc23 2014038609

Discounts are available for books ordered in bulk. Special consideration is given to state bars, CLE programs, and other bar-related organizations. Inquire at Book Publishing, ABA Publishing, American Bar Association, 321 N. Clark Street, Chicago, Illinois 60654-7598.

www.ShopABA.org

Este libro esta dedicado a mi abuela, Isolina Zambrano de Pérez,
12 de Julio de 1923–9 de Abril 2014.

Contents

Foreword

Many family law attorneys view detailed knowledge of the UCCJEA like most homeowners view alarm systems—a nice idea but not necessary at present. That's a dangerous approach.

Given that many UCCJEA cases start as emergencies, family law attorneys need to know the UCCJEA before a crisis hits. Marie Fahnert's book is a great step in that direction.

I'm a family law attorney in Illinois and a winning appellant in a UCCJEA case heard by the Michigan Supreme Court. I've seen firsthand the difference between an attorney who knows the UCCJEA and one who plods through it like a toddler crawling through a room full of razor blades. Make no mistake—this book is essential to navigating the nuances of a law that at times can create as many problems as it solves.

This book can help family law attorneys achieve three desirable goals. First, it will provide an understanding of the UCCJEA that will allow an attorney to hit the ground running when confronted with a complicated UCCJEA case. Second, it enables an attorney to have a go-to reference guide to help zero in on specific issues during the heat of battle. Third, and perhaps most importantly, Marie Fahnert's book can enable attorneys to employ foresight in preparing for the many dangerously nuanced potential pitfalls that plague many UCCJEA cases.

I strongly recommend this book to all the attorneys whom I will not face in a UCCJEA case.

—David Wolkowitz

Preface

My goal in writing this book was to provide family law practitioners with the knowledge and tools they need to analyze the Uniform Child Custody Jurisdiction and Enforcement Act (UCCJEA) and the Parental Kidnapping Prevention Act (PKPA). Case law in many states is evolving and will continue to evolve for the foreseeable future. Many states have yet to address significant portions of the UCCJEA and PKPA. Some sections, such as most of Article 3, Enforcement, of the UCCJEA, have yet to be addressed in depth by any state supreme court. Thus, family law practitioners should not depend solely on this book when making legal arguments in their jurisdictions.

In this book I primarily focus on state supreme court decisions because they are the law of the land in the state in which those decisions were issued and because state supreme court cases carry much more persuasive authority weight in sister states.

When determining how much weight to grant a sister state's decision, judges should keep in mind the purpose of the acts. The UCCJEA explicitly states in Section 401, Application and Construction, "[i]n applying and construing this Uniform Act, consideration must be given to the need to promote uniformity of the law with respect to its subject matter among states that enact it."[1] The PKPA was also drafted with the explicit purpose of creating uniformity across the states.

Ultimately, I hope that this book facilitates a uniform and consistent application of the UCCJEA and PKPA across the United States and that, in turn, more children involved in interstate custody disputes are able to maintain the stability necessary for a healthy childhood.

---

1. UCCJEA § 401.

Acknowledgments

Although I am technically the mastermind behind this book, I feel that it would have never been achieved without the faith and sacrifice of those around me. The following people deserve special thanks:

Isolina Zambrano de Pérez, my grandmother, for the support she gave me throughout my career and the pride she took in me during the writing of this book.

Katelyn Steiger, my former paralegal who, on top of her regular workload, single-handedly took over most of the law firm's managerial and administrative tasks while I devoted myself to writing. I could not have written this book without Katelyn's help.

Karmen Wong, my research assistant, who helped me through the arduous task of researching case law in 50 states and figuring out the format of this book.

Mélyse Mpiranya, my overachieving, hard-working, and disciplined paralegal who took it upon herself to help me finish drafting this book. She researched and mercilessly edited and critiqued my writing. This book is leaps and bounds better than it would have been without Mélyse's help. Her name has been added as coauthor of the first edition to reflect her contribution.

Bart Resnicoff, for his invaluable input into the content of this book and his endless patience as I extended deadline after deadline.

Gail Baker, the Family Law Book Board Chair, whose suggested addition to the introductory chapter was incorporated into this book.

Introduction

Prior to the 1960s, a state could assert jurisdiction over child custody if it had a "significant relationship to the child." A noncustodial parent who was not satisfied with a custody order from one state could move to another state and petition that court for modification. Often, judges would change custody to the home state litigant without even an appearance from the other side, which did nothing to deter but instead rewarded child snatching or retention after visitation.

The Uniform Child Custody Jurisdiction Act (UCCJA) and its successor, the Uniform Child Custody Jurisdiction and Enforcement Act (UCCJEA), were attempts to standardize the rules for jurisdictions to determine child custody.

The first attempt to standardize the rules and create uniformity in custody jurisdiction was the UCCJA proposed by the national conference of commissioners in the uniform state laws in 1968. The stated purposes of the UCCJA were to

1. discourage continued jurisdictional controversies between states;
2. deter child abductions;
3. promote uniformity in state jurisdictional laws;
4. promote interstate cooperation and communication in adjudicating child custody matters;
5. avoid relitigation of custody orders; and
6. facilitate the enforcement of custody decrees of sister states.

The UCCJA required strong ties with the forum state, litigants to provide information about possible pending jurisdiction in another state, and communication with other potential forums. If the courts could not agree, priority of filing prevailed. By 1984, all 50 states and the District of

Columbia had adopted the UCCJA, either by statute or by judicial decision making. While the UCCJA helped reduce interstate controversies, the version each state enacted was not always the same, and the UCCJA failed to eliminate the possibility of two states having concurrent jurisdiction at both the initial and modification stages and problems continued.

To alleviate these problems, Congress enacted the Parental Kidnapping Prevention Act of 1980 (PKPA), which provides a uniform approach to interpreting jurisdictional conflicts and improved the UCCJA in two ways:

1. Making home state a priority so that another state with significant connection may only take jurisdiction if there is no home state; and
2. Adopting the concept of exclusive continuing jurisdiction—if one state properly exercises jurisdiction it continues as long as the state remains the residence of any contestant or child.

The PKPA comes into play mainly with modification of sister state orders. Under the PKPA, the court of one state can modify a child custody order of another state only if (1) it has jurisdiction to make such a child custody determination, and (2) the court of the other state no longer has jurisdiction or has declined to exercise its jurisdiction. Jurisdictional preference is given to the state with continuing jurisdiction. The order of preference under the PKPA is:

1. continuing jurisdiction;
2. home state jurisdiction;
3. significant connection jurisdiction; and
4. jurisdiction when no other jurisdictional basis is available.

The PKPA of 1980 helped, but it did not fix the problems. Therefore, the UCCJEA was enacted in 1997 to replace the UCCJA and conform to the PKPA of 1980 and the Violence Against Women Act (VAWA). The UCCJEA sets out a three-step process to determine whether a state should assume jurisdiction of custody matters as follows:

1. Following the guidelines of the UCCJEA governing jurisdiction;
2. Determining which court is the more appropriate and convenient forum under the UCCJEA governing inconvenient forums; and
3. If the court accepts jurisdiction as the more convenient forum, the court must determine if the action to be taken is foreclosed by an order or judgment of the other state court.

Today, only Massachusetts uses the UCCJA. The remainder of the states and the District of Columbia have enacted some form of the UCCJEA. The UCCJEA also eliminates the determination of best interest of a child from a jurisdictional inquiry.

Constitutional Matters

No uniform set of laws regarding interstate recognition of child-custody orders existed prior to the passage of the UCCJA, the PKPA, and the UCCJEA. As a result, it was difficult to have the child-custody determination of one state be recognized in another state. If a parent was unsatisfied with a court's child-custody determination, that parent could take the child with him or her to another more sympathetic state and refile for custody there in the hopes of achieving a more favorable determination. These child-custody–related parental kidnappings were called child snatchings.

After a child snatching (what is now called parental kidnapping), the ensuing child-custody determinations entered by the new state often conflicted with the previous state's child-custody determination. Thus, even though stability is one of the most important things in a child's upbringing, final child-custody determinations remained elusive, and children's childhoods were often uprooted as a result.

Full Faith and Credit Clause

The U.S. Constitution's full faith and credit clause, as well as the parallel federal statute, is understood to oblige states to recognize and enforce a sister state's final judgment. However, child-custody determinations are never final, since they are always modifiable given a change in circumstances; thus, it has never been clear whether the full faith and credit clause applies to child-custody determinations.

The Constitution's full faith and credit clause, Article IV section 1, states:

> Full Faith and Credit shall be given in each State to the public Acts, records, and judicial proceedings of every other State. And the Congress may by general Laws prescribe the Manner in which such Acts, Records and Proceedings shall be proved, and the Effect thereof. [1]

The accompanying federal statute, 28 U.S.C. § 1738, reads as follows:

> Such Acts, records and judicial proceedings or copies thereof [of any State, territory, or Possession of the United States], so authenticated, shall have the same full faith and credit in every court within the United States and its Territories and Possessions as they have by law or usage in courts of such State, Territory or Possession from which they are taken.[2]

While the full faith and credit clause precludes a state from relitigating a case that has already been granted a final determination by a another state court, a state is free to use its own laws to enforce the sister state's judgment.[3] Interestingly, while there is well-developed case law regarding the enforcement of judgments, the applicability of the full faith and credit clause to state records, such as adoption decrees, has been largely ignored.[4]

Extending Full Faith and Credit

The UCCJA, UCCJEA, and PKPA attempt to extend the full faith and credit clause to child-custody determinations. By nature of only being a state law, the UCCJEA does not have the power to control states or territories that

1. U.S. CONST. art. IV, § 1.
2. 28 U.S.C. § 1738.
3. Adar v. Smith, 639 F.3d 146, 159 (5th Cir. 2011).
4. Elizabeth Page Redpath, *Between Judgment and Law: Full Faith and Credit, Public Policy, and State Records*, 62 EMORY L.J. 639 (2013).

have not yet enacted it. However, the PKPA, a federal law, was placed as an addendum to the full faith and credit statute.[5] The Utah Supreme Court noted in *In re Adoption of Baby E.Z.*:

> The United States Supreme Court has noted that a central purpose of the PKPA is to extend the requirements of the full faith and credit clause to custody determinations. In short, the PKPA was intended primarily as a full faith and credit statute.[6]

Thus, all states are now bound to recognize and enforce another state's child-custody judgment. Also, if a state chooses to issue a child-custody judgment defiant of the PKPA, then the PKPA provides that the state's child-custody judgment will not be entitled to full faith and credit in any other state.

Extending Full Faith to Tribes

There is no consensus among the states on the question of whether the PKPA applies to tribal courts. States have reached different conclusions, with some states giving full faith and credit to tribal child-custody orders and other states denying tribal orders full faith and credit.[7]

Case Law

Although the U.S. Supreme Court did not hear any child-custody cases during the earlier half of the 20th century, during this time the state courts were busy assessing whether the full faith and credit clause applied to child-custody determinations and, if so, under what circumstances. Some state courts found that when a child moved, the new state could enter a child-custody determination as if there had never been a previous determination.[8] Other state courts found that a court could modify another state's child-custody judgment in the child's best interests if there was a significant

---

5. 28 U.S.C. § 1738.
6. *In re* Adoption of Baby E.Z., 266 P.3d 702, 712 (Utah 2011), quoting Thompson v. Thompson, 484 U.S. 174, 183, 108 S. Ct. 513, 98 L. Ed. 2d 512 (1988) (quotations omitted).
7. Kelly Stoner & Richard A. Orona, *Full Faith and Credit, Comity, or Federal Mandate? A Path That Leads to Recognition and Enforcement of Tribal Court Orders, Tribal Protection Orders, and Tribal Child Custody Orders*, N.M. L. Rev. 6 (Spring 2004).
8. State v. Dist. Court of Tenth Judicial Dist. in & for Fergus Cnty., 46 Mont. 425 (1912).

change in circumstances.[9] A third court allowed the original court to retain jurisdiction.[10]

From 1942 to 1958, the U.S. Supreme Court issued a number of rulings that seemed to discourage granting full faith and credit to a sister state's child-custody determination. Of particular importance is the 1953 decision in *May v. Anderson*,[11] which found that the full faith and credit clause did not cover interstate recognition of child-custody determinations if the court which issued the initial child-custody determination did not have jurisdiction over both parents.

The Supreme Court rulings—together with increased mobility of the general American population and the rise in nontraditional families in the latter half of the 20th century—led to the epidemic of what was called at the time child snatchings and is now known as parental kidnapping. In an attempt to resolve the problem, the federal government passed the Parental Kidnapping Prevention Act of 1980, and states passed the Uniform Child Custody Jurisdiction Act (promulgated in 1968) and its successor, the Uniform Child Custody Jurisdiction Act (promulgated in 1997).

The following are the most important child-custody Supreme Court decisions between 1942 and 1958.

In *Williams v. State of North Carolina*,[12] the Supreme Court found that the full faith and credit clause forced states to recognize each other's divorce judgments. This was the case even if the issuing state did not have personal jurisdiction over the nonpetitioning spouse. Presumably, the results of more than one state having jurisdiction over a divorce proceeding resulted in more parallel divorce proceedings and the accompanying child-custody matters.

Five years after *Williams*, in 1947 in *New York ex rel Halvey v. Halvey*, the Supreme Court opined that, even if states gave full faith and credit to a child-custody determination, a succeeding state "has at least as much leeway to disregard the [original] judgment, to qualify it, or to depart from it as does the State where it was rendered."[13] Thus, a state could claim to

9. *Id.*
10. *Id.*
11. 345 U.S. 528 (1953).
12. 317 U.S. 287, 303–04 (U.S.N.C. 1942).
13. 330 U.S. 610, 615 (1947).

recognize the prior child-custody determination and yet find a change in circumstances that allowed it to modify the previous state's determination.

A decade later, the Supreme Court expanded on *Halvey* in the controversial *May* case:

> The question presented is whether, in a habeas corpus proceeding attacking the right of a mother to retain possession of her minor children, an Ohio court must give full faith and credit to a Wisconsin decree awarding custody of the children to their father when that decree is obtained by the father in an ex parte divorce action in a Wisconsin court which had no personal jurisdiction over the mother. For the reasons hereafter stated, our answer is no.[14]

Justice Frankfurter limited the majority *May* opinion by noting in his concurrence that the Supreme Court's ruling did not make a finding that it was unconstitutional to issue a child-custody determination when a state did not have personal jurisdiction over both parents. He concluded that states could choose to enact laws to give full faith and credit to another state's child-custody determination.

Due Process Clause

It is generally understood that to comply with the Due Process Clause of the 14th Amendment of the U.S. Constitution, a court needs to comply with "traditional notions of fair play and substantial justice."[15] The relevant part of Section 1 of the 14th Amendment states:

> No State shall make or enforce any law which shall abridge the privileges or immunities of citizens of the United States; nor shall any State deprive any person of life, liberty, or property, without due process of law; nor deny to any person within its jurisdiction the equal protection of the laws.[16]

14. 345 U.S. 528, 528–529 (1953).
15. Int'l Shoe Co. v. State of Wash., Office of Unemployment Comp. & Placement, 326 U.S. 310, 316 (1945).
16. U.S CONST. amend. XIV, § 1.

Personal jurisdiction over an individual is often considered essential to meeting requirements for due process. However, personal jurisdiction over a parent is not required under the PKPA and UCCJEA as long as the statute's requirements of notice are met. This is somewhat surprising since the *May* majority seemed clear in the need for personal jurisdiction over a parent when child custody was at issue:

> We have before us the elemental question whether a court of a state, where a mother is neither domiciled, resident nor present, may cut off her immediate right to the care, custody, management and companionship of her minor children without having jurisdiction over her in personam. Rights far more precious to appellant than property rights will be cut off if she is to be bound by the Wisconsin award of custody.[17]

The UCCJEA and the PKPA have discarded this statement as mere dictum. Acknowledging otherwise would make the UCCJEA as well as the PKPA unconstitutional. The drafters of the UCCJA, the PKPA, and UCCJEA "felt that a workable interstate custody law could not be built with or around the plurality opinion in *May v. Anderson*."[18] Ultimately the drafters interpreted *May* to mean what Justice Frankfurter's concurring opinion said it meant, that other states are authorized to pass laws recognizing as binding on their resident a custody decision of another state in which personal jurisdiction over this resident was not obtained.

All states that have addressed the constitutionality of the UCCJEA and the PKPA have found them to be constitutional, reasoning that child-custody matters qualify under the status exemption.

However, New York, recognizing the due process problem, has taken the precautionary step of amending UCCJEA Section 108, Notice to Persons Outside State (Section 75-g of New York's UCCJEA) to be more clearly compliant with the Constitution's due process clause. The relevant part of

17. 345 U.S. at 533 (1953).

18. Bridgette Bodenheimer, *The Uniform Child Custody Jurisdiction Act: A Legislative Remedy for Children Caught in the Conflict of Laws*, 22 VAND. L. REV. 1207, 1233 (1969). (Also see UCCJEA comments to Section 201 page 26, "As pointed out by Professor Bodenhaiemr, the reporter for the UCCJA, no 'workable interstate custody law could be built around [Justice] Burton's plurality opinion . . . '").

the comment to the "Notice" section of New York's statute is reproduced as follows:

> The original version of Section 75-g [L.2001, c. 386], which had been based on the national UCCJEA, authorized the Court to order almost any form of service to out-of-state persons. Given the risk of contravening procedural due process standards by sanctioning an ad hoc arrangement, in 2006 the Legislature wisely decided to amend subdivision 1 [L.2006, c. 184]. The revisions restore, virtually word by word, the prior UCCJA provisions that had been repealed in 2001. In effect, the legislature decided that, in this respect, the prior uniform act is preferable to the current version. Indeed, the amended (or restored) statute incorporates several elements which enhance accountability, not to mention the likelihood of effective notice. First, service outside New York cannot be utilized unless the person cannot be served within this state. Second, CPLR 313 is incorporated, thereby assuring that service is effected by an appropriate official. Last, the alternative of receipted mail notice is authorized, thereby permitting the most economical service method. Last, when attempts to effect personal service fail the section permits service by publication. In fact, the Trial Court's refusal to order service by publication may constitute reversible error; *Hofelich v. Garrow*, 69 A.D.3d 1254, 894 N.Y.S.2d 553 (3d Dept. 2010).[19]

Foreign Nationals and Due Process

Foreign nationals are entitled to additional due process protections under Article 37(b) ("Information in cases of death, guardianship or trusteeship, wrecks and air accidents") of the Vienna Convention on Consular Relations, which states:

> If the relevant information is available to the competent authorities of the receiving State, such authorities shall have the duty: . . . (b) to inform the competent consular post without delay of any case where the appointment of a guardian or trustee appears to be in the interests

19. N.Y. DOM. REL. LAW § 75-g (McKinney).

> of a minor or other person lacking full capacity who is a national of the sending State. The giving of this information shall, however, be without prejudice to the operation of the laws and regulations of the receiving State concerning such appointments.

The purpose of this section is to protect foreign nationals, who might be conspicuously ignorant of the American judicial system, by notifying their nation's consul of the proceeding and thereby giving the consul the opportunity to assist the foreign national.

The Vermont Supreme Court noted that compliance with the Vienna Convention was not optional when it quoted the Supremacy Clause:

> Pursuant to the Supremacy Clause, this treaty [the Vienna Convention] is "the supreme Law of the Land; and the Judges in every State shall be bound thereby, any Thing in the constitution or Laws of any State to the Contrary notwithstanding."[20]

However, while compliance is not optional, the treaty does not provide for any specific remedy to a violation. Therefore, it is unclear whether parents have an individual right of action when the treaty is not complied with.[21]

Status Exemption and Minimum Contacts

Dating back to *Pennoyer v. Neff* in 1877, the U.S. Supreme Court recognized that a state may determine the civil status of its own citizens toward a nonresident even when there is "no service of process or personal notice to the non-resident."[22] By way of example, the Court noted that a state "has absolute right to prescribe the conditions upon which the marriage relation between its own citizens shall be created, and the causes for which it may be dissolved."[23] However, the Supreme Court has yet to rule on what cases, apart from divorce, fall under the personal status exception.

---

20. *In re* R.W., 191 Vt. 108, 133 (2011) (quoting the Supremacy Clause, U.S. CONST. art. VI, cl. 2.).
21. Sanchez-Llamas v. Oregon, 548 U.S. 331 (2006); this case addressed the parallel statute Article 36 for criminal cases; however, Article 36 and Article 37 are so similar that the Supreme Court's reasoning for Article 37 likely applies to Article 36.
22. 95 U.S. 714, 734–35 (1877).
23. *Id.*

The Vermont Supreme Court, in finding that child custody was covered under the status exemption, opined:

> Much like the marriage relationship, severance of a parent's legal relationship to his or her child requires state intervention and is a matter of state concern. Thus, a child's home state has jurisdiction to adjudicate the status of a child present there even if the parents lack minimum contacts with the forum.[24]

This reasoning closely parallels the reasoning of the other states that have considered the issue.[25]

UCCJA, UCCJEA, and PKPA

While the UCCJA still holds importance when interpreting the current unaddressed issues in the UCCJEA, for clarity and brevity's sake, this book deals briefly with the UCCJA and focuses mainly on the UCCJEA and the PKPA, since all states (except Massachusetts, which has pending legislation as of 2014) have now substituted the UCCJA with the UCCJEA.

The UCCJEA and the PKPA are similar in that for both, except in emergency matters, a court may only decide a child-custody matter if the court qualifies for jurisdiction under one of four scenarios (which are discussed more thoroughly in Article 2, Jurisdiction):

1. Home state jurisdiction
2. Significant connection jurisdiction
3. More convenient forum jurisdiction
4. Default jurisdiction (or jurisdiction when no other jurisdictional basis is available)[26]

---

24. *In re* R.W., 191 Vt. 108, 125 (2011).
25. *See* State *ex rel.* W.A., 63 P.3d 607, 2002 UT 127, for a listing of jurisdictions that have considered the status exception as it relates to child-custody jurisdiction.
26. Thomas v. Avant, 370 Ark. 377, 382 (2007).

One of the main differences between the UCCJEA and the PKPA is that the PKPA is an addendum to the full faith and credit statute. Thus, by nature of being the one law that applies to all states, the PKPA brings national uniformity to interstate recognition of child-custody determinations. However, the PKPA is limited to extending full faith and credit to child-custody determinations. It does not address how a state may enforce a judgment or when a state has jurisdiction to issue an initial child-custody determination under its own laws.

The UCCJEA, on the other hand, is significantly broader than the PKPA. It covers state jurisdiction to enter an order, recognition of foreign child-custody orders, and enforcement of foreign child-custody orders. However, it lacks the PKPA's uniformity because the UCCJEA is enacted by each individual state, and some states have chosen to significantly alter it from its original draft. Case law has also affected the way each state interprets the statute. Thus, while the UCCJEA covers more ground than the PKPA, it is not uniformly adopted across the 50 states.

UCCJA (Promulgated in 1968)

The UCCJA was the first attempt to create a uniform set of laws among the states to contain the rising number of parental kidnappings throughout the United States. Before the UCCJEA replaced it, the UCCJA had been adopted by all 50 states. The UCCJA had some shortcomings that were later addressed through the PKPA and, ultimately, through the UCCJEA.

The UCCJA's main shortcoming was that states were still exercising concurrent jurisdiction due to

1. language in the UCCJA that allowed for concurrent jurisdiction between the states;
2. lack of uniformity due to divergent case law among states and significant modifications made to the proposed UCCJA draft by the states who adopted the statute; and
3. the UCCJA provided no "uniform method of enforcing custody and visitation orders validly entered in another [s]tate."[27]

27. UCCJEA prefatory note at 4 (quotation and citations omitted).

An additional problem was that the UCCJA drafters could not have foreseen the enactment of the PKPA in 1980. Once the PKPA was enacted, the slight but significant differences between the two acts were "technical enough to delight a medieval property lawyer."[28]

Parental Kidnapping Prevention Act (1980)

The PKPA was the federal government's response to the UCCJA's limitations. The most crucial section of the PKPA is the extension of the federal government's full faith and credit statute to child-custody determinations.

Although the PKPA has many sections, it is not uncommon for law review articles, court rulings, and experts to refer to 28 U.S.C.A. § 1738A (which extends the Full Faith and Credit Act to child-custody determinations) as the Parental Kidnapping and Prevention Act.

The full PKPA consists of five sections: (1) title; (2) findings and purposes; (3) full faith and credit given to child custody determination; (4) use of federal parental locator service in connection with the enforcement or determination of child-custody and in cases of parental kidnapping of a child; and (5) parental kidnapping.

Section 2: Findings and Purposes

Section 2 explains that the PKPA was drafted because it was difficult for child-custody determinations to receive full faith and credit, resulting in conflicting and inconsistent rulings across states on the same child-custody case. The purpose of the PKPA was to promote cooperation between the states in child-custody proceedings by

1. giving full faith and credit to child-custody determinations that were entered in the state that was best equipped to make decisions in the best interests of the child;
2. promoting the exchange of information and the enforcement of determinations between the states;

28. *Id.* at 2.

3. creating stability for children by avoiding the conflicting and inconsistent rulings that were limiting the ability of children to have stable childhoods; and
4. stopping parental kidnapings by removing the possibility of relitigating unfavorable child-custody determination in another state.

Section 3: Full Faith and Credit Given to Child-Custody Determinations

Section 3, 28 U.S.C.A. § 1738A, is an addendum to the full faith and credit statute, § 1738. It outlines the situations in which a state must recognize and enforce a foreign child-custody determination.

The UCCJEA and § 1738A of the PKPA closely parallel each other in that both acts give full faith and credit to child-custody determinations entered in a sister state. There are some important differences between the two acts: (1) the PKPA leaves enforcing state courts to their own laws in enforcing the foreign child-custody determinations; and (2) the PKPA does not have a mechanism for determining whether a state has jurisdiction to issue an initial child-custody determination.

Regardless, despite not explicitly controlling a state's jurisdiction to issue an initial child-custody determination, the PKPA does exert some control over whether a state claims jurisdiction over a child-custody determination by denying full faith and credit to those child-custody determinations that do not fulfill its requirements.

Section 4: Use of Federal Parental Locator Service in Connection with the Enforcement or Determination of Child-Custody and in Cases of Parental Kidnapping of a Child [29]

Section 4, 42 U.S.C.A § 663, expands the Parent Locator Service of the Department of Health and Human Services[30] by extending its coverage to "receive and transmit information concerning the whereabouts of any absent parent or child for purposes of (1) enforcing any State or Federal law with respect to the unlawful taking or restraing of a child; or (2) making or enforcing a child custody or visitation determination."[31]

29. 42 U.S.C.A. § 663.
30. *Id.* § 1073.
31. *Id.* § 663(a)(1)–(2) (West).

Section 5: Parental Kidnapping

In Section 5, Congress expresses its intent that the attorney general apply 18 U.S.C.A. § 1073 (its official title is "Flight to avoid prosecution or giving testimony," but it is also called the Fugitive Felon Act) to situations where a parent with a kidnapped child crosses interstate or international lines.

Under § 1073, a kidnapper may be "fined under this title and imprisoned not more than five years, or both" and will be prosecuted in the "Federal judicial district in which the original crime was alleged to have been committed."[32]

Congressional sponsors of the PKPA intended for the Justice Department to prosecute parental kidnappers under the Fugitive Felon Act with the same vigor that it prosecutes fugitive felons who cross state lines while committing felonies.[33] Despite congressional intent, the PKPA did not significantly alter how the attorney general and the Federal Bureau of Investigation (FBI) enforce the Fugitive Felon Act. As a result, the enforcement of this Act against parental kidnappers is still limited to extreme situations where the U.S. attorney has authorized the filing of a complaint, the federal arrest process is outstanding, and

1. there is probable clause to believe that the kidnapping parent has fled interstate or internationally to avoid prosecution or confinement;
2. there is an outstanding state warrant for the kidnapping parent, and this warrant charges the parent with a felony; and
3. state authorities are willing to extradite and prosecute the fugitive parent if the FBI finds that parent within the United States.[34]

---

32. 18 U.S.C.A. § 1073.

33. *Implementation of the Parental Kidnapping Prevention Act of 1980: Oversight Hearing Before the Subcomm. on Crime of the Comm. on the Judiciary House of Representatives*, 97th Cong., first session on implementation of the Parental Kidnapping Prevention Act of 1980, September 24, 1981, Serial No. 99.

34. *Family Child Abductions*, FBI, http://www.fbi.gov/about-us/investigate/vc_majorthefts/cac/family-abductions (last visited Aug. 3, 2014).

Conflicts with the UCCJEA

It is very unusual for a court to find that there is a conflict between the PKPA and the UCCJEA. However, if the two statutes were to conflict, the PKPA is preemptive.[35]

Conflicts with the Defense of Marriage Act

Like the PKPA, Section 2 of the Defense of Marriage Act (DOMA), Powers Reserved to the States, is an addendum to the full faith and credit clause. The PKPA's goal of interstate recognition of all child-custody judgments is seemingly at odds with DOMA's Section 2, which states:

> No State, territory, or possession of the United States, or Indian tribe, shall be required to give effect to any public act, record, or judicial proceeding of any other State, territory, possession or tribe respecting a relationship between persons of the same sex that is treated as a marriage under the laws of such other State, territory, possession, or tribe, or a right or claim arising from such a relationship.[36]

In 2013 in *United States v. Windsor*, the U.S. Supreme Court found unconstitutional Section 3, Definition of Marriage, of DOMA.[37] This section forbids the recognition of same-sex marriages by the federal government. In its ruling, the Supreme Court noted that DOMA interfered with the due process protections allowed to citizens under the 5th and 14th Amendments because DOMA's "avowed purpose and practical effect . . . are to impose a disadvantage, a separate status, and so a stigma upon all who enter into same-sex marriages made lawful by the unquestioned authority of the States"[38] and infringed upon a state's right to determine which of its citizens are to be treated as married persons.

While it remains to be determined if, or how, the *Windsor* ruling affects the seemingly mutually exclusive goals of DOMA's Section 3 and the PKPA,

35. Arkansas Dep't of Human Servs. v. Cox, 349 Ark. 205, 211 (2002).
36. 28 U.S.C.A. § 1738C.
37. 133 S. Ct. 2675 (2013).
38. *Id.* at 2681.

there is one state supreme court case that deals with whether DOMA forces a state to recognize a sister state's child-custody determination when that sister state's determination is in violation of the PKPA.

In *Miller-Jenkins v. Miller-Jenkins*,[39] two Vermont same-sex spouses filed for divorce in Vermont. After the initial child-custody ruling, the biological mother moved with the child to Virginia and filed for custody there. The Virginia court entered a child-custody determination finding that Vermont's civil union laws were "null and void"[40] under Virginia law and that the biological mother was the "sole biological and natural parent"[41] of the child. The biological mother then sought to have Vermont give full faith and credit to the Virginia judgment under DOMA.

The Vermont Supreme Court rejected the biological mother's argument, finding that

> unlike the PKPA, in no instance does DOMA require a court in one state to give full faith and credit to the decision of a court in another state. Its sole purpose is to provide an authorization *not* to give full faith and credit in the circumstances covered by the statute.[42]

It remains undetermined by any state supreme court whether a court may, under DOMA, fail to acknowledge a sister state's child-custody determination even if recognition is required under the PKPA.

UCCJEA (Promulgated in 1997)

Currently, 49 states[43]—as well as Guam, the District of Columbia, and the U.S. Virgin Islands, but not Puerto Rico[44]—have passed the UCCJEA. The

39. 180 Vt. 441 (2006).
40. *Id.* at 454.
41. *Id.* at 446.
42. *Id.* at 453.
43. Massachusetts is the only state that has not yet enacted the act because of concerns over how the UCCJEA may protect domestic violence victims. Fern L. Frolin, *Uniform Child Custody Jurisdiction Enforcement Act: A Better Child Custody Jurisdiction Law for Massachusetts*, 6 SEC. REV. 17 (2004), *available at* http://www.massbar.org/publications/section-review/2004/v6-n3/uniform-child-custody-jurisdiction-enforcement.
44. Puerto Rico is still subject to the PKPA.

UCCJEA was drafted and adopted in order to address the UCCJA's shortcomings. It did so as follows:

1. **Parallel jurisdiction.** The UCCJEA minimizes the chances of states exercising parallel jurisdiction by giving priority to the ways a state may acquire jurisdiction and omitting the "child's best interests" among the reasons a court may consider in determining jurisdiction (thereby avoiding the possibility that two states may consider that keeping jurisdiction over a case is in the "child's best interests").

   For example, a state may only claim UCCJEA jurisdiction in a child-custody matter where another state made a child-custody determination when (1) the parent, child, and any person acting as a parent has moved out of the original decree state; and (2) the state with exclusive, continuing jurisdiction declines to exercise jurisdiction under the grounds that another state is a more convenient forum.
2. **Temporary emergency jurisdiction.** The UCCJEA clarifies that, generally, emergency jurisdiction may only be exercised on a temporary basis. In addition, unlike its predecessor, the UCCJEA segregates temporary emergency jurisdiction away from the exclusive and continuing jurisdiction that is granted to a state exercising initial jurisdiction.
3. **Enforcement.** The UCCJEA adds an enforcement provision that was lacking in the UCCJA. The UCCJEA provides for (1) "a simple procedure for registering a custody determination in another State";[45] (2) swift remedies in the enforcement of the custody determination; and (3) the enforcing court to issue a warrant for the physical possession of the child if the court fears that the parent who has the child may flee or harm the child.
4. **Harmonization.** The UCCJEA harmonizes linguistically with the Uniform Interstate Family Support Act and the PKPA, thereby "simplifying the life of the family law practitioner" by making the law of interstate family proceedings as uniform as possible.[46]

45. UCCJEA prefatory note cmt. at 7.
46. *Id.* cmt. at 4.

Despite its achievements, there are limitations to the UCCJEA. For example, case law might lead to different outcomes on a UCCJEA case depending on the state that is litigating the matter. However, the greatest problem with the UCCJEA is that it is a state law that is designed to deal with a type of interstate problem (the recognition of foreign child-custody determinations) for which a federal law is better equipped.[47]

47. *In re* Marriage of Fontenot, 335 Mont. 79, 84–85 (2006).

Article 1

General Provisions

Section 101: Short Title

This section merely states that the UCCJEA may be cited as the "Uniform Child Custody Jurisdiction and Enforcement Act." The drafters' comments clarify the purposes of the statute, which are to

1. avoid jurisdictional competition between courts of different states;
2. promote cooperation between the courts on child-custody matters;
3. discourage the practice of using "the interstate system for continuing controversies over child custody";
4. deter the kidnapping of children;
5. avoid relitigating child-custody issues in other states; and
6. "facilitate the enforcement of custody decrees of other States."[1]

Section 102: Definitions

Section 102(1) Abandoned

The Uniform Child Custody Jurisdiction and Enforcement Act (UCCJEA) defines "abandoned" as "left without provision for reasonable and necessary care or supervision."[2]

---

1. UCCJEA § 101 cmt. at 7.
2. *Id.* § 102(1).

Courts have determined that for a child to be abandoned, there needs to be an element of willfulness. *Black's Law Dictionary* defines abandonment as "the relinquishing of a right or interest with the intention of never reclaiming it."[3] For example, when a mother gives up a child for adoption, that mother has abandoned that child.[4]

Section 102(2) Child

The UCCJEA defines a "child" as "an individual who has not attained 18 years of age."[5] The definition of child only covers children who are under the age of 18. It does not cover unborn infants.[6] It is irrelevant where the child was conceived.

Section 102(3) Child-Custody Determination and Section 102(4) Child-Custody Proceeding

Although child-custody determinations and proceedings are defined separately, they are intertwined because there cannot be a child-custody determination without a child-custody proceeding.

Proceedings and Determinations Covered under the UCCJEA

The UCCJEA and Parental Kidnapping Prevention Act's (PKPA) definition of "child-custody determination" has been interpreted broadly, and most courts have found that it encompasses almost any child-custody determination reached through a proceeding that qualifies as a UCCJEA child-custody proceeding. Most courts have found parenting time, adoptions, neglect and dependency proceedings, and guardianship proceedings to be covered under the UCCJEA.

Parenting-Time (Visitation) Proceedings

A parenting-time proceeding is covered under the UCCJEA even if the parents have reached an agreement on custody and the only issue before the court is visitation.[7]

3. Black's Law Dictionary.
4. White v. Adoption of Baby Boy D., 10 P.3d 212, 221 (Okla. 2000).
5. UCCJEA § 102(2).
6. *Arkansas Dep't of Human Servs.*, 349 Ark. 205, 214 (2002).
7. Castro v. Castro, 181 N.W.2d 753, 760 (N.D. 2012) ("Visitation issues involve more than a non-custodial parent's situation and those issues are not severable from a child-custody determination.").

Adoptions

Most states have determined that the UCCJEA applies to adoption proceedings.[8] Thus, even though adoption proceedings are excluded under Section 103, Proceedings Covered by Other Law, most states apply the UCCJEA to the termination of parental rights incident to an adoption. This book has a more detailed coverage of adoption as it relates to the UCCJEA under Section 103.

Neglect and Dependency Proceedings

The UCCJEA specifically expanded the limited reach of the UCCJA to cover child-abuse and neglect proceedings.[9] In listing neglect and dependency proceedings as those covered under the UCCJEA, the drafters sought to remove "any controversy about the types of proceedings where a custody determination can occur."[10]

However, some courts have held that the proceedings are not covered under the PKPA because

1. although the UCCJA explicitly applied to "neglect and dependency proceedings," the PKPA appears to have intentionally omitted parallel language;
2. the PKPA was drafted to prevent parental kidnappings; it was not drafted with the intent of interfering "with a state's protection of a dependent and neglected child"; and
3. the PKPA's section on continuing jurisdiction, Section 1738A(d), refers to a contestant, which in turn is defined in Section 1738A(b)(2) not to include the state.[11]

---

8. The majority of courts across the country addressing this issue have concluded that both the PKPA and the UCCJEA apply to adoption proceedings. *See, e.g.*, *In re* Adoption of Baby E.Z., 266 P.3d 702, 708 (recognizing the majority of jurisdictions apply PKPA to adoptions); Brookshire v. Blackwell, 384 S.C. 333, 682 S.E.2d 295, 298 (S.C. Ct. App. 2009) (recognizing that both PKPA and UCCJA apply to adoption cases); People *ex rel.* A.J.C., 88 P.3d 599 (Colo. 2004) (finding custody determinations included adoptions); Brown v. DeLapp, 312 P.3d 918 n.12 (Okla. 2013).
9. *In re* B.P., 343 Mont. 354, 350 (2008).
10. UCCJEA § 102 cmt., "child-custody proceeding."
11. Miller-Jenkins v. Miller-Jenkins, 180 Vt. 441, 452 (2006).

Guardianship Proceedings

The few state courts to have considered whether guardianship proceedings are covered under the UCCJEA have come to different conclusions. Alaska, for example, accepted without analysis that a California guardianship judgment would have qualified as a child custody determination under the UCCJEA if the order had still been in effect.[12] Maryland, on the other hand, found that a guardianship is different from a child-custody determination because child custody encompasses the

> care, control, and maintenance of the child . . . and is premised on the notion that the affection of a parent for a child is as strong and potent as any that springs from human relations and leads to desire and efforts to care properly for and raise the child, whereas a guardian's role in relation to the child is much more limited and the court defines the temporality, purpose, and authority of the appointment.[13]

Proceedings and Determinations Not Covered under the UCCJEA

While the UCCJEA's coverage of child-custody–related proceedings is extensive, there are some child-custody areas that are not covered, such as parentage stipulations (also called acknowledgment of parentage), parentage proceedings that are solely for the purpose of establishing paternity or child support, divorce judgments that do not address child-custody matters, and child-custody determinations that have expired.

Parentage Stipulations

Courts have found that a parental stipulation is not a child-custody determination because unlike a child-custody proceeding, a stipulation is not entered or filed by any court. Therefore, it is not a "judgment, decree, or other court order providing legal custody, physical custody, or parenting time with respect to a child."[14] Furthermore, unlike a real child-custody

12. S.B. v. State Dep't of Health & Soc. Servs., Div. of Family & Youth Servs., 61 P.3d 6, 11 (Alaska 2002).
13. Toland v. Futagi, 425 Md. 365, 388–89 (2012), *cert. denied*, 133 S. Ct. 265 (U.S. 2012) (citations and quotations omitted).
14. Foster v. Wolkowitz, 486 Mich. 356, 366–67 (2010).

determination that is entered by a court, the parentage stipulation is filed with the executive branch and kept in a parentage registry.

The reasoning behind the court's decision to exclude parentage stipulations applies even if

1. the state's parentage statute automatically awards custody to the mother;
2. the parental stipulation might be used in a child-custody proceeding; and
3. a parent subjected him- or herself to personal jurisdiction under state law by signing the parentage stipulation.[15]

Parentage Proceedings

If the proceeding is solely to determine parentage, then it is not subject to UCCJEA jurisdiction because a parentage proceeding in itself does not affect access to the child and therefore is more similar to child-support proceedings than to child-custody proceedings.[16] However, there is an exception if part of the relief requested in the parentage proceeding is custody or parenting time (visitation); then it is a child-custody proceeding covered under the UCCJEA.[17]

Divorce Judgments

Similar to a parentage proceeding, a divorce judgment is not covered under the UCCJEA unless it contains child-custody provisions. For example, merely naming the husband as the father of the children does not automatically make the divorce judgment a UCCJEA determination.[18] Ultimately, a divorce judgment that only establishes parentage and does not have any provisions for visitation or parenting time is the equivalent of a parentage action, which is not recognized by the courts to be a child-custody proceeding unless it involves the issues of child custody and parenting time.

---

15. *Id.* (2010) (the requirements for UCCJEA jurisdiction are different than those for personal jurisdiction).
16. Kessel v. Leavitt, 204 W. Va. 95, 171 (1998).
17. Greenhough v. Goforth, 354 Ark. 502, 508 (2003).
18. Hashberger v. Hashberger, 724 N.W.2d 148, 157 (N.D. 2006).

Expired Orders or Judgments

Orders or judgments that expired and can no longer be enforced, such as an expired temporary order of protection, are not covered under the UCCJEA even in cases where they were covered while the determination was still in effect. Similarly, a guardianship determination may not be covered if the guardian dies and the state does not "resuscitate" the guardianship proceeding to find a new guardian.[19]

Section 102(5) Commencement

The UCCJEA defines "commencement" as "the filing of the first pleading in a proceeding."[20] This definition applies in a straightforward way when no previous proceeding has been filed. In that situation, the proceeding commences on "the date the first pleading was filed." Therefore, for example, a motion to amend a parenting plan is not the commencement of a proceeding.[21] The definition of commencement, however, becomes more complex when a child-custody proceeding has begun in another state but that state no longer has exclusive, continuing jurisdiction because the parents and child have all moved out of state. In that situation, the proceeding commences when the first pleading is filed in a state with UCCJEA jurisdiction.[22]

Section 102(6) Court

The UCCJEA defines "court" as "an entity authorized under the law of a State to establish, enforce, or modify a child-custody determination."[23] The definition is more expansive than the *Black's Law* definition of "a governmental body consisting of one or more judges who sit to adjudicate disputes and administer justice."[24] The purpose of the drafters was likely to include child-custody determinations from foreign countries whose legal systems might not wholly match the American understanding of "court."

---

19. *S.B.*, 61 P.3d at 11.
20. UCCJEA § 102(5).
21. *In re* Marriage of Lloyd, 361 Mont. 22, 27–28 (2011).
22. Sidell v. Sidell, 18 A.3d 499, 506 (R.I. 2011).
23. UCCJEA § 102(6).
24. Black's Law Dictionary definition of "court."

Section 102(7) Home State

The UCCJEA defines "home state" as

> the state in which a child lived with a parent or a person acting as a parent for at least six consecutive months immediately before the commencement of a child-custody proceeding. In the case of a child less than six months of age, the term means the state in which the child lived from birth with any of the persons mentioned. A period of temporary absence of any of the mentioned persons is part of the period.[25]

There is a conflict between the definition of home state in this section and the jurisdiction-creating language of Section 201(1). Under Section 102(7), a state qualifies as home state only if a child has "lived with a parent or a person acting as a parent for at least six consecutive months *immediately* before the commencement of a child-custody proceeding."[26] However, the more expansive Section 201(1) states that a state qualifies for home state jurisdiction if the child has lived in the "home state *within* six months before the commencement of the proceeding."[27] States have resolved this conflict by holding that the more expansive description of Section 201(1) should be followed. See Section 201(a)(1) of this book for more information.

Temporary Absences

Temporary absences are often hotly contested in determining home state jurisdiction because temporary absences "do not interrupt the six-month pre-complaint residency period necessary to establish home state jurisdiction."[28] For instance, if a child is temporarily absent for eight months from his original home state, then the original state still has home state jurisdiction over the case and a stay-behind parent can file for custody in the original state, even though the child has been physically out of state for more than six months.[29]

25. UCCJEA § 102(7).
26. *Id.* (emphasis added).
27. *Id.* § 201(1) (emphasis added).
28. Ogawa v. Ogawa, 125 Nev. 660, 662 (2009).
29. *Id.* ("Although the children had been absent from the state for eight months when respondent filed her custody action, the testimony and evidence supported that the children left

Determining Temporary Absences

In determining temporary absence, courts have considered the following:[30]

1. the parent's purposes in removing the child from the state, rather than the length of the absence;
2. whether the parent remaining in the claimed home state believed the absence to be merely temporary;
3. whether the absence was of indefinite duration; and
4. the totality of the circumstances surrounding the child's absence.

Courts have found that court-ordered visitations, vacations, and business trips are temporary absences from the home state.[31] Temporary absences can turn into permanent absences because "an absence from a state is no longer 'temporary' once the intent is formed for the child to reside permanently in another state and is in fact doing so with such intent."[32]

In determining whether a move was intended to be permanent, there is a preference for objectively assessing a party's behavior rather than his or her alleged intent. When a parent moves with the children to a new state for his or her new spouse's job, that parent cannot later claim a temporary absence from the original state if that parent applies for his or her driver's license in the new state and enrolls the children in school in the new state.[33]

When the Child Is Less Than Six Months Old

The UCCJEA fails to specify the process for determining jurisdiction when a child who is less than six months of age has lived in different places since his or her birth. For example, if an infant was in State A for a few days during and following her birth but has lived most of her short life in State B,

---

Nevada for a temporary three-month vacation, and under the UCCJEA, temporary absences do not interrupt the six-month pre-complaint residency period necessary to establish home state jurisdiction. Thus, taking into account the temporary absence, the action was filed timely under the UCCJEA, and the Nevada district court had home-state jurisdiction in this matter.").

30. Sajjad v. Cheema, 428 N.J. Super., 160, 173 (App. Div. 2012).
31. *Ex parte* Siderius, 1120509, 2013 WL 6210834 (Ala. Nov. 27, 2013).
32. *In re* Marriage of Pereault, 829 N.W.2d 192 (Iowa Ct. App. 2013).
33. Powell v. Stover, 165 S.W.3d 322, 323 (Tex. 2005).

then neither State A nor State B has home state jurisdiction over the child for the commencement of a child-custody proceeding.[34]

Courts have found that following the exact language of the definition can lead to absurd results if the newborn child has spent his or her short life in one state as a result of a hospital stay incident to his or her birth.[35] However, the state claiming to be the newborn child's home state must follow proper procedure under Article 3, Enforcement, if it seeks to enforce its determination in the birth state.[36]

Section 102(8) Initial Determination

The UCCJEA defines "initial determination" as "the first child-custody determination concerning a particular child."[37] This definition is of particular relevance for Section 202, Exclusive, Continuing Jurisdiction. Despite the seemingly clear definition of initial determination, a case might have more than one initial determination. For example, if an initial determination expires in the state with UCCJEA jurisdiction under Section 202, then a new state might claim jurisdiction under Section 201 and issue a second initial determination.[38]

To be an initial determination, the determination made must be regarding a particular child. Previous child-custody determinations regarding a

34. *In re* Interest of Violet T., 286 Neb. 949, 955 (2013), and State *ex rel.* in Interest of R.P. v. Rosen, 966 S.W.2d 292, 300 (Mo. Ct. App. 1998).

35. *In re* D.S., 217 Ill. 2d 306, 317 (2005) ("The crucial question, of course, is what did the drafters of the UCCJEA mean by 'live,' a verb that can mean many different things depending upon the context. Did they mean, as respondents seem to suggest, nothing more than 'to be alive'? See Webster's Third New International Dictionary 1323 (1993). That, for purposes of the UCCJEA, a child 'lives' in every jurisdiction in which he or she draws a breath? Or did they mean, as the case law teaches, something more like 'to occupy a home'? See Webster's Third New International Dictionary 1323 (1993). We are convinced that they meant the latter. When people speak of where a mother and newborn baby 'live,' they do not speak of the maternity ward. Instead, they speak of the place to which the mother and baby return following discharge from the hospital. In many parts of Illinois, the mother's hospital of choice may be located in another city or even another state. Hoopeston mothers, we now know, may deliver in Champaign. Galena mothers may deliver in Dubuque. Yet no one would respond 'a hospital in Champaign' or 'a hospital in Dubuque' if asked where these mothers and babies live. Rather, they would respond 'Hoopeston' or 'Galena' because that *is* where these mothers and babies 'live,' as that term is commonly understood.").

36. *Cox*, 349 Ark. at 218 ("enforcement of foreign child-custody determinations is not a self-help process").

37. UCCJEA § 102(8).

38. Ronny M. v. Nanette H., 303 P.3d 302, 401 (Alaska 2013).

child's siblings do not count as "initial determinations" for purposes of establishing UCCJEA jurisdiction over the child's case.[39]

Section 102(9) Issuing Court

The UCCJEA defines "issuing court" as "the court that makes a child-custody determination for which enforcement is sought under this [Act]."[40] This definition is only used in Article 3.

Section 102(10) Issuing State

The UCCJEA defines "issuing state" as "the state in which a child-custody determination is made."[41] This definition is similar to the definition under the Uniform Interstate Family Support Act (UIFSA), with the exception that in UIFSA "it refers to the court that issued the support or parentage order."[42] This definition is only used in Article 3.

Section 102(11) Modification

The UCCJEA defines "modification" as "a child-custody determination that changes, replaces, supersedes, or is otherwise made after a previous determination concerning the same child, whether or not it is made by the court that made the previous determination."[43] This definition is especially relevant for Section 203, Jurisdiction to Modify Determination. It is important to note that despite the definition, a state may not modify a child-custody determination if the original determination has expired or is no longer enforceable.[44] In that situation, the new proceeding following the original expired determination should begin under Section 201, Initial Child-Custody Jurisdiction, and Section 202, Exclusive, Continuing Jurisdiction.

Section 102(12) Person

The UCCJEA defines "person" as "an individual, corporation, business trust, estate, trust, partnership, limited liability company, association, joint

39. *Arkansas Dep't of Human Servs.*, 349 Ark. 205, 212–13 (2002).
40. UCCJEA § 102(9).
41. *Id.* § 102(10).
42. *Id.* § 102 cmt. at 11.
43. Id. § 102(11).
44. *Ronny M.*, 303 P.3d at 401.

venture, government; governmental subdivision, agency, or instrumentality; public corporations; or any other legal or commercial entity."[45] Some of the entities covered under "person" are overly broad for the UCCJEA. This is because the definition is not specifically tailored to child-custody proceedings but rather "is the one that is mandated for all Uniform Acts."[46] Thus, the drafters did not purposefully include public corporations or a business trust as a "person" that could claim child custody over a child under the UCCJEA.

Section 102(13) Person Acting as a Parent

The UCCJEA defines "person acting as a parent" as a

> person, other than a parent, who: (A) has physical custody of the child or has had physical custody for a period of six consecutive months, including any temporary absence, within one year immediately before the commencement of a child-custody proceeding; and (B) has been awarded legal custody by a court or claims a right to legal custody under the law of this state.[47]

A person acting as a parent is someone who fits its commonsense definition. For example, when a grandparent takes care of a child during the weekdays because the mother is away at college, that grandparent is a person acting as a parent.

A caretaker is not in control of the determination of whether he or she is a person acting as a parent under the UCCJEA. The caretaker is a person acting as a parent if he or she fits the criteria.[48]

A government agency for child protective services may not qualify as a person acting as a parent if the neglect proceedings have terminated and the children have been placed in the permanent custody of a parent.[49]

45. UCCJEA § 102(12).
46. *Id.* § 102 cmt. at 11.
47. *Id.* § 102(13).
48. *In re* Custody of A.C., 165 Wash. 2d 568, 576 (2009).
49. *In re* B.P., 343 Mont. at 348.

Claim of Legal Custody under the Laws of the State

There are three elements—formality, timing, and plausibility—that states consider when determining whether a person "claims a right to legal custody under the laws of the state." They are:

1. *Formality.* Some states require that all persons seeking person-acting-as-a-parent status have petitioned the court for legal custody of the child. Other states do not require a formal application but merely require that the person acting as a parent has the right to claim legal custody under the laws of the state.
2. *Timing.* A few states allow nonparents to claim legal custody at any point in the proceeding. Most jurisdictions, however, require that the claim to legal custody be asserted before or at the time that the UCCJEA child-custody case is begun.
3. *Plausibility* (only considered by some courts). The claim to custody must be asserted in good faith and based on some plausible legal theory.[50]

Section 102(14) Physical Custody

The UCCJEA defines "physical custody" as "the physical care and supervision of a child."[51] The physical care, under this section, need not be court ordered. Thus, a person—any person or agency—who has control over the physical care and supervision of a child has physical custody of that child. This, of course, does not apply to schools or other entities that might have contractual temporary control of the child for a specific period of time but are operating under the control of the child's parents or persons acting as a parent.

Section 102(15) State

The UCCJEA defines "state" as "a state of the United States, the District of Columbia, Puerto Rico, the United States Virgin Islands, or any territory or insular possession subject to the jurisdiction of the United States."[52] This

50. Schirado v. Foote, 785 N.W.2d 235, 241 (N.D. 2010).
51. UCCJEA § 102(14).
52. *Id.* § 102(15).

definition is almost the same as the definition under the Uniform Interstate Family Support Act except that, under UIFSA, the issuing state is the state that issued the support or parentage order, whereas, under the UCCJEA, the issuing state is the state that "made the custody determination that is sought to be enforced."[53]

This section does not mean that a foreign country's child-custody proceedings or determination is excluded from the UCCJEA. In fact, Section 105, International Application of Act, states, "a court of this state shall treat a foreign country as if it were a state of the United States for the purpose of applying Article 1 [General Provisions] and Article 2 [Jurisdiction]."[54] You should review Section 105 when dealing with international cases.

Section 102(16) Tribe

The UCCJEA defines "tribe" as "an Indian tribe or band, or Alaskan Native village, which is recognized by federal law or formally acknowledged by a state."[55] This section is optional, but most states have adopted it. See Section 104, Application to Indian Tribes, later in this chapter for more information on how the UCCJEA and PKPA apply to Indian tribes.

Section 102(17) Warrant

The UCCJEA defines "warrant" as "an order issued by a court authorizing law enforcement officers to take physical custody of a child."[56] This definition is only used in Article 3, Enforcement.

Section 103: Proceedings Covered by Other Law

This section states "this [Act] does not govern an adoption proceeding or a proceeding pertaining to the authorization of emergency medical care for a child."[57]

53. *Id.* § 102 cmt. at 11.
54. *Id.* § 105.
55. *Id.* § 102(16).
56. *Id.* § 102(17).
57. *Id.* § 103.

The reason the UCCJEA specifically excludes adoption proceedings is because the drafters expected most states to pass the Uniform Adoption Act. Jurisdiction under that act is specifically tailored to the particular needs of adoption proceedings. Unfortunately, to date only a few states have passed the Uniform Adoption Act.

Regardless, the drafters acknowledged that even if the Uniform Adoption Act was enacted, there would still be some adoption situations in which the UCCJEA applies, such as instances where an adoption is denied or set aside.[58]

Most states to have considered whether adoption proceedings are covered under the UCCJEA have found that adoption proceedings are covered, at least as it refers to the termination of parental rights necessary for an adoption to succeed.[59] The Utah Supreme Court, in holding that the PKPA applied to adoption proceedings, reasoned:

> The PKPA defines "custody determination" broadly, as "a judgment decree, or other order of a court providing for the custody of a child, and includes permanent and temporary orders, initial orders and modifications." And the PKPA defines "physical custody" as "actual possession and control of the child." Reading the phrase "any proceedings for custody determination" together with the definitions of "custody determination" and "physical custody" we conclude that the phrase "any proceeding for a custody determination" includes all proceedings that establish who will have "actual possession and control of a child." In light of this conclusion, adoption proceedings fall within the "any proceeding for a custody determination" provision of the PKPA.[60]

A few states, such as Oklahoma, have determined that the UCCJEA does not cover termination of parental rights due to adoption proceedings, reasoning that, unlike the UCCJA, the UCCJEA explicitly excludes adoption proceedings.

---

58. *Id.* § 103 cmt. at 12.
59. Anthony H. v. Matthew G., 397 S.C. 447, 451 (Ct. App. 2012), *reh'g denied* (May 4, 2012) ("In order for an adoption action to proceed, the legal parents either consent to the adoption, relinquish their parental rights, or have their parental rights terminated.").
60. *In re* Adoption of Baby E.Z., 266 P3d 702, 707 (Utah 2011).

Section 104: Application to Indian Tribes

This section provides that the UCCJEA does not apply to child-custody proceeding governed by the Indian Child Welfare Act. The UCCJEA does not require states to recognize tribal child-custody determinations unless the states enacted the optional Sections 204(b) ("a court of this state shall treat a tribe as if it were a State of the United States for purposes of applying Articles 1 [General provisions] and 2 [Jurisdiction]") and (c) ("a child-custody determination made by a tribe under factual circumstances in substantial conformity with the jurisdictional standards of this [Act] must be recognized and enforced under Article 3 [Enforcement]"). There is a split among the courts about whether the PKPA requires states to recognize tribal child-custody determinations and tribal courts to recognize state determinations.

The *New Mexico Law Review* states of the applicability of the PKPA:

> While the PKPA's definition of "state" does not include Indian tribes specifically, many state courts have interpreted the PKPA to be applicable to Indians. . . . Some federal circuit courts[61] have also determined that the PKPA's full faith and credit provisions applies to tribes because tribal court orders, under certain circumstances, are entitled to full faith and credit, and tribes are similar to states for the purpose of sovereignty and jurisdiction. . . . However, many states have determined that there is enough of a parallel between Indian tribes and foreign nations to satisfy this requirement of comity.[62]

It is possible, under the UCCJEA and PKPA, for an Indian tribe and a state court to both have jurisdiction over the same case.[63] This is the only exception to the "exclusive and continuing jurisdiction" clause possible under the UCCJEA.

---

61. Since *Thompson v. Thompson* (federal circuit courts no longer hear PKPA cases because *Thompson* held that the PKPA does not entitle a party to a federal cause of action).
62. Kelly Stoner & Richard A. Orona, *Full Faith and Credit, Comity, or Federal Mandate? A Path That Leads to Recognition and Enforcement of Tribal Court Orders, Tribal Protection Orders, and Tribal Child-Custody Orders*, N.M. L. REV. 382, 399 (Spring 2004).
63. Garcia v. Gutierrez, 147 N.M. 105, 121 (2009).

Section 105: International Application of [Act]

A state must treat a foreign country as if it were a state of the United States as long as that country's child-custody jurisdictional determination is in "substantial conformity of this act"[64] and that foreign country's child-custody laws do not violate fundamental principles of human rights.

To have its child-custody proceeding or determination recognized under the UCCJEA, a foreign court need not be in full compliance with the UCCJEA.[65] However, a court must consider at least some of the relevant factors under the UCCJEA in determining to exercise jurisdiction over a child-custody matter.

In determining whether to recognize a foreign country's child-custody proceeding or determination, a state court that has enacted the UCCJEA must take into consideration whether "the child custody law of a foreign country violates fundamental principles of human rights."[66] However, the court need only consider how those laws were applied to the particular foreign child-custody proceeding and, if it is a pre-decree matter, the state court need not extrapolate how the foreign court might rule in the future.[67]

Section 106: Effect of Child-Custody Determination

This section clarifies that everyone who was served under Section 108, Notice to Persons Outside the State, is bound by a state court's child-custody determination if that determination was made in compliance with the UCCJEA.

Section 106 applies even if all parties in the child-custody proceeding live in the same state and there is no foreign child-custody judgment.[68] However, it does not cover a situation when the court that enters the

64. UCCJEA § 105.
65. Bellew v. Larese, 288 Ga. 495, 499 (2011).
66. UCCJEA § 105 cmt. at 14.
67. *Toland*, 425 Md. 365, 390 (2012), *cert. denied*, 133 S. Ct. 265 (U.S. 2012).
68. Arthur v. Arthur, 54 So. 3d 454, 457 (Fla. 2010).

child-custody determination does not have jurisdiction to do so under the UCCJEA.

Section 107: Priority

Section 107 clarifies that "if a question of existence or exercise of jurisdiction under this [Act] is raised in a child-custody proceeding, the question, upon request of a party, must be given priority on the calendar and handled expeditiously."[69] This section is central to the UCCJEA in that, by prioritizing the determination of jurisdiction, it ensures that the parties will not have to waste time and resources unnecessarily litigating the same case in parallel states.

Section 108: Notice to Persons Outside the State

Section 108 raises constitutional questions in that, under *May v. Anderson*,[70] it does not conform with traditional understanding that personal jurisdiction is required to meet the constitutional due process requirement because, while it recognizes a state *may* give notice in a "manner prescribed by the law of this State for service of process or by the law of the State in which the service is made," it also allows for service by publication if other means are not effective. At least one state, New York, rewrote this section to address "the risk of contravening procedural due process standards by sanctioning [the UCCJEA's] ad hoc arrangement."[71]

In international cases, a person seeking to give proper notice should consult the Hague Convention on Service Abroad of Judicial and Extrajudicial

69. UCCJEA § 107.
70. 345 U.S. 528 (1953).
71. N.Y. DOM. REL. LAW § 75-g (McKinney). (Added L.2001, c. 386, § 1, eff. April 28, 2002. Amended L.2006, c. 184, § 1, eff. July 26, 2006.)

Documents in Civil or Commercial Matters,[72] because "countries have their own rules on service which must usually be followed."[73]

Section 109: Appearance and Limited Immunity

This section establishes that a party who participates in a child-custody proceeding will not automatically subject him- or herself to the court's jurisdiction where "personal jurisdiction over the individual is required."[74] This protection extends to presence required under Article 3, Enforcement. The purpose of this section is to prevent a party from having to choose between representing him- or herself in a child-custody proceeding and "protecting a right not to be subject to monetary judgment by a court with no other relationship to the party."[75]

This section is of particular importance for those situations where, since the entry of the judgment, the residential parent has moved to a new state and the nonresidential parent has moved to another state. In this situation, the state where the residential parent lives would have UCCJEA (child-custody) jurisdiction, and the state where the nonresidential parent lives would have UIFSA (child-support) jurisdiction. If it were not for this section, the residential parent could change UIFSA jurisdiction by initiating a child-custody proceeding in the child's home state and then serving the nonresidential parent when that parent appeared to represent him- or herself in the child-custody proceeding.[76]

Section 110: Communication Between Courts

Communication between the courts of different states is encouraged by the UCCJEA and "is required under Sections 204 [Temporary emergency

72. 20 U.S.T. 36, T.I.A.S. 6638 (1965).
73. UCCJEA § 108 cmt. at 16.
74. *Id.* § 109 cmt. at 17.
75. *Id.*
76. *Id.*

jurisdiction], 206 [Simultaneous proceedings], and 306 [Enforcement of registered determination] and strongly suggested in applying Section 207 [Inconvenient forum]."[77] However, the courts are not limited to only communicating under these sections. They may choose to communicate any time they deem it necessary.

Communication between the courts is important because, for example, the communication may alert

> the issuing state to a potential loss of exclusive continuing jurisdiction, based on residence, before the new state assumes jurisdiction to modify the issuing state's child-custody order. It also alerts the new state to any pending actions in the issuing state and helps to develop a factual record in the matter of jurisdiction.[78]

Although it is preferable for the parties to be present when the courts communicate, the UCCJEA drafters understood that matching both court's schedules with the litigants and their attorneys would sometimes be impossible. Thus, the drafters allowed for communication between the courts outside of the presence of the parties. To prevent any confusion or ex parte communication, the courts must maintain a record of their communications and "the parties must be informed promptly of the communication and granted access to the record."[79]

If a judge from one state attempts to communicate with the judge of a court of another state, that other state's judge may not disregard the communication attempt. The other state's judge is required to facilitate and participate in the communication.[80]

The UCCJEA does not provide for a penalty to a state court that refuses to communicate with another state court. However, as always, the appellate court may choose to publicly name the offending judge

77. *Id.* §109.
78. Brandt v. Brandt, 368 P.3d 406, 413 (Colo. 2012).
79. UCCJEA § 110 cmt. at 18.
80. *In re* Sophia G.L., 229 Ill. 2d 143, 172 (2008).

in the hopes of using the possibility of future public embarrassment as a deterrent.[81]

Section 111: Taking Testimony in Another State

A party to a child-custody proceeding may offer the testimony of a witness in another state through deposition in addition to any other means available in the state holding the hearing. The court may facilitate ordering "that the testimony of a person be taken in another state and . . . prescribe the manner in which and the terms upon which the testimony is taken."[82]

The court may also facilitate the presentation of evidence by allowing a witness who lives in another state to be deposed or testify by telephone, audiovisual means, or other electronic means before a designated court or at another location in that state.

The drafters of the UCCJEA seem to have been ahead of their time, since some states, such as Illinois, have only recently begun to allow litigants who are unable to attend court to testify through audiovisual means such as Skype or FaceTime. This, needless to say, may result in significant savings for the parties and on more relevant evidence being presented to the court.

Section 112: Cooperation Between the Courts; Preservation of Records

This section provides for the proper exchange between the courts for the acquisition of information necessary for a proper child-custody determination.

Under Section 112(a), a court proceeding under the UCCJEA may order a court of another state to

81. *Id.*
82. UCCJEA § 111.

1. hold an evidentiary hearing;
2. order a person to produce or give evidence pursuant to procedures of that State;
3. order that an evaluation be made with respect to the custody of a child involved in a pending proceeding;
4. forward to the court of this State a certified copy of the transcript of the record of the hearing, the evidence otherwise presented, and any evaluation prepared in compliance with the request; and
5. order a party to a child-custody proceeding or any person having physical custody of the child to appear in the proceeding with or without the child.[83]

A court of another state that is ordered to hold an evidentiary hearing under Section 112(a)(1) must comply with that order.[84]

The court with jurisdiction under Section 202, Exclusive, Continuing Jurisdiction, may also order that the parties pay for the "necessary and reasonable expenses" that were incurred for proceedings under this subsection against the parties as provided under state law.[85]

This section does address the possibility of assessing costs against the state when that state happens to be a party in the child-custody proceeding. However, local law may assess that issue.

Finally, the statute provides that the court shall preserve all the "pleadings, orders, decrees, records of hearings, evaluations, and other pertinent records with respect to a child-custody proceeding until the child attains 18 years of age."[86] Upon request, the court shall provide a copy of those records to a court or law enforcement official of another state.

83. *Id.* § 112.
84. *Id.* § 112(b).
85. *Id.* § 112(c).
86. *Id.* § 112(d).

Article 2

Jurisdiction

Subject-Matter Jurisdiction or Statutory Limitation?

The courts are split on whether Uniform Child Custody Jurisdiction and Enforcement Act (UCCJEA) and Parental Kidnapping Prevention Act (PKPA) jurisdiction is subject-matter jurisdiction or merely a statutory limitation. The drafters of the UCCJEA clarified what they meant by jurisdiction in Section 201, Initial Child-Custody Jurisdiction, when they noted that the parties could not waive UCCJEA jurisdiction because "jurisdiction to make a child custody determination is subject-matter jurisdiction" and therefore "an agreement of the parties to confer jurisdiction on a court that would not otherwise have jurisdiction under this Act is ineffective."[1] Some states have followed the UCCJEA drafters' lead and view UCCJEA jurisdiction as subject-matter jurisdiction. Other states view UCCJEA jurisdiction as merely placing a statutory limitation upon the court.

Knowing how a state interprets UCCJEA jurisdiction is important because if a state interprets it as subject-matter jurisdiction, litigants may not waive their rights under the UCCJEA and PKPA. Judgments from courts that do not have subject-matter jurisdiction are void.[2] Also, in this situation a state may allow a litigant to bring up the issue of UCCJEA jurisdiction for the

1. UCCJEA § 202 cmt. at 28.
2. Weller v. Weller, 960 P.2d 493, 496 (Wyo. 1998) ("Lack of subject matter jurisdiction constitutes a fundamental defect in a proceeding which cannot be cured by waiver or consent by the parties. Nor may it be cured by the passage of time.") (internal quotations and citations omitted).

first time on appeal and might even allow the trial or appellate court to raise the issue sua sponte.[3]

On the other hand, a child-custody court determination may be valid even if the court erroneously assumed jurisdiction over the proceeding in those states that believe that UCCJEA and PKPA jurisdiction is merely a limitation on a court's power.[4]

Section 201: Initial Child-Custody Jurisdiction

Section 201(a)(1) Home State Jurisdiction

Like the PKPA, the UCCJEA prioritizes home state jurisdiction over all other kinds of jurisdiction.[5] Home state jurisdiction continues for six months after a child has been removed from the home state as long as a parent or person acting as a parent remains in the home state.

When determining jurisdiction after a child has been removed, it does not matter "why a child has been removed"[6] or the child's best interests. The only inquiry relates to the status of the person left behind. The original state retains home state jurisdiction for six months after a child moves to another state if at the time the child moved, the child had been living for six months or more in the original state and a parent or person acting as a parent remains in that state. If a parent or person acting as a parent does not file for custody within six months of the child moving out of the original state, then that state loses its exclusive and continuing jurisdiction, and the new state may assume initial jurisdiction under this section.

---

3. SC v. State, Dep't of Family Servs., 2013 WY 2 (Wyo. 2013) ("We recognize two exceptions to [the rule that this Court normally does not address issues raised for the first time on appeal], however, and will consider the issue if it raises jurisdictional questions or if it is of such a fundamental nature that it must be considered. Because application of the UCCJEA is a jurisdictional question, we will address it.").

4. *In re* Adoption of Baby E.Z., 266 P.3d 702, 712 (Utah 2011) ("Unlike claims of subject-matter jurisdiction, full-faith-and-credit claims are subject to waiver if not raised in a timely fashion.").

5. UCCJEA § 201 cmt. at 24.

6. *Id.*

"Home State" Definition versus "Home State" Jurisdiction

There is a conflict between how "home state" is defined in Article 1, Section 102, Definitions, and its use in the jurisdiction-creating language of Section 201(1). When we insert Section 102's definition of home state into Section 201(1) we get:

> Except as otherwise provided in Section 204 [Emergency Jurisdiction] a court of this State has jurisdiction to make an initial child-custody determination only if:
>
> (1) this State is the [State in which a child lived with a parent or a person acting as a parent for at least six consecutive months immediately before the commencement of a child-custody proceeding] on the date of the commencement of the proceeding, or was the [State in which a child lived with a parent or a person acting as a parent for at least six consecutive months immediately before the commencement of a child-custody proceeding] within six months before the commencement of the proceeding and the child is absent from this State but a parent or person acting as a parent continues to live in this State.[7]

Under Section 102(7), for a state to qualify as home state, a child needs to have "lived with a parent or a person acting as a parent for at least six consecutive months *immediately* before the commencement of a child-custody proceeding."[8] However, under Section 201(1), a state qualifies for home state jurisdiction if the child has lived in the "home state *within* six months before the commencement of the proceeding."[9]

States that have addressed the home state definition/jurisdiction conundrum have found that the more expansive definition in Section 201 should be followed because either "Section 201(a)(1) modifies and enlarges the definition of home state"[10] or "to construe [home state] otherwise would

7. *Id.* § 201(1) using § 102(7)'s definition of "home state."
8. *Id.* § 102(7) (emphasis added).
9. *Id.* § 201(1) (emphasis added).
10. *In re* K.R., 229 W. Va. 733, 741 (2012) (citations omitted).

render the 'within six months' language in Section 201(a)(1) meaningless"[11] and would lead to absurd results. Also, Section 201's expansive definition "carries forward the clear intent of the UCCJEA that expressly incorporated the 'six-month extended home state provision'" from the UCCJA.[12]

Section 201(a)(2) Significant Connection Jurisdiction

If no state has home state jurisdiction under Section 201(1), a state may claim "significant connection jurisdiction" under Section 201(2). This section allows a "significant connection state" to "assume jurisdiction only when there is no home State or when the home state decides that the significant-connection state would be a more appropriate forum under Section 207 or 208."[13]

Some examples of what has been considered in determining whether a child has significant connection with a state has been whether (1) the father and his family reside in the state, (2) parenting time is exercised in the state, and (3) the child attends church and Bible school in the state.[14] Generally, "if the remaining parent continues to assert and exercise his visitation rights, then the parent-child relationship has not deteriorated sufficiently to terminate jurisdiction."[15]

Under this section a court must also consider if there is "substantial evidence" in the state. Substantial evidence is discussed more thoroughly in Section 202, Exclusive, Continuing Jurisdiction, later in this article.

Section 201(a)(3) More Appropriate Forum Jurisdiction

A state may also have jurisdiction over a case if all courts having home state or significant connection jurisdiction have declined to exercise jurisdiction because they believe that particular state is the more appropriate forum to hear the child-custody proceeding and issue the child-custody determination. This situation might arise when there are siblings living in different

11. *Id.*
12. *Ex parte* Siderius, 1120509, 2013 WL 6210834 (Ala. Nov. 27, 2013).
13. UCCJEA § 201 cmt. at 25.
14. *Thomas,* 370 Ark. 377, 388 (2007).
15. Watson v. Watson, 272 Neb. 647, 654 (2006) (quoting Graham v. Superior Court, 132 Cal. App. 4th 1193, 1198–99, 34 Cal. Rptr. 3d 270, 274 (2005)).

states and it is more appropriate for only one state to deal with the child-custody proceedings of all the children.

Section 201(a)(4) Default Jurisdiction

When no state qualifies under the previous initial jurisdictions, then a state may claim default jurisdiction. This situation occasionally occurs when a marriage dissolves abroad after a family has been living outside the United States for several years. In such a situation, sometimes the foreign country, for whatever reason, cannot hear child-custody proceedings. The only option available to the parties is to conduct the child-custody proceeding in a state with default jurisdiction.

Section 202: Exclusive, Continuing Jurisdiction and Section 203: Jurisdiction to Modify Termination

Under these sections a state with exclusive and continuing jurisdiction must decline jurisdiction when that state determines that neither the child nor the child and a parent have a significant connection with that state.[16]

Sections 202 and 203 complement each other in that they both clarify the process that a non-decree–granting court must go through to determine whether it has jurisdiction to modify a child-custody determination.

Under Section 202(a)(1), the original decree state maintains exclusive, continuing jurisdiction over a child-custody case if it had jurisdiction to begin the child-custody proceeding under Section 201, Initial Child-Custody Jurisdiction. This means that no other state may issue rulings related to the case unless it is to enforce the determination under Article 3, Enforcement, or in an emergency under Section 204, Temporary, Emergency Jurisdiction.

The party seeking to terminate a state's exclusive, continuing jurisdiction under Sections 202 or 203 has the burden of proof.[17] That parent

16. Watson v. Watson, 272 Neb. 647, 654 (2006); *but see* Devine v. Martens, 371 Ark. 60, 69 (2007).
17. *Brandt*, 268 P.3d 406, 408 (Colo. 2012).

"bears the burden of proving, not only that the new state would have jurisdiction to enter an initial child-custody order [under Section 201], but that the issuing state has lost or declined to exercise jurisdiction as well."[18]

Similarly, before determining that a decree-granting state has lost jurisdiction, a court must hold an evidentiary hearing and make a finding that the requirements under Section 202 and 203 have been met.[19]

No Significant Connection or Substantial Evidence

A state's exclusive, continuing jurisdiction terminates when that state determines that "the relationship between the child and the person remaining in the state with exclusive, continuing jurisdiction [is] so attenuated that the court [can] no longer find significant connections and substantial evidence."[20] This determination is reached if two requirements are met, "the child and at least one parent no longer have a significant connection with [the state] and that substantial evidence is no longer available in [the state] concerning the child's care, protection, training, and personal relationships."[21] In declining jurisdiction, it is not enough for the court with exclusive, continuing jurisdiction to find that there is no significant connection. The state must find that there is no significant connection *and* no substantial evidence within the state.[22] However, in retaining jurisdiction, the court need only establish that a significant connection remains and need not address the substantial evidence issue.[23]

18. *Id.* at 413.
19. *Id.* at 412–13 (Colo. 2012) ("[T]he UCCJEA specifically requires action by the state of potential modification before exclusive continuing jurisdiction in the issuing state ceases." The court held that "[a]n automatic loss of jurisdiction, without any factual determination, would add uncertainty, diminish oversight ability of the courts, and increase conflicts between the states.") (quotations and citations omitted).
20. UCCJEA § 202 cmt. at 27.
21. Benson v. Benson, 677 N.W.2d 582, 585–86 (N.D. 2003).
22. *Thomas*, 370 Ark at 383–84 ("Once it is determined that a significant connection remains, it is unnecessary under section . . . 202(a) to also determine whether there is substantial evidence available in this state.").
23. *Thomas*, 370 Ark. 377, 384 (2007) ("[O]nce it is determined that a significant connection remains, it is unnecessary under section . . . 202(a) to also determine whether there is substantial evidence available in this state.").

Substantial Evidence

The most important factor in determining whether evidence is substantial is determining how the evidence relates to the issue before the court (i.e., the child's "care, protection, training, and personal relationships"[24]). Thus, in a case dealing with the children's visitation with the noncustodial parent, evidence assisting the court in making the following determinations was deemed to be substantial:

1. Whether the children are exposed to illegal drug use in the parent's home
2. Whether a parent's mentally unstable sister (who has threatened the children) lives with the parent
3. Whether the parent has an extensive criminal history
4. Whether the parent has the means to hide the children and has done so in the past[25]

Only the state with exclusive, continuing jurisdiction may make the determination that it no longer has jurisdiction under Section 202(a)(1). Even if the child moves to a new state, the state with exclusive, continuing jurisdiction "may not be divested of exclusive continuing jurisdiction by another state unless no party presently resides in the issuing state."[26] This provision parallels the PKPA and neutralizes the perverse incentive a parent may have to take the child to another state to relitigate custody in the new state.

The Nebraska Supreme Court stated the same concept as follows:

> So long as one parent, or person acting as a parent, remains in the state that made the original custody determination, only that state can determine when the relationship between the child and the left-behind parent has deteriorated sufficiently so that jurisdiction is lost.[27]

24. UCCJEA § 201(a)(2)(B).
25. Steven v. Nicole, 308 P.3d 875, 880 (Alaska 2013).
26. *Brandt*, 268 P.3d 406, 412 (Colo. 2012).
27. *Watson*, 272 Neb. at 654 (citations and quotations omitted).

The only exception, of course, is under Section 204, Emergency Jurisdiction, where a state that does not have exclusive and continuing jurisdiction may exercise jurisdiction on a temporary, emergency basis.[28]

It depends on the circumstances whether a court must decline jurisdiction even if there is no pending proceeding elsewhere. The Montana Supreme Court, for example, reached two very different outcomes in two cases dealing with this issue. In the first case, the father registered the original child-custody determination in another state and the mother sought the declination of jurisdiction of the case in Montana so she could pursue the action in the new state. The Montana Supreme Court found that the original court abused its discretion when it did not decline jurisdiction despite knowing that all the parties had moved out ("the District Court was obligated to apply this statute, make such a determination and relinquish jurisdiction over this matter").[29]

In the second case, the parties had moved out of state, but the relevant entities in the new state made it clear that they would refuse jurisdiction over the case. In this case, the court ruled that "any obligation to relinquish jurisdiction to another court under the 'exclusive, continuing jurisdiction' provision of the UCCJEA requires a pending proceeding in the other state. The original state's court is not obligated to seek out a sister state's court and demand initiation of a proceeding."[30]

The state with original and exclusive, continuing jurisdiction or the new state, however, may terminate the original state's jurisdiction by finding that the "child, the child's parents, and any person acting as a parent do not presently reside in [the original] state."[31] However, the original state's jurisdiction may not be terminated if there is an ongoing proceeding.[32]

28. *In re* NC, 294 P.3d 866, 874 (Wyo. 2013).
29. *In re* B.P., 343 Mont. 345, 355 (2008).
30. *In re* A.R.B., 312 P.3d 425, 428 (Mont. 2013).
31. UCCJEA § 202(a)(2).
32. *Id.* § 202 cmt. at 28 ("Unless a modification proceeding has been commenced, when the child, the parents and all persons acting as parents physically leave the State to live elsewhere, the exclusive, continuing jurisdiction ceases.").

Definition of Reside

There is a split among the states on how to interpret "presently reside." As stated in *Brandt v. Brandt*, "some states take the view that a person resides only where physically present when a petition for assumption of modification jurisdiction is filed."[33] Other states have found that courts should do a totality of circumstances analysis in determining jurisdiction. Colorado, for example, outlined the factors to be included in this analysis:

1. The length and reasons for the parents' and the child's absence from the issuing state
2. Their intent in departing from the state and returning to it
3. Reserve and active military assignments affecting one or both parents
4. Where they maintain a home, car, driver's license, job, professional licensure, and voting registration
5. Where they pay taxes
6. The issuing state's determination of residency based on the facts and the issuing state's law
7. Any other circumstances demonstrated by evidence in the case[34]

The states are also split on whether a transfer due to a military assignment terminates or continues someone's residence. Some states consider it a temporary absence,[35] while others consider it a permanent absence.[36] The Nebraska Supreme Court stated as follows:

> The fact that [son] was in Japan because of [Father]'s military obligations is of no consequence. The UCCJEA does not specifically address the meaning of "temporary absence" as used in [Section 101]. But it is clear that time spent living in another state or country due to a permanent military duty assignment is not considered a "temporary absence" simply because it was motivated by such an assignment.[37]

33. *Brandt*, 268 P.3d at 414.
34. *Id.* at 408.
35. *Id.*
36. Carter v. Carter, 276 Neb. 840, 848 (2008).
37. *Id.*

A state court considering claiming jurisdiction must consider whether the original decree-granting state has lost jurisdiction under Section 202(1)(b) as well as the original state's laws in reaching the determination.[38]

Sections 202 and 203 are not the only situation in which a non-decree–granting state may assume custody over a child-custody matter in a nonemergency situation. A non-decree–granting court may also assume jurisdiction over a child-custody proceeding if the state with exclusive, continuing jurisdiction declines to exercise it under Section 207, Inconvenient Forum, and Section 208, Jurisdiction Declined by Reason of Conduct.

States are split on whether an original decree-granting state loses its exclusive and continuing child-custody jurisdiction once the temporary child-custody order ends with no further proceeding relating to the matter immediately established in the original state (such as when a temporary order of protection ends).

For example, the Alaska Supreme Court held that Alaska had child-custody jurisdiction even though another state had previously entered child-custody orders because "all three orders [entered by the original decree granting state] were no longer effective or enforceable"[39] at the time the new proceedings were begun in Alaska. Thus, there was no existing, ongoing child-custody determination, and it was proper for the Alaska trial court to assume jurisdiction. In this situation, Alaska would assume jurisdiction under Section 201 as if there had been no previous child-custody order entered in another state regarding the particular child.

However, other states have reached the opposite conclusion. The Washington Supreme Court, for example, has found that a decree-granting state keeps its exclusive, continuing jurisdiction even if it begins and then dismisses a parental termination case against a parent (thereby ending the state's temporary protective custody over the child) because the order met the definition of an initial child-custody determination by giving custody to the parent.[40]

38. Ronny M. v. Nanette H., 303 P.3d 302 (Alaska 2013).
39. *Id.* at 401.
40. *In re* Custody of A.C., 165 Wash. 2d 568, 575–76 (2009) ("The definitions of the UCCJEA are quite broad. The definition of 'child-custody determination' includes 'a judgment, decree, parenting plan, or other order of the court providing for the legal custody, physical custody, or visitation with respect to a child,' and includes even temporary orders. . . . The statutory

Section 204: Temporary Emergency Jurisdiction

Section 204 was drafted for those extreme circumstances where a state that is not the home state or the state with exclusive, continuing jurisdiction must step in to protect a child. The jurisdiction and orders entered under this section are supposed to be only temporary although, under very specific circumstances, the order may become final and the state may obtain exclusive continuing jurisdiction over the case.

Although this section is meant for emergency situations, the requirement of proper service is not waived, and a litigant seeking an order under this section must ensure that "there has been notice and a reasonable opportunity to be heard as set out in Section 205."[41] Similarly, despite the emergency nature of proceedings under this section, a party must comply with Section 209 by letting the emergency court know if another state may claim jurisdiction under Sections 201–203. If there is a court with exclusive, continuing jurisdiction, the party must also inform that court of the emergency proceeding in the new state.

In determining whether it has temporary emergency jurisdiction, after issuing the initial emergency custody determination, a court may hold a second, evidentiary hearing to determine if an emergency exists.[42]

Section 204(a) may be interpreted in different ways, due to its failure to properly use commas when using the words "and" and "or." On the one hand, some states have found there needs to be a child-related emergency for a state to properly exercise emergency jurisdiction under this section.[43] On the other hand, the Arkansas Supreme Court has found that the court has temporary emergency jurisdiction pursuant to Section 204 if the child

definition of modification is similarly broad and includes any child-custody determination that 'changes, replaces, supersedes, or is otherwise made after a previous determination concerning the same child.'").

41. UCCJEA § 204 cmt. at 34.

42. *In re* NC, 294 P.3d at 877.

43. *Id.* at 874 ("[A state with exclusive continuing jurisdiction has jurisdiction unless] the child is present in another state *and* it is necessary for the other state to exercise emergency jurisdiction for the child's protection.").

is present in the non-decree–granting state and has been abandoned, even if there is no immediate danger to the child.[44]

While "abandoned" has been defined in Section 102 of the UCCJEA ("left without provision for reasonable and necessary care or supervision"), the UCCJEA has failed to define "abuse" or "mistreatment." When determining the meaning of these words, states should use their own laws.[45]

Another issue left unaddressed by the UCCJEA is how serious the threat to the child must be to qualify as an emergency. Courts have found that to obtain jurisdiction under this section, the threat must be immediate. For example, a parent may not attempt to gain jurisdiction under this section by claiming that the "selection of an alternate therapist" for the child is an emergency.[46] Similarly, a parent's "allegations that the child feared returning to Nigeria because of ongoing violence there" is not enough to qualify for UCCJEA emergency jurisdiction.[47]

At the initial emergency hearing, the court may assume jurisdiction based upon a party's allegation.[48] However, a court should hold a follow-up evidentiary hearing where the parties may present evidence to support their positions.[49]

Once a state court determines that it has emergency jurisdiction, it may still only issue orders relating to the immediate well-being of the child. The orders should have a termination date if there is a state with exclusive, continuing jurisdiction under Section 202.[50] However, "if a child custody proceeding has not been or is not commenced in a court of a state having jurisdiction under sections 201–203, a child custody determination made

44. Devine v. Martens, 371 Ark. 60, 68 (2007) ("[A] court has temporary emergency jurisdiction [pursuant to Section 204, Emergency jurisdiction] if the child is present in [State b] and has been abandoned or an emergency exists to protect the child because the child is subjected to or threatened with mistreatment or abuse.").

45. *In re* NC, 294 P.3d at 875 ("The UCCJEA does not define the terms mistreatment or abuse. Other states have observed that a court exercising emergency jurisdiction is acting in its capacity as parents patriae to protect a child within that state's borders. We agree with this observation, and in this capacity, we believe it makes the most sense to apply [State law] in determining what constitutes abuse for the purpose of determining emergency jurisdiction under the UCCJEA.").

46. Button v. Waite, 208 S.W.3d 366, 369–70 (Tenn. 2006).

47. Jackson v. Sanomi, 202 Ga. 888, 890 (2013).

48. *In re* NC, 294 P.3d at 875.

49. *Id.* at 876–77.

50. UCCJEA § 204(c).

under this section becomes a final determination" if the emergency state becomes the home state of the child.[51] Thus, unlike with Section 201, Initial Child-Custody Jurisdiction, where a state gains home state jurisdiction if it was the child's home state at the time of the filing of the proceeding, under this section a state may gain jurisdiction even if it was not the child's home state at the filing of the emergency motion.

Some orders are outside the scope covered under this section. They include orders

1. administering the parties' property;
2. awarding child support payments;
3. requiring that a parent attend "battering intervention and prevention programs";
4. making format adjudications of abuse or neglect;
5. requiring paternity (DNA) tests; and
6. subjecting the parties to evaluations, counseling, or psychological services.[52]

Corrections

The UCCJEA was promulgated in 1997, and since then the Violence Against Women Act has been edited. The drafters' comments state that "although the Violence Against Women Act (VAWA), does provide an independent basis for the granting of full faith and credit to protective orders, it expressly excludes 'custody' orders from the definition of protective orders."[53]

However, the current VAWA defines "protection order" as follows:

> Any support, child custody or visitation provisions, orders, remedies or relief issued as part of a protection order, restraining order, or injunction pursuant to State, tribal, territorial, or local law authorizing the issuance of protection orders, restraining orders, or intentions for the protection of victims of domestic violence, sexual assault, dating violence, or stalking.[54]

51. *Id.* § 204(b).
52. *In re* NC, 294 P.3d 866.
53. UCCJEA § 204 cmt at 34.
54. VAWA, 18 U.S.C.A. § 2266(B).

Thus, protection orders are covered under the both the UCCJEA and VAWA.

The drafters of the UCCJEA envisioned that once an emergency order is entered in a new state, the state with exclusive continuing jurisdiction would hold its own hearing to address the emergency and issue an order on the matter. Presumably, in many of these cases there would be an element of danger in the litigants returning to the home state. To address this issue, the drafters clarify that "any hearing in the state with jurisdiction under Section 201–203 on the temporary emergency determination is subject to the provisions of Section 111 and 112 . . . [that] facilitate the presentation of testimony and evidence taken out of state."[55]

Finally, the court of the emergency state and the court with continuing exclusive jurisdiction have a duty to communicate with each other immediately upon learning that the other court is exercising concurrent jurisdiction. The purpose of the communication is to "resolve the emergency, protect the safety of the parties and the child, and determine a method for the duration of the temporary order."[56]

Section 205: Notice; Opportunity to Be Heard; Joinder

This section does not limit who is entitled to notice in a child-custody proceeding. Rather, this section ensures that, apart from any other person who may be entitled to notice under state law, "any parent whose parental rights have not been previously terminated, and any person having physical custody of the child"[57] will receive notice of a UCCJEA proceeding.

If proper notice is not given pursuant to this section, then a child-custody order even if entered by a state with exclusive continuing jurisdiction is not enforceable under the UCCJEA.[58] The PKPA has a nearly identical section that only allows for a custody determination to be entitled to full faith and credit if there has been "reasonable notice and an opportunity to be heard."[59]

55. UCCJEA § 204 cmt.. at 33.
56. *Steven*, 308 P.3d 875, 883 (Alaska 2013).
57. UCCJEA § 205(a).
58. *Id.* § 205(b).
59. PKPA § 1738(e).

A person is not entitled to notice merely by sharing the same roof with a child. There must be evidence that the person is responsible for the "physical care and supervision of [the] child."[60] It follows then that a biological father is not entitled to notice merely by living with a child. To be entitled to notice, the assumed father must go through the legal process of establishing parentage or at least meet the statutory requirements to be legally considered a "presumed father." As the Illinois Supreme Court stated,

> We will not construe the UCCJEA to require [a new state] court to recognize any judgment that would effectively deprive the father, who has previously established paternity, of his parental rights without notice or hearing. To do so would violate the explicit language of the UCCJEA, which states: "[t]his Act does not govern the enforceability of a child custody determination made without notice or an opportunity to be heard."[61]

Thus, if a father establishes parentage in the middle of a child-custody proceeding, he is entitled to notice on any additional proceedings related to the child.[62]

Section 206: Simultaneous Proceedings

Although the UCCJEA was drafted specifically with the intent of preventing simultaneous proceedings, the drafters acknowledged that there would be situations in which two states might be in a position to exercise parallel jurisdiction.

At the time the UCCJEA was promulgated, the drafters felt that there was really only one situation where the two simultaneous proceedings might arise: "when there is no home state, no state with exclusive, continuing jurisdiction and more than one significant connection state."[63] Unfortu-

60. *In re* Sophia G.L., 229 Ill. 2d 143, 167 (2008).
61. *Id.* at 171.
62. *Id.* at 169.
63. UCCJEA § 206 cmt. at 37.

nately, the issue of conflicting jurisdiction arises much more often than the drafters expected because they were overly optimistic in their expectation that states would uniformly interpret Sections 201 and 202.

According to Section 206, a court may not exercise jurisdiction in a child-custody case if another state with jurisdiction under Section 202 has already begun a child-custody proceeding and there is no emergency under Section 204. The only exception to this rule is when a proceeding was begun in the other state but that proceeding has been terminated or that court has decided to decline jurisdiction under Section 207 because this state is a more convenient forum.

This section, however, not only deals with concurrent jurisdiction. It also aims to prevent states from inadvertently assuming jurisdiction when there is another child-custody proceeding in another state. This section requires a court to attempt to determine whether another proceeding has previously begun in another state before beginning its own child-custody proceeding. If a nonenforcement child-custody proceeding has indeed begun, the court shall stay proceedings and communicate with the court of the other state.

If the proceeding is to modify a child-custody determination and the court determines that an enforcement proceeding has already begun in a different state, the court seeking to modify that termination may

> (1) stay a proceeding for modification pending the entry of an order of the court of the other state enforcing, staying, denying, or dismissing the preceding for enforcement; (2) enjoin the parties from continuing with a proceeding for enforcement; or (3) proceed with the modification under conditions it considers appropriate.[64]

It is not mandatory that the new court communicate with the enforcement court.[65] The opposite is true, however, under Section 306, where the enforcement court must communicate with the modification court "in order to determine what action the modification court wishes the enforcement court to take."[66]

64. *Id.* § 206(c)(1)–(3).
65. *Id.* § 206 cmt. at 37–38 ("However, communication is not mandatory.").
66. *Id.* § 206 cmt. at 3.

Occasionally, a state will erroneously assert jurisdiction and begin a child-custody proceeding when it does not have jurisdiction. Most states have found that the proper way of dealing with this is to correct the mistake by either not enforcing the decree resulting from the erroneous assumption of jurisdiction or, if the case is pre-decree, transferring the case to the correct state.

The Colorado Supreme Court, for example, found that it was not bound in any way by a child-custody determination by Nebraska when that determination was made without Nebraska having UCCJEA jurisdiction. They reasoned that because Nebraska failed to exercise jurisdiction in accordance with the requirements of the PKPA, the PKPA does not require Colorado to give full faith and credit to the Nebraska custody determination.[67]

Like the Colorado Supreme Court, the Texas Supreme Court dealt with a case where Texas court improperly assumed jurisdiction and the New Mexico trial court erroneously ceded jurisdiction to Texas.[68] The Texas Supreme Court determined that the Texas and New Mexico courts should communicate with each other to determine if New Mexico should decline jurisdiction pursuant to Sections 207 or 208.[69]

The Texas case was of particular interest because the Texas Supreme Court opined that under Section 206(b), the Texas court was bound to communicate with the court that was dealing with the New Mexico case, which was then New Mexico Court of Appeals.[70]

The Georgia Supreme Court made a similar determination to the Colorado and Texas courts when it found that "the trial court [that] had jurisdiction to determine questions of child custody . . . was not required under the UCCJEA to stay its proceedings in favor of any proceedings in [the state with no UCCJEA jurisdiction]."[71]

One state, Wyoming, reached a different outcome from the cases just described. Wyoming found that, given certain circumstances, it could assume jurisdiction over a case if no other child-custody proceeding had been filed

67. *In re* L.S., 257 P.3d 201, 202 (Colo. 2011).
68. *In re* Dean, 393 S.W.3d 741 (Tex. 2012), *reh'g denied* (Jan. 18, 2013).
69. *Id.* at 744.
70. *Id.* at 750.
71. Black v. Black, 292 Ga. 291, 294 (2013).

in a state with UCCJEA jurisdiction. The facts of the case give rise to the inference that there might have been an argument that the children had no home state at the time that the Wyoming trial court assumed jurisdiction. However, this was not addressed by the Wyoming Supreme Court.[72]

Section 207: Inconvenient Forum

This section is for the unusual scenario where the state with exclusive, continuing jurisdiction is not the best state to hear a child-custody case. In this situation, the state with exclusive, continuing jurisdiction may decline to exercise jurisdiction.

This section is particularly useful for those situations where different states have jurisdiction under Section 201 over different siblings. Rather than argue the same issues in different states, it makes sense for only one state to hear the child-custody proceeding over all the related siblings.

The list of factors under this section that a court must consider in making the determination to decline jurisdiction are

1. whether domestic violence has occurred and is likely to continue in the future and which state could best protect the parties and the child;
2. the length of time the child has resided outside of State A;
3. the distance between the court of this state and the court of the state that would assume jurisdiction;
4. the relative financial circumstances of the parties;
5. any agreement of the parties as to what state should assume jurisdiction;
6. the nature and location of the evidence required to resolve the pending litigation, including testimony of the child;
7. the ability of the court of the state to decide the issue expeditiously and the procedures necessary to protect the evidence; and
8. the familiarity of the court of each state with the facts and issues in the pending litigation.[73]

72. Harignordoquy v. Barlow, 313 P.3d 1265, 1268 (Wyo. 2013).
73. UCCJEA § 207.

While the drafters of the UCCJEA were clear that the list of factors to be considered was "not meant to be exclusive,"[74] the courts have not been generous in allowing a court to expand upon these factors. For example, courts may not take into consideration

1. the state in which it would be more affordable to litigate the child-custody case;[75]
2. whether a new state has exercised jurisdiction over the case when another state's assumption of jurisdiction seems to be in violation of the UCCJEA;[76] or
3. whether it would be in the child's best interest to litigate in one state versus another state.[77]

It is up to the court with exclusive, continuing jurisdiction how to weigh the factors. So, in a case where there was more evidence in the state with exclusive, continuing jurisdiction but the credibility of that evidence was less likely to be questioned than the credibility of the evidence in another state ("the credibility of witnesses such as doctors is less likely to be questioned in the same way that the credibility of relatives [which live in State B] is, potentially making personal observation of relatives and other lay witnesses more important in assessing credibility"), a court may give more weight to Section 207(b)(6) ("nature and location of the evidence required to resolve the pending litigation, including testimony of the child") than to the other factors.[78]

In reaching its determination, the court with exclusive, continuing jurisdiction must take into consideration the whole child-custody proceeding and not just the particular issue currently pending before the court.[79] For example, a court may not decline jurisdiction merely because all evidence

74. *Id.* § 207.
75. Mikesell v. Waterman, 197 P.3d 184, 192 (Alaska 2008).
76. *Watson*, 272 Neb. at 658.
77. *In re* Marriage of Fontenot, 335 Mont. 79, 81–82 (2006).
78. *Mikesell*, 197 P.3d 184.
79. *Id.* ("However, in declining jurisdiction under this section, a court must take into consideration that the declination is permanent and that child-custody issues and, therefore, evidence necessary, may change as the case progresses.").

necessary for the particular issue before the court (such as whether a non-residential parent is an alcoholic) is present in the other state.[80]

A court must at least make it clear on the order that declines jurisdiction for inconvenient forum that it declined jurisdiction under Section 207 and list the factors it took into consideration. It should avoid vague findings that make it impossible for a reviewing court to know exactly under which section the court declined jurisdiction and how the court reached its decision.[81]

The order-declining jurisdiction should be reviewed closely by the court seeking to assume jurisdiction. This is because under Section 203, a new court may only assume jurisdiction under Section 207 if the court with exclusive, continuing jurisdiction determines that "a court of [the other state] would be a more convenient forum under Section 207."[82] Thus, if a new state assumes jurisdiction without the original state explicitly declining jurisdiction under Section 207, then the new state does not have jurisdiction under its own laws over the child-custody case. This, in turn, creates an interstate enforceability problem for any child-custody determination entered by the new state because under both the PKPA and the UCCJEA, full faith and credit may only be given to child-custody determinations when those orders were entered by a state having child-custody jurisdiction under its own laws.

The same problem was described by the Colorado Supreme Court in *In re the Parental Responsibilities of L.S.*:

80. *Castro*, 181 N.W.2d 753, 759 (N.D. 2012). Compare *Castro*'s interpretation of Section 207 with *Steven*'s (308 P.3d at 884) interpretation of Section 202. Both cases dealt with evidence related to the noncustodial parent who lived in State B. In *Castro*, the court abused its discretion by declining jurisdiction. In *Steven*, the court did not abuse its discretion by retaining jurisdiction under Section 202.

81. *Benson*, 667 N.W.2d 582, 585 (N.D. 2003) ("The district court concluded 'the State of Texas would have jurisdiction in this case.' In light of this statement and after reviewing the record, we are unable to determine whether the court concluded it had exclusive, continuing jurisdiction but declined to exercise jurisdiction . . . , whether the court concluded [State A] did not have jurisdiction, or whether it determined [State B] would be the more appropriate forum."); *Steven*, 308 P3d at 884 ("Without a sufficiently thorough discussion of the superior court's reasoning, it is difficult to determine whether the court abused its discretion, that is, to determine whether it considered the statutory factors, or what interpretation it placed on the facts.").

82. UCCJEA § 203(1).

> Because we determine that the Nebraska district court did not have jurisdiction over this custody determination under its own law—as it was not the child's home state, and the home state did not decline jurisdiction—we therefore conclude that the PKPA does not obligate Colorado to accord the Nebraska determination full faith and credit.[83]

The UCCJEA is clear that a new state may not claim UCCJEA jurisdiction merely by declaring the state with exclusive, continuing jurisdiction to be an inconvenient forum.[84] This issue has repeatedly been dealt with by various states that have reached the same conclusion ("only the state that originally entered the custody order may decide that another forum would be more convenient."[85]).

Finally, declining jurisdiction is an option, not a duty. Even if the list of factors under Section 207(b) shows that it would be more appropriate for the court of another state to exercise jurisdiction, the state with exclusive, continuing jurisdiction may still choose to keep the case and not decline jurisdiction.[86]

Section 208: Jurisdiction Declined by Reason of Conduct

This section is intended to cripple a parent's attempt at forum shopping when that parent's unjustifiable conduct results in a state having UCCJEA jurisdiction over a child-custody proceeding. This section does not affect jurisdiction in those situations where a state already had jurisdiction under Sections 201, 202, or 203 before the parent engaged in unjustifiable conduct.

---

83. 257 P.3d 201, 207 (Colo. 2011).
84. *See* UCCJEA §§ 202, 203, and 207.
85. *Brandt*, 268 P.3d 406, 414 (Colo. 2012). *See also* Rosen v. Celebrezze, 117 Ohio St. 3d 241 (2008); Rosen v. Rosen, 222 W. Va. 402 (2008); Powell v. Stover, 165 S.W.3d 322 (Tex. 2005); and *Watson*, 272 Neb. 647.
86. Rosen v. Rosen, 644 S.E.2d 743, 750 (2008) (Section 207 "gives the court possession jurisdiction permissive discretion to determine whether or not it wishes to decline to exercise jurisdiction if it determines that it is an inconvenient forum under the circumstances and the court of another state is a more appropriate forum. An elementary principle of statutory construction is that the word 'may' is inherently permissive in nature and connotes discretion."). *See also Steven*, 308 P.3d at 884.

Unjustifiable conduct is not defined in this section but is to be interpreted in context. Examples of unjustifiable conduct include "removing, secreting, retaining, or restraining the child."[87] "Technically illegal" behavior does not rise to the level of unjustifiable conduct.[88] For example, temporarily violating a visitation order to prevent physical harm to the child or a parent is not unjustifiable conduct.

Unlike Section 207, where a state may *choose* to decline jurisdiction, declining jurisdiction under Section 208 is not optional. A state with exclusive, continuing jurisdiction *must* decline jurisdiction if the jurisdiction was obtained as a result of a parent's unjustifiable conduct, unless

1. the parents and all persons acting as parents have acquiesced in the exercise of jurisdiction;[89]
2. a court with UCCJEA jurisdiction declines jurisdiction because the state that obtained jurisdiction through unjustifiable conduct is a more appropriate forum;[90] or
3. *no court of any other state would have jurisdiction* under the criteria specified in Sections 201, 202, and 203.[91]

The drafters of the UCCJEA intended for this section to be rarely used since under Section 201 a state retains initial child-custody jurisdiction for six months after the child has moved out of state, and six months should give the left-behind parent enough time to begin proceedings in the home state. The drafters also reasoned that, in a scenario where the left-behind parent obtains home-state jurisdiction, Sections 202 and 203 prevent another state from exerting or usurping the original state's jurisdiction over the child-custody proceeding. Thus, there would be few possibilities (apart from the left-behind parent missing the deadline to file for home state jurisdiction) where this section would apply.

87. UCCJEA § 208 cmt. at 42.
88. *Id.* at 43.
89. *Id.* § 208(1), (2), and (3).
90. *Id.* § 208(2).
91. *Id.* § 208(3).

The drafters' comments mention two ways in which a parent may acquiescence to the jurisdiction of the court that obtained jurisdiction through unjustifiable conduct:

1. By filing a pleading submitting the jurisdiction; and
2. By not filing in the court that would otherwise have jurisdiction under this act.[92]

It would have been advisable for the drafters to offer more detailed examples, since these particular examples are open to interpretation for those who would not read them in the proper context. For example, a pleading that submits a party to the "jurisdiction of the court" should be for the explicit purpose of clarifying that the parent will not be asking the court to decline jurisdiction under Section 208. A pleading arguing for or against a child-custody determination should not be interpreted as waiving the jurisdictional argument, since a parent should never be put in the position of choosing whether to argue for declining of jurisdiction under this section or risk being defaulted in the child-custody proceeding.

Similarly, a parent should not automatically loose his or her right to argue for declination of jurisdiction under this section merely because the parent did not file "in the court that would otherwise have jurisdiction under [Section 208]."[93] Interpreting waiver in such a way would defeat the purpose of Section 208(b), which grants the court that gained jurisdiction through unjustifiable conduct the option of fashioning "an appropriate remedy . . . including staying the proceeding until a child-custody proceeding is commenced in a court having jurisdiction under Sections 201 through 203."[94]

Thus, a parent should only lose jurisdiction for failing to file "in the court that would otherwise have jurisdiction under this act" if

1. the parent extensively participates in a child-custody proceeding and later asks for a Section 208 ruling in an attempt to move the child-custody proceeding to a more favorable forum; or

92. *Id.* § 208 cmt. at 42.
93. *Id.* § 208 cmt. at 42.
94. *Id.* § 208(b).

2. a court makes a finding of unjustifiable conduct under this section and dismisses the petition or stays proceedings, and the wronged parent does not follow through by filing for child-custody determination in the proper state.

Under Section 208, the court must hold two hearings.[95] The first one is to determine whether it has jurisdiction under Section 201. If the court does have jurisdiction under Section 201, then the court must hold a second hearing to determine whether the accused party's unjustifiable conduct resulted in the court having jurisdiction over the child-custody proceeding. If the court finds that the party engaged in unjustifiable conduct, then the court must decline jurisdiction.

Once a court has declined jurisdiction under this section, it must assess reasonable attorney's fees and expenses in favor of the wronged party and against the party who engaged in unjustifiable conduct.[96]

Section 209: Information to Be Submitted to Court

Section 209 outlines the information that each party in the child-custody proceeding must comply with to assist the court in determining whether it has jurisdiction under the UCCJEA to hear a child-custody proceeding. Many courts have template forms to assist the parties.

Each party to the child-custody proceeding must file a pleading or affidavit stating whether the party

1. has participated, as a party or witness or in any other capacity, in any other proceeding concerning the custody of or visitation with the child and, if so, identify the court, the case number, and the date of the child-custody determination, if any;

95. R.M. v. J.S., 20 A.3d 496, 509 (Pa. Super. Ct. 2011).
96. UCCJEA § 208 cmt. at 42 ("The attorney's fees standard for this section is patterned after the International Child Abduction Remedies Act, 42 U.S.C. § 11607(b)(3). The assessed costs and fees are to be paid to the respondent who established that jurisdiction was based on unjustifiable conduct.").

2. knows of any proceeding that could affect the current proceeding, including proceedings for enforcement and proceedings relating to domestic violence, protective orders, termination of parental rights, and adoptions and, if so, identify the court, the case number, and the nature of the proceeding; and
3. knows the names and addresses of any person not a party to the proceeding with physical custody of the child or claims rights of legal custody or physical custody of, or visitation with, the child and, if so, the names and addresses of those persons.[97]

The term "proceeding" is not limited to child-custody proceedings. It encompasses any proceeding related to the child that might affect the court's assumption or declination of jurisdiction or the child-custody proceeding. For example, both parties would be obligated to inform the court of a parent's criminal prosecution "for child abuse or custodial interference."[98] The parties have a continuing obligation to notify the court of any additional proceedings in the state or in another state that may affect the child-custody proceeding before the court.[99]

Most states have enacted Section 209(e), which provides that if a party "alleges in an affidavit or pleading under oath that the health, safety, or liberty of a party or child would be jeopardized by disclosure of identifying information, the information must be sealed and may not be disclosed to the other party."[100] There is no need for the court to hold a hearing on whether the information should be sealed. The only requirement is that the party allege the requisite information in an affidavit or pleading. However, the court is required to hold a hearing if a party seeking access to the information requests it. In deciding to disclose the information, the court must find that "disclosure is in the interest of justice" after taking into consideration "the health, safety, or liberty of the party or child."[101]

97. *Id.* § 209(a)(1)–(3).
98. *Id.* § 209 cmt. at 45.
99. *Id.* § 209(d).
100. *Id.* § 209(e).
101. *Id.* § 209(e).

Although this section makes it clear that the parties must apprise the court of any legal proceedings and information that might affect the court's jurisdiction or determination, the court does not loose subject-matter jurisdiction over a case if the parties fail to comply with this section.[102] However, the court may use its power to "stay the proceedings until the information is furnished"[103] and, if necessary, request that the parties provide additional information about any proceeding they may have disclosed to the court.

Section 210: Appearance of Parties and Child

This section provides that "in a child-custody proceeding . . . the court may order a *party to the proceeding who is in this state* to appear before the court in person with or without the child."[104] Similarly, the court may order a person "who is in this state and who has physical custody or control of the child to appear in person with the child."[105]

There is also a provision for when the party or the party and the child are outside of this state. If the court wants that party to appear with or without the child, the court must give "notice pursuant to Section 108 include a statement directing the party to appear in person with or without the child and informing the party that a failure to appear may result in a decision adverse to the party."[106]

There is no provision for a court to order an out-of-state person who is not part of a proceeding but has physical custody or control of the child to bring the child to the court.

If a court orders a party who is outside of the state to appear in court with or without the child, the court may order that "another party . . . pay

102. Brush v. Davis, 315 P.3d 648, 653 (Wyo. 2013) ("Although the requirement is mandatory, the statute does not indicate it is jurisdictional. To the contrary, § 20–5–309(b) states that the court **may stay** the proceeding until the information is furnished, but it is not required to do so. The statute certainly does not say that the district court does not have jurisdiction over the matter if the requisite statement is omitted. The district court had subject matter jurisdiction over Father's petition.") *See also In re* A.R.G., 361 N.C. 392, 399 (2007).

103. UCCJEA § 209(b).

104. *Id.* § 210(a).

105. *Id.* § 210(a) (emphasis added).

106. *Id.* § 210(b).

reasonable and necessary travel and other expenses of the party"[107] that was ordered to appear.

While there are no published appellate cases dealing with this section of the UCCJEA, there is one appellate case dealing with the parallel section of the old UCCJA. In that case, *Perez v. Perez*,[108] the Connecticut court issued a decision adverse to the grandparents, who were parties to the case and had physical control of the child, because the grandparents violated a court order by failing to appear in court with the child. The grandparents claimed that they could not appear because Puerto Rico, who was exercising parallel jurisdiction over the case, had ordered that the child not leave Puerto Rico. The Connecticut court found the argument unpersuasive because the Puerto Rico order had been entered after the Connecticut court ordered that the grandparents appear with the child.

This provision only applies once child-custody jurisdiction has been established. Thus, this section of the UCCJEA does not grant a court the authority to order a party to bring a child to a UCCJEA jurisdictional hearing.

107. *Id.* § 210(d).
108. 212 Conn. 63 (1989).

Article 3

Enforcement

Section 301: Definitions

Section 301 of the Uniform Child Custody Jurisdiction and Enforcement Act (UCCJEA) is necessary to clarify the meaning of "petitioner" and "respondent" in the notice and hearing sections of Article 3, Enforcement.

A petitioner is a person who seeks to enforce a child-custody determination or, if it is an international case, "a person who seeks an enforcement of an order for the return of a child under the Hague Convention on the Civil Aspects of International Child-Abduction."[1] A respondent is a person against whom the enforcement proceeding is begun.

Section 302: Enforcement under Hague Convention

This section authorizes a court to "enforce an order for the return of the child made under the Hague Convention on the Civil Aspects of International Child-Abduction as if it were a child-custody determination"[2] if the enforcing court has a duty to enforce under Section 303, Duty to Enforce.

1. UCCJEA § 301(a).
2. *Id.* § 302.

Section 303: Duty to Enforce

This section requires that every state grant full faith and credit to a child-custody determination issued by another state[3] but only if the state that issued the determination exercised jurisdiction in substantial conformity with its own laws[4] and the UCCJEA or "the determination was made under factual circumstances meeting the jurisdictional standards of this [Act] and the determination has not been modified in accordance with this Act."[5]

The enforcing state may use any means of enforcement that it would use if it were enforcing a determination issued in the enforcing state. This means that the state is not limited by the remedies available under Article 3, and the state may also use any other local law to enforce the foreign child-custody decree.

Section 304: Temporary Visitation

In exercising its duty to enforce a foreign child-custody order, an enforcing court may issue a temporary order whose purpose is to enforce

1. a visitation schedule made by a court of another state; or
2. the visitation provisions of a child-custody determination of another state that does not provide for a specific visitation schedule.[6]

If the enforcing court exercises the second option, then as with Section 204, the court should "specify in the order a period that it considers adequate to allow the petitioner to obtain an order from a court" that has jurisdiction under Section 202.[7] The order entered by the enforcing court expires upon the first of (1) the court with jurisdiction under Section 202 issues a

3. *In re* Marriage of Lloyd, 361 Mont. 22, 28 (2011).
4. 28 U.S.C.A. § 1738A(c)(1) (PKPA).
5. UCCJEA § 303(a).
6. *Id.* § 304(a).
7. *Id.* § 304(b).

visitation schedule order, or (2) the expiration date on the visitation order entered by the enforcing state.[8]

Section 305: Registration of Child-Custody Determination

When dealing with the registration of a child-custody determination, this section takes precedence over any general state laws regarding the enforcement of foreign judgments.[9] Also, confirmation of a registered order only means that the court may give full faith and credit to the foreign decree. It is not a determination that the court has jurisdiction under Article 2 to make or modify a child-custody determination.[10]

For a custody determination to be entitled to recognition by a foreign court under the UCCJEA, it must be registered in the appropriate court of the foreign state. The appropriate court varies from state to state and may sometimes even vary from county to county within a state.[11]

A person may register the determination even if he or she is not immediately seeking to modify it under Section 203 or enforce it under Article 3. This is in compliance with Article 26 of the 1996 Hague Convention on Jurisdiction, Applicable Law, Recognition and Cooperation in Respect of Parental Responsibility and Measures for the Protection of Children, which "requires those States which accede to the Convention to provide such a procedure."[12] In practice this means that a "custodial parent under a foreign custody order can receive an advance determination of whether that order would be recognized and enforced before sending the child to the United States for visitation."[13]

This section specifies

8. *Id.* § 304(b).
9. Kostrzewski v. Frisinger, 680 N.W.2d 271, 273 (N.D. 2004) ("A specific statute governs over a more general statute as a general rule of statutory construction.").
10. *Id.* at 274.
11. UCCJEA § 305, Alabama statutory comments.
12. *Id.* § 305 cmt. at 54.
13. *Id.*

1. the registration procedure that a party must follow to register the foreign judgment;
2. the registering court's procedure once it receives the documents; and
3. the steps that a party must take when seeking to contest the validity of a registered determination.

The person seeking to register the foreign judgment must send to the enforcing state

1. a letter or other document requesting registration of the child-custody determination;
2. two copies, including one certified copy, of the determination sought to be registered, and a statement under penalty of perjury that to the best of the knowledge and belief of the person seeking registration the order has not been modified; and
3. except as otherwise provided in Section 209, the name and address of the person seeking registration and any parent or person acting as a parent who has been awarded custody or visitation in the child-custody determination sought to be registered.[14]

Once the registering court receives these documents, the court shall

1. file as a foreign judgment the child-custody determination, together with one copy of any accompanying documents and information, regardless of their form; and
2. serve notice (pursuant to Section 309) upon the persons named in the letter or document registering the judgment and provide the recipient an opportunity to contest the registration in accordance with Section 305.

The registering court's notice must state that

14. *Id.* § 305(a).

1. a registered determination is enforceable as of the date of the registration in the same manner as a determination issued by a court of that state;
2. a hearing to contest the validity of the registered determination must be requested within 20 days after service of notice; and
3. failure to contest the registration will result in confirmation of the child-custody determination and preclude further contest of that determination with respect to any matter that could have been asserted.

A party may only make the following arguments when contesting the validity registration:

1. the issuing court did not have jurisdiction under [Article] 2;
2. the child-custody determination sought to be registered has been vacated, stayed, or modified by a court having jurisdiction to do so under [Article] 2; or
3. the person contesting registration was entitled to notice, but notice was not given in accordance with the standards of Section 108, Notice to Persons Outside the State, in the proceedings before the court that issued the order for which registration is sought.[15]

Within reason, people may waive their right to argue that they did not receive notice in accordance with the standards of Section 108. Notice in compliance with Section 108 is not necessary if the litigant had "actual" notice of the proceedings and had opportunity to raise the issue in the court that issued the custody determination.[16]

A contesting party only has 20 days[17] after service of notice to contest the validity of the registration.[18] If the party misses the deadline, that party is precluded from attacking the order under any of the arguments listed above in a hearing under Section 310, Hearing and Order.[19]

---

15. *Kostrzewski*, 680 N.W.2d at 273.
16. Chick v. Chick, 164 N.C. App. 444, 452–53 (2004).
17. Alabama, for one, has extended the original 20 days to 30 days to be more consistent with "the timeline generally allowed in Alabama." UCCJEA § 305, Alabama statutory comments.
18. UCCJEA § 305(e).
19. *Id.* § 305(f).

Section 306: Enforcement of Registered Determination

Just as with the enforcement of any foreign judgment entitled to full faith and credit, an enforcing state may enforce the determination as if it had been entered in the enforcing state. However, the enforcing state has no authority to modify the determination unless it has jurisdiction to do so under Article 2.

Section 307: Simultaneous Proceedings

An enforcement court has an affirmative duty to communicate with the court with jurisdiction under Section 202 or jurisdiction to modify under Section 203.

The language of this section states that "the proceeding for enforcement continues unless the enforcing court, after consultation with the modifying court, stays or dismisses the proceeding."[20] This would imply that ultimate authority regarding the enforcement of the determination lies with the enforcement court. However, the drafter's comments state the opposite: "The ultimate decision rests with the court having exclusive, continuing jurisdiction under Section 202, or if there is no State with exclusive, continuing jurisdiction, then the decision rests with the State that would have jurisdiction to modify under Section 203."[21]

Section 308: Expedited Enforcement of Child-Custody Determination

A person may seek to enforce a child-custody determination even if that determination has not been registered under Section 305.

The following is a checklist for a petition seeking the enforcement of the child-custody determination under this section. The petition must state:

20. *Id.* § 307.
21. *Id.* § 307 cmt. 55.

1. whether the court that issued the determination identified the jurisdictional basis it relied upon in exercising jurisdiction and, if so, what the basis was;
2. whether determination for which enforcement is sought has been vacated, stayed, or modified by a court whose decision must be enforced under this [Act] and, if so, identify the court, the case number, and the nature of the proceeding;
3. whether any proceeding has been commenced that could affect the current proceeding, including proceedings relating to domestic violence, protective orders, termination of parental rights, and adoptions and, if so, identify the court, the case number, and the nature of the proceeding;
4. the present physical address of the child and the respondent, if known;
5. whether relief in addition to the immediate physical custody of the child and attorney's fees is sought, including a request for assistance from [law enforcement officials] and, if so, the relief sought; and
6. if child-custody determination has been registered and confirmed under Section 305, Registration of Child-Custody Determination, and, if so, the date and place of registration.[22]

The petition for enforcement of the child-custody determination must be verified and include attached certified copies (or a certified copy of an order) of all child-custody determinations sought to be enforced, and the order, if any, confirming registration under Section 305.

When a petition under this section is filed, the court shall issue an order that states the following:

> On [date and time of hearing], [the Respondent] shall appear in person [with or without the child] for a hearing pursuant to Section 310 of the UCCJEA.
>
> At the hearing the court will order that:

22. *Id.* § 308(b)(1)–(6).

1. The Petitioner may take immediate physical custody of the child,
2. The payment of fees, costs, and expenses under Section 312 [of the UCCJEA], and
3. If necessary, schedule a hearing to determine if further relief is appropriate.[23]

[The Respondent] may contest the court's authority to enforce the child-custody determination entered on ________ in [the issuing court] and avoid the ruling described above by appearing and establishing under Section 310 of the UCCJEA that

1. The child-custody determination has not been registered and confirmed under Section 305 and that:
    a) The issuing court did not have jurisdiction under [Article] 2;
    b) The child-custody determination for which enforcement is sought has been vacated, stayed, or modified by a court having jurisdiction to do so under [Article] 2; or
    c) [The Respondent] was entitled to notice, but notice was not given in accordance with the standards of Section 108, in the proceedings before the court that issued the order for which enforcement is sought; or
2. the child-custody determination for which enforcement is sought was registered and confirmed under Section 304, but has been vacated, stayed, or modified by a court of a State having jurisdiction to do so under [Article] 2.[24]

This section makes it clear that unless the petitioner requests otherwise, the enforcement hearing must be held on the next judicial day after service of the order unless that date is impossible. "Next judicial day . . . means the next day when a judge is at the courthouse."[25] If the petitioner does not request a different date, but it is impossible to hold the hearing on the next

23. *Id.* § 308(d) (this is what the order should look like based on this section but is not an exact quote of the section).
24. *Id.* § 308(d)(1)–(2) (this is what the order should look like based on this section but is not an exact quote of the section).
25. *Id.* § 308 cmt. at 58.

judicial day after service of the order, then the court shall set the hearing on the first judicial day possible.

Since it is generally impossible for a court to know exactly when a person is going to be served, the requirement under Section 308(c) that a hearing be held on the "next judicial day after service" clashes with Section 308(d), which requires that the order issued by the court state "the time and place" of the hearing. The drafter's comments do not provide guidance in this area, but logic dictates that the court should have the option of choosing to order the respondent to either (1) appear in court on a specific date and time, or (2) appear in court the next judicial day after service of the order.

Section 309: Service of Petition and Order

Although this section does not explicitly cite Section 308, it appears to be drafted for the purpose of addressing that section's notice requirements: "Except as otherwise provided in Section 311, this petition and order must be served, by any method authorized [by the law of this State], upon respondent and any person who has physical custody of the child."[26]

It is important to note that this section does not address how notice should be given under Section 305.

Section 310: Hearing and Order

A hearing under this section is for the sole purpose of determining whether the issuing court had UCCJEA jurisdiction to enter the child-custody determination.[27] If the enforcing court finds that the foreign court did have UCCJEA jurisdiction, then the enforcing court must issue an order enforcing that foreign child-custody determination.

26. *Id.* § 309.

27. *Brandt*, 268 P.3d 406, 413 (Colo. 2012) ("It is imperative that an out-of-state court tasked with enforcing a custody order has clear factual record, either by stipulation or from the taking of evidence, on which to assess whether jurisdiction was properly asserted by the court which entered the order.").

At the heart of this section is the quick enforcement of foreign orders. A court must, upon finding that the foreign child-custody determination entitles a parent to the immediate physical custody of a child, "order that the petitioner may take immediate physical custody of the child."[28]

The burden of proof for the petitioner is relatively light in that "the certified copy, or a copy of the certified copy, or the custody determination . . . is prima facie evidence of the issuing court's jurisdiction to enter the order."[29] Once the petitioner meets his or her burden, the burden then shifts to the respondent to show that the custody determination is not entitled to enforcement.

The respondent may prove the court that entered the child-custody determination did not have UCCJEA jurisdiction to issue the determination by establishing that "the child-custody determination for which enforcement is sought was registered and confirmed under Section 305 but has been vacated, stayed, or modified by a court of a State having jurisdiction to do so under [Article] 2" or

> the child-custody determination has not been registered and confirmed under Section 305 and:
>
> (1) the issuing court did not have jurisdiction under [Article] 2;
>
> (2) the child-custody determination sought to be registered has been vacated, stayed, or modified by a court having jurisdiction to do so under [Article] 2; or
>
> (3) the person contesting registration was entitled to notice, but notice was not given in accordance with the standards of Section 108, in the proceedings before the court that issued the order for which registration is sought.[30]

The last argument is of particular interest, since it takes into consideration the law of the decree-granting state:

28. UCCJEA § 310(a).

29. *Id.* § 310 cmt. at 60. Although Section 311 does not make it explicitly clear, it may be inferred from the requirement that the order include Section 308(b) language, that a Section 310 hearing is still required even after the court has taken physical custody of the child.

30. *Id.* § 310(1).

> Thus, if the defense of lack of notice would not be available under local law if the Respondent purposely hid from the petitioner, took deliberate steps to avoid service of process or elected not to participate in the initial proceedings, the defense also would not be available under this Act.[31]

The respondent may not make any other arguments to contest the enforcement of the order other than the ones allowed under this section.[32]

After determining that the issuing state had UCCJEA jurisdiction to issue the child-custody decree and that the decree was being violated by the respondent the court may

1. award fees, costs, and expenses authorized under Section 312;
2. grant additional relief (such as the assistance of law enforcement officials); and
3. set an additional hearing date to determine if additional relief is appropriate.

The last two subsections, dealing with the privilege and against self-incrimination and spousal privileges and immunities, seem somewhat out of place. This is because they were derived from the Uniform Interstate Family Support Act (UIFSA) Section 312, and their intent is to keep child-custody and child-support proceedings as similar as possible.[33]

Section 311: Warrant to Take Physical Custody of Child

If a petitioner believes that the child is in immediate physical harm or likely to be removed from the state, he or she may need to apply for the issuance of a warrant to take physical custody of the child along with the petition to enforce a foreign child-custody judgment through Section 308.

The main difference between Section 308 and Section 311 lies in that under Section 308, the court may not take action to protect the child until

31. *Id.* § 310 cmt. at 60.
32. Kostrzewski v. Frisinger, 680 N.W.2d 271, 273 (N.D. 2004).
33. UCCJEA § 310 cmt. at 60.

a Section 310 hearing is held. Under Section 311, the court may take physical custody of the child without giving any notice to the respondent and then hold a Section 310 hearing at the earliest opportunity.

To apply for a warrant a petitioner must file

1. a Section 308 petition seeking enforcement of a child-custody determination; and
2. a verified application for the issuance of a warrant to take physical custody of the child stating that the child is immediately likely to suffer serious physical harm or be removed from the state, and also stating the requirements under Section 308(b), which require a Petitioner to state whether
   - the court that issued the determination identified the jurisdictional basis it relied upon in exercising jurisdiction and, if so, what the basis was;
   - the determination for which enforcement is sought has been vacated, stayed, or modified by a court whose decision must be enforced under the UCCJEA and, if so, identify the court, the case number, and the nature of the proceeding;
   - any proceeding has been commenced that could affect the current proceeding, including proceedings relating to domestic violence, protective orders, termination of parental rights, and adoptions and, if so, identify the court, the case number, and the nature of the proceeding;
   - the present physical address of the child and the respondent, if known;
   - relief sought in addition to the immediate physical custody of the child and attorney's fees, including a request for assistance from law enforcement officials and, if so, the relief sought; and
   - the child-custody determination has been registered and confirmed under Section 305 and, if so, the date and place of registration.

Before issuing the warrant, the court must hear the testimony of the petitioner or other witnesses and find that the child is imminently likely to suffer serious physical harm or be removed from the state if a warrant is not issued.

An affidavit making the required allegations is not enough for a court to issue a warrant. The court must hear testimony from the petitioner or other witnesses. In those situations where the petitioner may not personally appear, the petitioner may testify long distance pursuant to Section 111 or any other local law.[34]

"Harm" has not been defined in this section because the drafters believed that, "as in the issuance of temporary restraining orders, the appropriate issuance of the warrant is left to the circumstances of the case."[35]

Some examples listed by the UCCJEA drafters of where the court might be authorized to issue a warrant are situations where giving notice might cause a negative reaction, such as when the respondent is secreting the child in violation of a court order, abusing the child, or a flight risk.

If the court determines that the requirements for a warrant to take physical custody of the child have been met, the court must

- recite the facts upon which a conclusion of imminent serious physical harm or removal from the jurisdiction is based;
- direct law enforcement officers to take physical custody of the child immediately; and
- provide for the placement of the child pending final relief under Section 310.

Upon issuing the warrant, the court must also hold that the Section 308 petition must be heard on the next judicial day after the warrant is executed or the earliest day possible after the execution of a warrant.

It is generally expected that the child will be placed with the petitioner. However, the court may provide the child with any "appropriate placement authorized under the laws of the court's State."[36] For example, a court may choose to err on the side of caution and place the child with a child-welfare agency if the court suspects that the petitioner may choose to flee the state once the child is under his or her control. Similarly, if the petitioner is not

34. *Id.* § 311 cmt. at 63.
35. *Id.* § 311 cmt. at 62.
36. *Id.* § 311 cmt. at 63.

currently near the child, it may be impossible to immediately reunite parent and child.

The warrant issued by a court under this section is enforceable throughout the state. The court's warrant may allow for law enforcement, in attempting to obtain custody of the child, to enter private property or even make forcible entry at any hour.

The very last subsection is somewhat enigmatic in that it states "the court may impose conditions upon placement of a child to ensure the appearance of the child and the child's custodian."[37] The choice of the word "custodian" is somewhat perplexing, since that word is not defined in the UCCJEA and, in Article 3, the words "petitioner" and "respondent" are generally used to refer to the litigants.

Deepening the mystery, the drafters' commentary fails to refer to a custodian while stating as follows:

> This section authorizes the court to utilize whatever means are available under local law to ensure the appearance of the petitioner and the child at the enforcement hearing [under Section 310]. Such means might include cash bonds, a surrender of a passport, or whatever the court determines is necessary.[38]

While the choice of language raises some questions, it appears that the very last subsection was the drafters' attempt to thwart the plans of unscrupulous petitioners who might attempt to abscond with the child by exploiting this section's lowered evidentiary standards.

Section 312: Costs, Fees, and Expenses

This section is taken from the International Child-Abduction Remedies Act[39] and ensures that the prevailing party in an enforcement proceeding

37. *Id.* § 311(f).
38. *Id.* § 211 cmt. at 63.
39. 42 U.S.C. § 11607(b)(3).

shall be awarded "necessary and reasonable" expenses incurred as a result of the litigation, including:

1. costs,
2. communication expenses,
3. attorney's fees,
4. investigative fees,
5. expenses for witnesses,
6. travel expenses, and
7. child care during the course of the proceedings.

This section does not clarify the definition of "prevailing party," but it is expected that each state provide its own standard.[40]

The only way for the party who did not prevail to avoid these fees is for that party to show that the award would be "clearly inappropriate." An example of a clearly inappropriate award would be if payment of the award would so harm a parent and child that they would need public assistance.

The last section parallels UIFSA's Section 313 and is intended to prevent any fee awards against a state unless otherwise authorized by law.

Section 313: Recognition and Enforcement

This section ensures that all states give each other's child-custody enforcement orders full faith and credit as long as those orders were entered in consistency with Article 3 of the UCCJEA and that the order sought to be enforced has not been "vacated, stayed or modified by a court having jurisdiction to do so under Article 2 [Jurisdiction]."[41]

40. UCCJEA § 312 cmt. at 64.
41. *Id.* § 313.

Section 314: Appeals

This section allows for appeals from final orders in a child-custody enforcement proceeding under Article 3. If the enforcing court feels that it must, under Section 310, enforce a child-custody determination that might result in harm to the child, the court may assume emergency jurisdiction under Section 204 to stay the enforcement proceeding while the appellate court considers an appeal regarding the enforceability of the child-custody order entered under this Article 3.

The final order must be appealed in accordance with the state's expedited appellate procedures in other civil cases. Many states have special expedited appellate procedures for child-custody cases of which the appellant should be taken advantage.

Finally, a litigant may also attempt to obtain extraordinary remedies "such as mandamus or prohibition from an appellate court to stay the court's enforcement action."[42]

Section 315: Role of the Public Prosecutor

This section allows a prosecutor or other appropriate public official to take any action under Article 3 or other civil proceedings under state law to (1) locate a child, (2) obtain the return of a child, or (3) enforce a child-custody determination. The prosecutor or other public official does not act on behalf of either party but on behalf of the enforcing court.

The drafters intended for the states to change the language of which public authority is allowed to take action. Some states have substituted the original "prosecutor or other appropriate public official" to "state's attorney" (Illinois), "district attorney" (Oklahoma), "prosecuting attorney" (Arkansas), and "attorney general or county prosecuting attorney" (Hawaii). It is important that a party seeking assistance under this section check his or her state statute to know which state public authority to contact for assistance.

42. *Id.* § 314 cmt. at 65.

The purpose of this section is to

1. encourage the parties to "abide by the terms of the court order"[43] by involving public authorities;
2. make remedies under Article 3 available to people of limited means who might not be able to otherwise afford enforcement of a child-custody determination; and
3. make use of resources available to the public authority (such as making use of law enforcement under Section 316) that might not be available to a private attorney.

The drafters, recognizing that "there is only so much time and money available for enforcement proceedings,"[44] intended for the public authority to develop guidelines to prioritize cases. Similarly, they intended for the public authorities to only become involved when there is

1. an existing child-custody determination;
2. a request to do so from a court in a pending child-custody proceeding;
3. a reasonable belief that a criminal statute has been violated; or
4. a reasonable belief that the child has been wrongfully removed or retained in violation of the Hague Convention on the Civil Aspects of International Child-Abduction.[45]

Expanding the range of relief generally available to the public agency (particularly if it is a prosecutor) from criminal procedures to civil procedures should provide a "more economical and less disruptive means of solving problems of criminal abduction and retention"[46] than with the use of criminal procedures alone.

A public official seeking to enforce this section and a criminal statute should be aware of his or her state's ethical rules, since some ethical rules disapprove of a lawyer threatening criminal action to gain an advantage

43. *Id.* § 315 cmt. at 66.
44. *Id.* § 315 cmt. at 67.
45. *Id.* § 315(a)(1)–(4).
46. *Id.* § 315 cmt. at 67.

in a civil case. The drafters, discarding the ethical concern, made it clear in their comments that they did not intend for this section to detract from the enforcement of criminal provisions in child-abduction cases.[47]

Section 316: Role of Law Enforcement

This section allows for a public official in his or her capacity under Section 315 to direct a law enforcement officer to "take any lawful action reasonably necessary to locate a child or a party and assist"[48] the public official with his or her duties under Section 315.

Section 317: Costs and Expenses

Under this section, if the respondent does not prevail (presumably under a Section 310 hearing), the court may order that the respondent pay the "direct expenses and costs incurred by the [prosecutor or other appropriate public official] and [law enforcement officers] under Section 315 or 316."[49]

47. *Id.* § 315 cmt. at 67. (The drafters discarded this concern as follows: "the prohibition relates to threats that are solely to gain advantage in a civil case. If the prosecutor has a good faith reason for pursuing the criminal action there is no basis for concern.")
48. *Id.* § 316.
49. *Id.* § 317.

Article 4

Miscellaneous Provisions

All the sections in Article 4 are commonly included in uniform laws if they are applicable.

Section 401: Application and Construction

Section 401 confirms that the drafters of the Uniform Child Custody Jurisdiction and Enforcement Act (UCCJEA) intended for the persuasive authority of sister state determinations to be given significant weight among the states when it states that "in applying and construing this Uniform Act, consideration must be given to the need to promote uniformity of the law with respect to its subject matter among States that enact it."[1]

Section 402: Severability Clause

Section 402 merely clarifies that, if any part of the UCCJEA is held invalid, that invalidity does not extend to other parts of the UCCJEA if those parts "can be given effect without the invalid provision of application."[2]

1. UCCJEA § 401.
2. *Id.* § 402.

Section 403: Effective Dates

Section 403 states the effective date of the act.

Section 404: Repeals

Section 404 states which statute is being repealed. All states had to repeal the Uniform Child Custody Jurisdiction Act (UCCJA) to enter the UCCJEA.

Section 405: Transitional Provision

Section 405 clarifies that when the UCCJEA is enacted, the motions that were filed before its enactment will be heard under the UCCJA.

Violence Against Women Reauthorization Act of 2013

S. 47

One Hundred Thirteenth Congress of the United States of America

AT THE FIRST SESSION

Begun and held at the City of Washington on Thursday, the third day of January, two thousand and thirteen

An Act

To reauthorize the Violence Against Women Act of 1994.

Be it enacted by the Senate and House of Representatives of the United States of America in Congress assembled,

SECTION 1. SHORT TITLE.

This Act may be cited as the "Violence Against Women Reauthorization Act of 2013".

SEC. 2. TABLE OF CONTENTS.

The table of contents for this Act is as follows:

S. 47—2

SEC. 3. UNIVERSAL DEFINITIONS AND GRANT CONDITIONS.

(a) DEFINITIONS.—Subsection (a) of section 40002 of the Violence Against Women Act of 1994 (42 U.S.C. 13925(a)) is amended—

(1) by striking paragraphs (5), (17), (18), (23), (29), (33), (36), and (37);

(2) by redesignating—

(A) paragraphs (34) and (35) as paragraphs (41) and (42), respectively;

(B) paragraphs (30), (31), and (32) as paragraphs (36), (37), and (38), respectively;

(C) paragraphs (24) through (28) as paragraphs (30) through (34), respectively;

(D) paragraphs (21) and (22) as paragraphs (26) and (27), respectively;

(E) paragraphs (19) and (20) as paragraphs (23) and (24), respectively;

(F) paragraphs (10) through (16) as paragraphs (13) through (19), respectively;

S. 47—4

(G) paragraphs (6), (7), (8), and (9) as paragraphs (8), (9), (10), and (11), respectively; and

(H) paragraphs (1), (2), (3), and (4) as paragraphs (2), (3), (4), and (5), respectively;

(3) by inserting before paragraph (2), as redesignated, the following:

"(1) ALASKA NATIVE VILLAGE.—The term 'Alaska Native village' has the same meaning given such term in the Alaska Native Claims Settlement Act (43 U.S.C. 1601 et seq.).";

(4) in paragraph (3), as redesignated, by striking "serious harm." and inserting "serious harm to an unemancipated minor.";

(5) in paragraph (4), as redesignated, by striking "The term" through "that—" and inserting "The term 'community-based organization' means a nonprofit, nongovernmental, or tribal organization that serves a specific geographic community that—";

(6) by inserting after paragraph (5), as redesignated, the following:

"(6) CULTURALLY SPECIFIC.—The term 'culturally specific' means primarily directed toward racial and ethnic minority groups (as defined in section 1707(g) of the Public Health Service Act (42 U.S.C. 300u–6(g)).

"(7) CULTURALLY SPECIFIC SERVICES.—The term 'culturally specific services' means community-based services that include culturally relevant and linguistically specific services and resources to culturally specific communities.";

(7) in paragraph (8), as redesignated, by inserting "or intimate partner" after "former spouse" and "as a spouse";

(8) by inserting after paragraph (11), as redesignated, the following:

"(12) HOMELESS.—The term 'homeless' has the meaning provided in section 41403(6).";

(9) in paragraph (18), as redesignated, by inserting "or Village Public Safety Officers" after "governmental victim services programs";

(10) in paragraph (19), as redesignated, by inserting at the end the following:

"Intake or referral, by itself, does not constitute legal assistance.";

(11) by inserting after paragraph (19), as redesignated, the following:

"(20) PERSONALLY IDENTIFYING INFORMATION OR PERSONAL INFORMATION.—The term 'personally identifying information' or 'personal information' means individually identifying information for or about an individual including information likely to disclose the location of a victim of domestic violence, dating violence, sexual assault, or stalking, regardless of whether the information is encoded, encrypted, hashed, or otherwise protected, including—

"(A) a first and last name;

"(B) a home or other physical address;

"(C) contact information (including a postal, e-mail or Internet protocol address, or telephone or facsimile number);

"(D) a social security number, driver license number, passport number, or student identification number; and

"(E) any other information, including date of birth, racial or ethnic background, or religious affiliation, that would serve to identify any individual.

"(21) POPULATION SPECIFIC ORGANIZATION.—The term 'population specific organization' means a nonprofit, nongovernmental organization that primarily serves members of a specific underserved population and has demonstrated experience and expertise providing targeted services to members of that specific underserved population.

"(22) POPULATION SPECIFIC SERVICES.—The term 'population specific services' means victim-centered services that address the safety, health, economic, legal, housing, workplace, immigration, confidentiality, or other needs of victims of domestic violence, dating violence, sexual assault, or stalking, and that are designed primarily for and are targeted to a specific underserved population.";

(12) in paragraph (23), as redesignated, by striking "services" and inserting "assistance";

(13) by inserting after paragraph (24), as redesignated, the following:

"(25) RAPE CRISIS CENTER.—The term 'rape crisis center' means a nonprofit, nongovernmental, or tribal organization, or governmental entity in a State other than a Territory that provides intervention and related assistance, as specified in section 41601(b)(2)(C), to victims of sexual assault without regard to their age. In the case of a governmental entity, the entity may not be part of the criminal justice system (such as a law enforcement agency) and must be able to offer a comparable level of confidentiality as a nonprofit entity that provides similar victim services.";

(14) in paragraph (26), as redesignated—

(A) in subparagraph (A), by striking "or" after the semicolon;

(B) in subparagraph (B), by striking the period and inserting "; or"; and

(C) by inserting at the end the following:

"(C) any federally recognized Indian tribe.";

(15) in paragraph (27), as redesignated—

(A) by striking "52" and inserting "57"; and

(B) by striking "150,000" and inserting "250,000";

(16) by inserting after paragraph (27), as redesignated, the following:

"(28) SEX TRAFFICKING.—The term 'sex trafficking' means any conduct proscribed by section 1591 of title 18, United States Code, whether or not the conduct occurs in interstate or foreign commerce or within the special maritime and territorial jurisdiction of the United States.

"(29) SEXUAL ASSAULT.—The term 'sexual assault' means any nonconsensual sexual act proscribed by Federal, tribal, or State law, including when the victim lacks capacity to consent.";

(17) by inserting after paragraph (34), as redesignated, the following:

"(35) TRIBAL COALITION.—The term 'tribal coalition' means an established nonprofit, nongovernmental Indian organization, Alaska Native organization, or a Native Hawaiian organization that—

"(A) provides education, support, and technical assistance to member Indian service providers in a manner that enables those member providers to establish and maintain culturally appropriate services, including shelter and rape crisis services, designed to assist Indian women and the dependents of those women who are victims of domestic violence, dating violence, sexual assault, and stalking; and

"(B) is comprised of board and general members that are representative of—

"(i) the member service providers described in subparagraph (A); and

"(ii) the tribal communities in which the services are being provided.";

(18) by inserting after paragraph (38), as redesignated, the following:

"(39) UNDERSERVED POPULATIONS.—The term 'underserved populations' means populations who face barriers in accessing and using victim services, and includes populations underserved because of geographic location, religion, sexual orientation, gender identity, underserved racial and ethnic populations, populations underserved because of special needs (such as language barriers, disabilities, alienage status, or age), and any other population determined to be underserved by the Attorney General or by the Secretary of Health and Human Services, as appropriate.

"(40) UNIT OF LOCAL GOVERNMENT.—The term 'unit of local government' means any city, county, township, town, borough, parish, village, or other general purpose political subdivision of a State."; and

(19) by inserting after paragraph (42), as redesignated, the following:

"(43) VICTIM SERVICE PROVIDER.—The term 'victim service provider' means a nonprofit, nongovernmental or tribal organization or rape crisis center, including a State or tribal coalition, that assists or advocates for domestic violence, dating violence, sexual assault, or stalking victims, including domestic violence shelters, faith-based organizations, and other organizations, with a documented history of effective work concerning domestic violence, dating violence, sexual assault, or stalking.

"(44) VICTIM SERVICES OR SERVICES.—The terms 'victim services' and 'services' mean services provided to victims of domestic violence, dating violence, sexual assault, or stalking, including telephonic or web-based hotlines, legal advocacy, economic advocacy, emergency and transitional shelter, accompaniment and advocacy through medical, civil or criminal justice, immigration, and social support systems, crisis intervention, short-term individual and group support services, information and referrals, culturally specific services, population specific services, and other related supportive services.

"(45) YOUTH.—The term 'youth' means a person who is 11 to 24 years old.".

(b) GRANTS CONDITIONS.—Subsection (b) of section 40002 of the Violence Against Women Act of 1994 (42 U.S.C. 13925(b)) is amended—

(1) in paragraph (2)—

(A) in subparagraph (B), by striking clauses (i) and (ii) and inserting the following:

"(i) disclose, reveal, or release any personally identifying information or individual information collected in connection with services requested, utilized, or denied through grantees' and subgrantees' programs, regardless of whether the information has been encoded, encrypted, hashed, or otherwise protected; or

"(ii) disclose, reveal, or release individual client information without the informed, written, reasonably time-limited consent of the person (or in the case of an unemancipated minor, the minor and the parent or guardian or in the case of legal incapacity, a court-appointed guardian) about whom information is sought, whether for this program or any other Federal, State, tribal, or territorial grant program, except that consent for release may not be given by the abuser of the minor, incapacitated person, or the abuser of the other parent of the minor.

If a minor or a person with a legally appointed guardian is permitted by law to receive services without the parent's or guardian's consent, the minor or person with a guardian may release information without additional consent.";

(B) by amending subparagraph (D), to read as follows:

"(D) INFORMATION SHARING.—

"(i) Grantees and subgrantees may share—

"(I) nonpersonally identifying data in the aggregate regarding services to their clients and nonpersonally identifying demographic information in order to comply with Federal, State, tribal, or territorial reporting, evaluation, or data collection requirements;

"(II) court-generated information and law enforcement-generated information contained in secure, governmental registries for protection order enforcement purposes; and

"(III) law enforcement-generated and prosecution-generated information necessary for law enforcement and prosecution purposes.

"(ii) In no circumstances may—

"(I) an adult, youth, or child victim of domestic violence, dating violence, sexual assault, or stalking be required to provide a consent to release his or her personally identifying information as a condition of eligibility for the services provided by the grantee or subgrantee;

"(II) any personally identifying information be shared in order to comply with Federal, tribal, or State reporting, evaluation, or data collection requirements, whether for this program or any other Federal, tribal, or State grant program.";

(C) by redesignating subparagraph (E) as subparagraph (F);

(D) by inserting after subparagraph (D) the following:

"(E) STATUTORILY MANDATED REPORTS OF ABUSE OR NEGLECT.—Nothing in this section prohibits a grantee or subgrantee from reporting suspected abuse or neglect, as those terms are defined and specifically mandated by the State or tribe involved."; and

S. 47—8

(E) by inserting after subparagraph (F), as redesignated, the following:

"(G) CONFIDENTIALITY ASSESSMENT AND ASSURANCES.—Grantees and subgrantees must document their compliance with the confidentiality and privacy provisions required under this section.";

(2) by striking paragraph (3) and inserting the following:

"(3) APPROVED ACTIVITIES.—In carrying out the activities under this title, grantees and subgrantees may collaborate with or provide information to Federal, State, local, tribal, and territorial public officials and agencies to develop and implement policies and develop and promote State, local, or tribal legislation or model codes designed to reduce or eliminate domestic violence, dating violence, sexual assault, and stalking.";

(3) in paragraph (7), by inserting at the end the following: "Final reports of such evaluations shall be made available to the public via the agency's website."; and

(4) by inserting after paragraph (11) the following:

"(12) DELIVERY OF LEGAL ASSISTANCE.—Any grantee or subgrantee providing legal assistance with funds awarded under this title shall comply with the eligibility requirements in section 1201(d) of the Violence Against Women Act of 2000 (42 U.S.C. 3796gg–6(d)).

"(13) CIVIL RIGHTS.—

"(A) NONDISCRIMINATION.—No person in the United States shall, on the basis of actual or perceived race, color, religion, national origin, sex, gender identity (as defined in paragraph 249(c)(4) of title 18, United States Code), sexual orientation, or disability, be excluded from participation in, be denied the benefits of, or be subjected to discrimination under any program or activity funded in whole or in part with funds made available under the Violence Against Women Act of 1994 (title IV of Public Law 103–322; 108 Stat. 1902), the Violence Against Women Act of 2000 (division B of Public Law 106–386; 114 Stat. 1491), the Violence Against Women and Department of Justice Reauthorization Act of 2005 (title IX of Public Law 109–162; 119 Stat. 3080), the Violence Against Women Reauthorization Act of 2013, and any other program or activity funded in whole or in part with funds appropriated for grants, cooperative agreements, and other assistance administered by the Office on Violence Against Women.

"(B) EXCEPTION.—If sex segregation or sex-specific programming is necessary to the essential operation of a program, nothing in this paragraph shall prevent any such program or activity from consideration of an individual's sex. In such circumstances, grantees may meet the requirements of this paragraph by providing comparable services to individuals who cannot be provided with the sex-segregated or sex-specific programming.

"(C) DISCRIMINATION.—The authority of the Attorney General and the Office of Justice Programs to enforce this paragraph shall be the same as it is under section 3789d of title 42, United States Code.

"(D) CONSTRUCTION.—Nothing contained in this paragraph shall be construed, interpreted, or applied to supplant, displace, preempt, or otherwise diminish the responsibilities and liabilities under other State or Federal civil rights law, whether statutory or common.

"(14) CLARIFICATION OF VICTIM SERVICES AND LEGAL ASSISTANCE.—Victim services and legal assistance under this title also include services and assistance to victims of domestic violence, dating violence, sexual assault, or stalking who are also victims of severe forms of trafficking in persons as defined by section 103 of the Trafficking Victims Protection Act of 2000 (22 U.S.C. 7102).

"(15) CONFERRAL.—

"(A) IN GENERAL.—The Office on Violence Against Women shall establish a biennial conferral process with State and tribal coalitions and technical assistance providers who receive funding through grants administered by the Office on Violence Against Women and authorized by this Act, and other key stakeholders.

"(B) AREAS COVERED.—The areas of conferral under this paragraph shall include—

"(i) the administration of grants;

"(ii) unmet needs;

"(iii) promising practices in the field; and

"(iv) emerging trends.

"(C) INITIAL CONFERRAL.—The first conferral shall be initiated not later than 6 months after the date of enactment of the Violence Against Women Reauthorization Act of 2013.

"(D) REPORT.—Not later than 90 days after the conclusion of each conferral period, the Office on Violence Against Women shall publish a comprehensive report that—

"(i) summarizes the issues presented during conferral and what, if any, policies it intends to implement to address those issues;

"(ii) is made available to the public on the Office on Violence Against Women's website and submitted to the Committee on the Judiciary of the Senate and the Committee on the Judiciary of the House of Representatives.

"(16) ACCOUNTABILITY.—All grants awarded by the Attorney General under this Act shall be subject to the following accountability provisions:

"(A) AUDIT REQUIREMENT.—

"(i) IN GENERAL.—Beginning in the first fiscal year beginning after the date of the enactment of this Act, and in each fiscal year thereafter, the Inspector General of the Department of Justice shall conduct audits of recipients of grants under this Act to prevent waste, fraud, and abuse of funds by grantees. The Inspector General shall determine the appropriate number of grantees to be audited each year.

"(ii) DEFINITION.—In this paragraph, the term 'unresolved audit finding' means a finding in the final audit report of the Inspector General of the Department of Justice that the audited grantee has utilized grant funds for an unauthorized expenditure or otherwise unallowable cost that is not closed or resolved within 12 months from the date when the final audit report is issued.

"(iii) MANDATORY EXCLUSION.—A recipient of grant funds under this Act that is found to have an unresolved audit finding shall not be eligible to receive grant funds under this Act during the following 2 fiscal years.

"(iv) PRIORITY.—In awarding grants under this Act, the Attorney General shall give priority to eligible entities that did not have an unresolved audit finding during the 3 fiscal years prior to submitting an application for a grant under this Act.

"(v) REIMBURSEMENT.—If an entity is awarded grant funds under this Act during the 2-fiscal-year period in which the entity is barred from receiving grants under paragraph (2), the Attorney General shall—

"(I) deposit an amount equal to the grant funds that were improperly awarded to the grantee into the General Fund of the Treasury; and

"(II) seek to recoup the costs of the repayment to the fund from the grant recipient that was erroneously awarded grant funds.

"(B) NONPROFIT ORGANIZATION REQUIREMENTS.—

"(i) DEFINITION.—For purposes of this paragraph and the grant programs described in this Act, the term 'nonprofit organization' means an organization that is described in section 501(c)(3) of the Internal Revenue Code of 1986 and is exempt from taxation under section 501(a) of such Code.

"(ii) PROHIBITION.—The Attorney General may not award a grant under any grant program described in this Act to a nonprofit organization that holds money in offshore accounts for the purpose of avoiding paying the tax described in section 511(a) of the Internal Revenue Code of 1986.

"(iii) DISCLOSURE.—Each nonprofit organization that is awarded a grant under a grant program described in this Act and uses the procedures prescribed in regulations to create a rebuttable presumption of reasonableness for the compensation of its officers, directors, trustees and key employees, shall disclose to the Attorney General, in the application for the grant, the process for determining such compensation, including the independent persons involved in reviewing and approving such compensation, the comparability data used, and contemporaneous substantiation of the deliberation and decision. Upon request, the Attorney General shall make the information disclosed under this subsection available for public inspection.

"(C) CONFERENCE EXPENDITURES.—

"(i) LIMITATION.—No amounts authorized to be appropriated to the Department of Justice under this Act may be used by the Attorney General, or by any individual or organization awarded discretionary funds through a cooperative agreement under this Act, to host or support any expenditure for conferences that uses more than $20,000 in Department funds, unless the Deputy Attorney General or such Assistant Attorney Generals, Directors, or principal deputies as the Deputy Attorney General may designate, provides prior written authorization that the funds may be expended to host a conference.

"(ii) WRITTEN APPROVAL.—Written approval under clause (i) shall include a written estimate of all costs associated with the conference, including the cost of all food and beverages, audiovisual equipment, honoraria for speakers, and any entertainment.

"(iii) REPORT.—The Deputy Attorney General shall submit an annual report to the Committee on the Judiciary of the Senate and the Committee on the Judiciary of the House of Representatives on all approved conference expenditures referenced in this paragraph.

"(D) ANNUAL CERTIFICATION.—Beginning in the first fiscal year beginning after the date of the enactment of this Act, the Attorney General shall submit, to the Committee on the Judiciary and the Committee on Appropriations of the Senate and the Committee on the Judiciary and the Committee on Appropriations of the House of Representatives, an annual certification that—

"(i) all audits issued by the Office of the Inspector General under paragraph (1) have been completed and reviewed by the appropriate Assistant Attorney General or Director;

"(ii) all mandatory exclusions required under subparagraph (A)(iii) have been issued;

"(iii) all reimbursements required under subparagraph (A)(v) have been made; and

"(iv) includes a list of any grant recipients excluded under subparagraph (A) from the previous year.".

SEC. 4. EFFECTIVE DATE.

Except as otherwise specifically provided in this Act, the provisions of titles I, II, III, IV, VII, and sections 3, 602, 901, and 902 of this Act shall not take effect until the beginning of the fiscal year following the date of enactment of this Act.

TITLE I—ENHANCING JUDICIAL AND LAW ENFORCEMENT TOOLS TO COMBAT VIOLENCE AGAINST WOMEN

SEC. 101. STOP GRANTS.

Title I of the Omnibus Crime Control and Safe Streets Act of 1968 (42 U.S.C. 3711 et seq.) is amended—

(1) in section 1001(a)(18) (42 U.S.C. 3793(a)(18)), by striking "$225,000,000 for each of fiscal years 2007 through 2011" and inserting "$222,000,000 for each of fiscal years 2014 through 2018";

S. 47—12

(2) in section 2001(b) (42 U.S.C. 3796gg(b))—
(A) in the matter preceding paragraph (1)—
(i) by striking "equipment" and inserting "resources"; and
(ii) by inserting "for the protection and safety of victims," after "women,";
(B) in paragraph (1), by striking "sexual assault" and all that follows through "dating violence" and inserting "domestic violence, dating violence, sexual assault, and stalking, including the appropriate use of nonimmigrant status under subparagraphs (T) and (U) of section 101(a)(15) of the Immigration and Nationality Act (8 U.S.C. 1101(a))";
(C) in paragraph (2), by striking "sexual assault and domestic violence" and inserting "domestic violence, dating violence, sexual assault, and stalking";
(D) in paragraph (3), by striking "sexual assault and domestic violence" and inserting "domestic violence, dating violence, sexual assault, and stalking, as well as the appropriate treatment of victims";
(E) in paragraph (4)—
(i) by striking "sexual assault and domestic violence" and inserting "domestic violence, dating violence, sexual assault, and stalking"; and
(ii) by inserting ", classifying," after "identifying";
(F) in paragraph (5)—
(i) by inserting "and legal assistance" after "victim services";
(ii) by striking "domestic violence and dating violence" and inserting "domestic violence, dating violence, and stalking"; and
(iii) by striking "sexual assault and domestic violence" and inserting "domestic violence, dating violence, sexual assault, and stalking";
(G) by striking paragraph (6) and redesignating paragraphs (7) through (14) as paragraphs (6) through (13), respectively;
(H) in paragraph (6), as redesignated by subparagraph (G), by striking "sexual assault and domestic violence" and inserting "domestic violence, dating violence, sexual assault, and stalking";
(I) in paragraph (7), as redesignated by subparagraph (G), by striking "and dating violence" and inserting "dating violence, and stalking";
(J) in paragraph (9), as redesignated by subparagraph (G), by striking "domestic violence or sexual assault" and inserting " domestic violence, dating violence, sexual assault, or stalking";
(K) in paragraph (12), as redesignated by subparagraph (G)—
(i) in subparagraph (A), by striking "triage protocols to ensure that dangerous or potentially lethal cases are identified and prioritized" and inserting "the use of evidence-based indicators to assess the risk of domestic and dating violence homicide and prioritize dangerous or potentially lethal cases"; and
(ii) by striking "and" at the end;

(L) in paragraph (13), as redesignated by subparagraph (G)—

(i) by striking "to provide" and inserting "providing";

(ii) by striking "nonprofit nongovernmental";

(iii) by striking the comma after "local governments";

(iv) in the matter following subparagraph (C), by striking "paragraph (14)" and inserting "paragraph (13)"; and

(v) by striking the period at the end and inserting a semicolon; and

(M) by inserting after paragraph (13), as redesignated by subparagraph (G), the following:

"(14) developing and promoting State, local, or tribal legislation and policies that enhance best practices for responding to domestic violence, dating violence, sexual assault, and stalking;

"(15) developing, implementing, or enhancing Sexual Assault Response Teams, or other similar coordinated community responses to sexual assault;

"(16) developing and strengthening policies, protocols, best practices, and training for law enforcement agencies and prosecutors relating to the investigation and prosecution of sexual assault cases and the appropriate treatment of victims;

"(17) developing, enlarging, or strengthening programs addressing sexual assault against men, women, and youth in correctional and detention settings;

"(18) identifying and conducting inventories of backlogs of sexual assault evidence collection kits and developing protocols and policies for responding to and addressing such backlogs, including protocols and policies for notifying and involving victims;

"(19) developing, enlarging, or strengthening programs and projects to provide services and responses targeting male and female victims of domestic violence, dating violence, sexual assault, or stalking, whose ability to access traditional services and responses is affected by their sexual orientation or gender identity, as defined in section 249(c) of title 18, United States Code; and

"(20) developing, enhancing, or strengthening prevention and educational programming to address domestic violence, dating violence, sexual assault, or stalking, with not more than 5 percent of the amount allocated to a State to be used for this purpose.";

(3) in section 2007 (42 U.S.C. 3796gg–1)—

(A) in subsection (a), by striking "nonprofit nongovernmental victim service programs" and inserting "victim service providers";

(B) in subsection (b)(6), by striking "(not including populations of Indian tribes)";

(C) in subsection (c)—

(i) by striking paragraph (2) and inserting the following:

"(2) grantees and subgrantees shall develop a plan for implementation and shall consult and coordinate with—

"(A) the State sexual assault coalition;

S. 47—14

"(B) the State domestic violence coalition;
"(C) the law enforcement entities within the State;
"(D) prosecution offices;
"(E) State and local courts;
"(F) Tribal governments in those States with State or federally recognized Indian tribes;
"(G) representatives from underserved populations, including culturally specific populations;
"(H) victim service providers;
"(I) population specific organizations; and
"(J) other entities that the State or the Attorney General identifies as needed for the planning process;";
(ii) by redesignating paragraph (3) as paragraph (4);
(iii) by inserting after paragraph (2), as amended by clause (i), the following:
"(3) grantees shall coordinate the State implementation plan described in paragraph (2) with the State plans described in section 307 of the Family Violence Prevention and Services Act (42 U.S.C. 10407) and the programs described in section 1404 of the Victims of Crime Act of 1984 (42 U.S.C. 10603) and section 393A of the Public Health Service Act (42 U.S.C. 280b–1b).";
(iv) in paragraph (4), as redesignated by clause (ii)—
(I) in subparagraph (A), by striking "and not less than 25 percent shall be allocated for prosecutors";
(II) by redesignating subparagraphs (B) and (C) as subparagraphs (C) and (D);
(III) by inserting after subparagraph (A), the following:
"(B) not less than 25 percent shall be allocated for prosecutors;"; and
(IV) in subparagraph (D) as redesignated by subclause (II) by striking "for" and inserting "to"; and
(v) by adding at the end the following:
"(5) not later than 2 years after the date of enactment of this Act, and every year thereafter, not less than 20 percent of the total amount granted to a State under this subchapter shall be allocated for programs or projects in 2 or more allocations listed in paragraph (4) that meaningfully address sexual assault, including stranger rape, acquaintance rape, alcohol or drug-facilitated rape, and rape within the context of an intimate partner relationship.";
(D) by striking subsection (d) and inserting the following:
"(d) APPLICATION REQUIREMENTS.—An application for a grant under this section shall include—
"(1) the certifications of qualification required under subsection (c);
"(2) proof of compliance with the requirements for the payment of forensic medical exams and judicial notification, described in section 2010;

"(3) proof of compliance with the requirements for paying fees and costs relating to domestic violence and protection order cases, described in section 2011 of this title;

"(4) proof of compliance with the requirements prohibiting polygraph examinations of victims of sexual assault, described in section 2013 of this title;

"(5) an implementation plan required under subsection (i); and

"(6) any other documentation that the Attorney General may require.";

(E) in subsection (e)—

(i) in paragraph (2)—

(I) in subparagraph (A), by striking "domestic violence and sexual assault" and inserting "domestic violence, dating violence, sexual assault, and stalking"; and

(II) in subparagraph (D), by striking "linguistically and"; and

(ii) by adding at the end the following:

"(3) CONDITIONS.—In disbursing grants under this part, the Attorney General may impose reasonable conditions on grant awards to ensure that the States meet statutory, regulatory, and other program requirements.";

(F) in subsection (f), by striking the period at the end and inserting ", except that, for purposes of this subsection, the costs of the projects for victim services or tribes for which there is an exemption under section 40002(b)(1) of the Violence Against Women Act of 1994 (42 U.S.C. 13925(b)(1)) shall not count toward the total costs of the projects."; and

(G) by adding at the end the following:

"(i) IMPLEMENTATION PLANS.—A State applying for a grant under this part shall—

"(1) develop an implementation plan in consultation with the entities listed in subsection (c)(2), that identifies how the State will use the funds awarded under this part, including how the State will meet the requirements of subsection (c)(5); and

"(2) submit to the Attorney General—

"(A) the implementation plan developed under paragraph (1);

"(B) documentation from each member of the planning committee as to their participation in the planning process;

"(C) documentation from the prosecution, law enforcement, court, and victim services programs to be assisted, describing—

"(i) the need for the grant funds;

"(ii) the intended use of the grant funds;

"(iii) the expected result of the grant funds; and

"(iv) the demographic characteristics of the populations to be served, including age, disability, race, ethnicity, and language background;

"(D) a description of how the State will ensure that any subgrantees will consult with victim service providers during the course of developing their grant applications in order to ensure that the proposed activities are designed

S. 47—16

to promote the safety, confidentiality, and economic independence of victims;

"(E) demographic data on the distribution of underserved populations within the State and a description of how the State will meet the needs of underserved populations, including the minimum allocation for population specific services required under subsection (c)(4)(C);

"(F) a description of how the State plans to meet the regulations issued pursuant to subsection (e)(2);

"(G) goals and objectives for reducing domestic violence-related homicides within the State; and

"(H) any other information requested by the Attorney General.

"(j) REALLOCATION OF FUNDS.—A State may use any returned or remaining funds for any authorized purpose under this part if—

"(1) funds from a subgrant awarded under this part are returned to the State; or

"(2) the State does not receive sufficient eligible applications to award the full funding within the allocations in subsection (c)(4)";

(4) in section 2010 (42 U.S.C. 3796gg–4)—

(A) in subsection (a), by striking paragraph (1) and inserting the following:

"(1) IN GENERAL.—A State, Indian tribal government, or unit of local government shall not be entitled to funds under this subchapter unless the State, Indian tribal government, unit of local government, or another governmental entity—

"(A) incurs the full out-of-pocket cost of forensic medical exams described in subsection (b) for victims of sexual assault; and

"(B) coordinates with health care providers in the region to notify victims of sexual assault of the availability of rape exams at no cost to the victims.";

(B) in subsection (b)—

(i) in paragraph (1), by inserting "or" after the semicolon;

(ii) in paragraph (2), by striking "; or" and inserting a period; and

(iii) by striking paragraph (3); and

(C) by amending subsection (d) to read as follows:

"(d) NONCOOPERATION.—

"(1) IN GENERAL.—To be in compliance with this section, a State, Indian tribal government, or unit of local government shall comply with subsection (b) without regard to whether the victim participates in the criminal justice system or cooperates with law enforcement.

"(2) COMPLIANCE PERIOD.—States, territories, and Indian tribal governments shall have 3 years from the date of enactment of this Act to come into compliance with this section."; and

(5) in section 2011(a)(1) (42 U.S.C. 3796gg–5(a)(1))—

(A) by inserting "modification, enforcement, dismissal, withdrawal" after "registration," each place it appears;

(B) by inserting ", dating violence, sexual assault, or stalking" after "felony domestic violence"; and

(C) by striking "victim of domestic violence" and all that follows through "sexual assault" and inserting "victim of domestic violence, dating violence, sexual assault, or stalking".

SEC. 102. GRANTS TO ENCOURAGE ARREST POLICIES AND ENFORCEMENT OF PROTECTION ORDERS.

(a) IN GENERAL.—Part U of title I of the Omnibus Crime Control and Safe Streets Act of 1968 (42 U.S.C. 3796hh et seq.) is amended—

(1) in section 2101 (42 U.S.C. 3796hh)—

(A) in subsection (b)—

(i) in the matter preceding paragraph (1), by striking "States," and all that follows through "units of local government" and inserting "grantees";

(ii) in paragraph (1), by inserting "and enforcement of protection orders across State and tribal lines" before the period;

(iii) in paragraph (2), by striking "and training in police departments to improve tracking of cases" and inserting "data collection systems, and training in police departments to improve tracking of cases and classification of complaints";

(iv) in paragraph (4), by inserting "and provide the appropriate training and education about domestic violence, dating violence, sexual assault, and stalking" after "computer tracking systems";

(v) in paragraph (5), by inserting "and other victim services" after "legal advocacy service programs";

(vi) in paragraph (6), by striking "judges" and inserting "Federal, State, tribal, territorial, and local judges, courts, and court-based and court-related personnel";

(vii) in paragraph (8), by striking "and sexual assault" and inserting "dating violence, sexual assault, and stalking";

(viii) in paragraph (10), by striking "non-profit, non-governmental victim services organizations," and inserting "victim service providers, staff from population specific organizations,"; and

(ix) by adding at the end the following:

"(14) To develop and implement training programs for prosecutors and other prosecution-related personnel regarding best practices to ensure offender accountability, victim safety, and victim consultation in cases involving domestic violence, dating violence, sexual assault, and stalking.

"(15) To develop or strengthen policies, protocols, and training for law enforcement, prosecutors, and the judiciary in recognizing, investigating, and prosecuting instances of domestic violence, dating violence, sexual assault, and stalking against immigrant victims, including the appropriate use of applications for nonimmigrant status under subparagraphs (T) and (U) of section 101(a)(15) of the Immigration and Nationality Act (8 U.S.C. 1101(a)(15)).

"(16) To develop and promote State, local, or tribal legislation and policies that enhance best practices for responding to the crimes of domestic violence, dating violence, sexual assault, and stalking, including the appropriate treatment of victims.

"(17) To develop, implement, or enhance sexual assault nurse examiner programs or sexual assault forensic examiner programs, including the hiring and training of such examiners.

"(18) To develop, implement, or enhance Sexual Assault Response Teams or similar coordinated community responses to sexual assault.

"(19) To develop and strengthen policies, protocols, and training for law enforcement officers and prosecutors regarding the investigation and prosecution of sexual assault cases and the appropriate treatment of victims.

"(20) To provide human immunodeficiency virus testing programs, counseling, and prophylaxis for victims of sexual assault.

"(21) To identify and inventory backlogs of sexual assault evidence collection kits and to develop protocols for responding to and addressing such backlogs, including policies and protocols for notifying and involving victims.

"(22) To develop multidisciplinary high-risk teams focusing on reducing domestic violence and dating violence homicides by—

"(A) using evidence-based indicators to assess the risk of homicide and link high-risk victims to immediate crisis intervention services;

"(B) identifying and managing high-risk offenders; and

"(C) providing ongoing victim advocacy and referrals to comprehensive services including legal, housing, health care, and economic assistance.";

(B) in subsection (c)—

(i) in paragraph (1)—

(I) in the matter preceding subparagraph (A), by inserting "except for a court," before "certify"; and

(II) by redesignating subparagraphs (A) and (B) as clauses (i) and (ii), and adjusting the margin accordingly;

(ii) in paragraph (2), by inserting "except for a court," before "demonstrate";

(iii) in paragraph (3)—

(I) by striking "spouses" each place it appears and inserting "parties"; and

(II) by striking "spouse" and inserting "party";

(iv) in paragraph (4)—

(I) by inserting ", dating violence, sexual assault, or stalking" after "felony domestic violence";

(II) by inserting "modification, enforcement, dismissal," after "registration," each place it appears;

(III) by inserting "dating violence," after "victim of domestic violence,"; and

(IV) by striking "and" at the end;

(v) in paragraph (5)—

(I) in the matter preceding subparagraph (A), by striking ", not later than 3 years after January 5, 2006";

(II) by inserting ", trial of, or sentencing for" after "investigation of" each place it appears;

(III) by redesignating subparagraphs (A) and (B) as clauses (i) and (ii), and adjusting the margin accordingly;

(IV) in clause (ii), as redesignated by subclause (III) of this clause, by striking "subparagraph (A)" and inserting "clause (i)"; and

(V) by striking the period at the end and inserting "; and";

(vi) by redesignating paragraphs (1) through (5), as amended by this subparagraph, as subparagraphs (A) through (E), respectively;

(vii) in the matter preceding subparagraph (A), as redesignated by clause (v) of this subparagraph—

(I) by striking the comma that immediately follows another comma; and

(II) by striking "grantees are States" and inserting the following: "grantees are—

"(1) States"; and

(viii) by adding at the end the following:

"(2) a State, tribal, or territorial domestic violence or sexual assault coalition or a victim service provider that partners with a State, Indian tribal government, or unit of local government that certifies that the State, Indian tribal government, or unit of local government meets the requirements under paragraph (1).";

(C) in subsection (d)—

(i) in paragraph (1)—

(I) in the matter preceding subparagraph (A), by inserting ", policy," after "law"; and

(II) in subparagraph (A), by inserting "and the defendant is in custody or has been served with the information or indictment" before the semicolon; and

(ii) in paragraph (2), by striking "it" and inserting "its"; and

(D) by adding at the end the following:

"(f) ALLOCATION FOR TRIBAL COALITIONS.—Of the amounts appropriated for purposes of this part for each fiscal year, not less than 5 percent shall be available for grants under section 2001 of title I of the Omnibus Crime Control and Safe Streets Act of 1968 (42 U.S.C. 3796gg).

"(g) ALLOCATION FOR SEXUAL ASSAULT.—Of the amounts appropriated for purposes of this part for each fiscal year, not less than 25 percent shall be available for projects that address sexual assault, including stranger rape, acquaintance rape, alcohol or drug-facilitated rape, and rape within the context of an intimate partner relationship."; and

(2) in section 2102(a) (42 U.S.C. 3796hh–1(a))—

(A) in paragraph (1), by inserting "court," after "tribal government,"; and

(B) in paragraph (4), by striking "nonprofit, private sexual assault and domestic violence programs" and inserting "victim service providers and, as appropriate, population specific organizations".

S. 47—20

(b) AUTHORIZATION OF APPROPRIATIONS.—Section 1001(a)(19) of title I of the Omnibus Crime Control and Safe Streets Act of 1968 (42 U.S.C. 3793(a)(19)) is amended—

(1) by striking "$75,000,000" and all that follows through "2011." and inserting "$73,000,000 for each of fiscal years 2014 through 2018."; and

(2) by striking the period that immediately follows another period.

SEC. 103. LEGAL ASSISTANCE FOR VICTIMS.

Section 1201 of the Violence Against Women Act of 2000 (42 U.S.C. 3796gg–6) is amended—

(1) in subsection (a)—

(A) in the first sentence, by striking "arising as a consequence of" and inserting "relating to or arising out of"; and

(B) in the second sentence, by inserting "or arising out of" after "relating to";

(2) in subsection (b)—

(A) in the heading, by inserting "AND GRANT CONDITIONS" after "DEFINITIONS"; and

(B) by inserting "and grant conditions" after "definitions";

(3) in subsection (c)—

(A) in paragraph (1), by striking "victims services organizations" and inserting "victim service providers"; and

(B) by striking paragraph (3) and inserting the following:

"(3) to implement, expand, and establish efforts and projects to provide competent, supervised pro bono legal assistance for victims of domestic violence, dating violence, sexual assault, or stalking, except that not more than 10 percent of the funds awarded under this section may be used for the purpose described in this paragraph.";

(4) in subsection (d)—

(A) in paragraph (1), by striking "this section has completed" and all that follows and inserting the following: "this section—"

"(A) has demonstrated expertise in providing legal assistance to victims of domestic violence, dating violence, sexual assault, or stalking in the targeted population; or

"(B)(i) is partnered with an entity or person that has demonstrated expertise described in subparagraph (A); and

"(ii) has completed, or will complete, training in connection with domestic violence, dating violence, stalking, or sexual assault and related legal issues, including training on evidence-based risk factors for domestic and dating violence homicide;"; and

(B) in paragraph (2), by striking "stalking organization" and inserting "stalking victim service provider"; and

(5) in subsection (f) in paragraph (1), by striking "this section" and all that follows and inserting the following: "this section $57,000,000 for each of fiscal years 2014 through 2018.".

SEC. 104. CONSOLIDATION OF GRANTS TO SUPPORT FAMILIES IN THE JUSTICE SYSTEM.

(a) IN GENERAL.—Title III of division B of the Victims of Trafficking and Violence Protection Act of 2000 (Public Law 106–386;

114 Stat. 1509) is amended by striking the section preceding section 1302 (42 U.S.C. 10420), as amended by section 306 of the Violence Against Women and Department of Justice Reauthorization Act of 2005 (Public Law 109–162; 119 Stat. 316), and inserting the following:

"SEC. 1301. GRANTS TO SUPPORT FAMILIES IN THE JUSTICE SYSTEM.

"(a) IN GENERAL.—The Attorney General may make grants to States, units of local government, courts (including juvenile courts), Indian tribal governments, nonprofit organizations, legal services providers, and victim services providers to improve the response of all aspects of the civil and criminal justice system to families with a history of domestic violence, dating violence, sexual assault, or stalking, or in cases involving allegations of child sexual abuse.

"(b) USE OF FUNDS.—A grant under this section may be used to—

"(1) provide supervised visitation and safe visitation exchange of children and youth by and between parents in situations involving domestic violence, dating violence, child sexual abuse, sexual assault, or stalking;

"(2) develop and promote State, local, and tribal legislation, policies, and best practices for improving civil and criminal court functions, responses, practices, and procedures in cases involving a history of domestic violence or sexual assault, or in cases involving allegations of child sexual abuse, including cases in which the victim proceeds pro se;

"(3) educate court-based and court-related personnel and court-appointed personnel (including custody evaluators and guardians ad litem) and child protective services workers on the dynamics of domestic violence, dating violence, sexual assault, and stalking, including information on perpetrator behavior, evidence-based risk factors for domestic and dating violence homicide, and on issues relating to the needs of victims, including safety, security, privacy, and confidentiality, including cases in which the victim proceeds pro se;

"(4) provide appropriate resources in juvenile court matters to respond to dating violence, domestic violence, sexual assault (including child sexual abuse), and stalking and ensure necessary services dealing with the health and mental health of victims are available;

"(5) enable courts or court-based or court-related programs to develop or enhance—

"(A) court infrastructure (such as specialized courts, consolidated courts, dockets, intake centers, or interpreter services);

"(B) community-based initiatives within the court system (such as court watch programs, victim assistants, pro se victim assistance programs, or community-based supplementary services);

"(C) offender management, monitoring, and accountability programs;

"(D) safe and confidential information-storage and information-sharing databases within and between court systems;

S. 47—22

"(E) education and outreach programs to improve community access, including enhanced access for underserved populations; and

"(F) other projects likely to improve court responses to domestic violence, dating violence, sexual assault, and stalking;

"(6) provide civil legal assistance and advocacy services, including legal information and resources in cases in which the victim proceeds pro se, to—

"(A) victims of domestic violence; and

"(B) nonoffending parents in matters—

"(i) that involve allegations of child sexual abuse;

"(ii) that relate to family matters, including civil protection orders, custody, and divorce; and

"(iii) in which the other parent is represented by counsel;

"(7) collect data and provide training and technical assistance, including developing State, local, and tribal model codes and policies, to improve the capacity of grantees and communities to address the civil justice needs of victims of domestic violence, dating violence, sexual assault, and stalking who have legal representation, who are proceeding pro se, or who are proceeding with the assistance of a legal advocate; and

"(8) to improve training and education to assist judges, judicial personnel, attorneys, child welfare personnel, and legal advocates in the civil justice system.

"(c) CONSIDERATIONS.—

"(1) IN GENERAL.—In making grants for purposes described in paragraphs (1) through (7) of subsection (b), the Attorney General shall consider—

"(A) the number of families to be served by the proposed programs and services;

"(B) the extent to which the proposed programs and services serve underserved populations;

"(C) the extent to which the applicant demonstrates cooperation and collaboration with nonprofit, nongovernmental entities in the local community with demonstrated histories of effective work on domestic violence, dating violence, sexual assault, or stalking, including State or tribal domestic violence coalitions, State or tribal sexual assault coalitions, local shelters, and programs for domestic violence and sexual assault victims; and

"(D) the extent to which the applicant demonstrates coordination and collaboration with State, tribal, and local court systems, including mechanisms for communication and referral.

"(2) OTHER GRANTS.—In making grants under subsection (b)(8) the Attorney General shall take into account the extent to which the grantee has expertise addressing the judicial system's handling of family violence, child custody, child abuse and neglect, adoption, foster care, supervised visitation, divorce, and parentage.

"(d) APPLICANT REQUIREMENTS.—The Attorney General may make a grant under this section to an applicant that—

"(1) demonstrates expertise in the areas of domestic violence, dating violence, sexual assault, stalking, or child sexual abuse, as appropriate;

"(2) ensures that any fees charged to individuals for use of supervised visitation programs and services are based on the income of those individuals, unless otherwise provided by court order;

"(3) for a court-based program, certifies that victims of domestic violence, dating violence, sexual assault, or stalking are not charged fees or any other costs related to the filing, petitioning, modifying, issuance, registration, enforcement, withdrawal, or dismissal of matters relating to the domestic violence, dating violence, sexual assault, or stalking;

"(4) demonstrates that adequate security measures, including adequate facilities, procedures, and personnel capable of preventing violence, and adequate standards are, or will be, in place (including the development of protocols or policies to ensure that confidential information is not shared with courts, law enforcement agencies, or child welfare agencies unless necessary to ensure the safety of any child or adult using the services of a program funded under this section), if the applicant proposes to operate supervised visitation programs and services or safe visitation exchange;

"(5) certifies that the organizational policies of the applicant do not require mediation or counseling involving offenders and victims being physically present in the same place, in cases where domestic violence, dating violence, sexual assault, or stalking is alleged;

"(6) certifies that any person providing legal assistance through a program funded under this section has completed or will complete training on domestic violence, dating violence, sexual assault, and stalking, including child sexual abuse, and related legal issues; and

"(7) certifies that any person providing custody evaluation or guardian ad litem services through a program funded under this section has completed or will complete training developed with input from and in collaboration with a tribal, State, territorial, or local domestic violence, dating violence, sexual assault, or stalking victim service provider or coalition on the dynamics of domestic violence and sexual assault, including child sexual abuse, that includes training on how to review evidence of past abuse and the use of evidenced-based theories to make recommendations on custody and visitation.

"(e) AUTHORIZATION OF APPROPRIATIONS.—There is authorized to be appropriated to carry out this section, $22,000,000 for each of fiscal years 2014 through 2018. Amounts appropriated pursuant to this subsection shall remain available until expended.

"(f) ALLOTMENT FOR INDIAN TRIBES.—

"(1) IN GENERAL.—Not less than 10 percent of the total amount available under this section for each fiscal year shall be available for grants under the program authorized by section 3796gg–10 of this title.

"(2) APPLICABILITY OF PART.—The requirements of this section shall not apply to funds allocated for the program described in paragraph (1).".

(b) TECHNICAL AND CONFORMING AMENDMENT.—Subtitle J of the Violence Against Women Act of 1994 (42 U.S.C. 14043 et seq.) is repealed.

S. 47—24

SEC. 105. SEX OFFENDER MANAGEMENT.

Section 40152(c) of the Violence Against Women Act of 1994 (42 U.S.C. 13941) is amended by striking "$5,000,000" and all that follows and inserting "$5,000,000 for each of fiscal years 2014 through 2018.".

SEC. 106. COURT-APPOINTED SPECIAL ADVOCATE PROGRAM.

Subtitle B of title II of the Crime Control Act of 1990 (42 U.S.C. 13011 et seq.) is amended—

(1) in section 216 (42 U.S.C. 13012), by striking "January 1, 2010" and inserting "January 1, 2015";

(2) in section 217 (42 U.S.C. 13013)—

(A) by striking "Code of Ethics" in section (c)(2) and inserting "Standards for Programs"; and

(B) by adding at the end the following:

"(e) REPORTING.—An organization that receives a grant under this section for a fiscal year shall submit to the Administrator a report regarding the use of the grant for the fiscal year, including a discussion of outcome performance measures (which shall be established by the Administrator) to determine the effectiveness of the programs of the organization in meeting the needs of children in the child welfare system."; and

(3) in section 219(a) (42 U.S.C. 13014(a)), by striking "fiscal years 2007 through 2011" and inserting "fiscal years 2014 through 2018".

SEC. 107. CRIMINAL PROVISION RELATING TO STALKING, INCLUDING CYBERSTALKING.

(a) INTERSTATE DOMESTIC VIOLENCE.—Section 2261(a)(1) of title 18, United States Code, is amended—

(1) by inserting "is present" after "Indian Country or"; and

(2) by inserting "or presence" after "as a result of such travel";

(b) STALKING.—Section 2261A of title 18, United States Code, is amended to read as follows:

"§ 2261A. Stalking

"Whoever—

"(1) travels in interstate or foreign commerce or is present within the special maritime and territorial jurisdiction of the United States, or enters or leaves Indian country, with the intent to kill, injure, harass, intimidate, or place under surveillance with intent to kill, injure, harass, or intimidate another person, and in the course of, or as a result of, such travel or presence engages in conduct that—

"(A) places that person in reasonable fear of the death of, or serious bodily injury to—

"(i) that person;

"(ii) an immediate family member (as defined in section 115) of that person; or

"(iii) a spouse or intimate partner of that person; or

"(B) causes, attempts to cause, or would be reasonably expected to cause substantial emotional distress to a person described in clause (i), (ii), or (iii) of subparagraph (A); or

"(2) with the intent to kill, injure, harass, intimidate, or place under surveillance with intent to kill, injure, harass, or intimidate another person, uses the mail, any interactive computer service or electronic communication service or electronic communication system of interstate commerce, or any other facility of interstate or foreign commerce to engage in a course of conduct that—

"(A) places that person in reasonable fear of the death of or serious bodily injury to a person described in clause (i), (ii), or (iii) of paragraph (1)(A); or

"(B) causes, attempts to cause, or would be reasonably expected to cause substantial emotional distress to a person described in clause (i), (ii), or (iii) of paragraph (1)(A),

shall be punished as provided in section 2261(b) of this title.".

(c) INTERSTATE VIOLATION OF PROTECTION ORDER.—Section 2262(a)(2) of title 18, United States Code, is amended by inserting "is present" after "Indian Country or".

SEC. 108. OUTREACH AND SERVICES TO UNDERSERVED POPULATIONS GRANT.

Section 120 of the Violence Against Women and Department of Justice Reauthorization Act of 2005 (42 U.S.C. 14045) is amended to read as follows:

"SEC. 120. GRANTS FOR OUTREACH AND SERVICES TO UNDERSERVED POPULATIONS.

"(a) GRANTS AUTHORIZED.—

"(1) IN GENERAL.—Of the amounts appropriated under the grant programs identified in paragraph (2), the Attorney General shall take 2 percent of such appropriated amounts and combine them to award grants to eligible entities described in subsection (b) of this section to develop and implement outreach strategies targeted at adult or youth victims of domestic violence, dating violence, sexual assault, or stalking in underserved populations and to provide victim services to meet the needs of adult and youth victims of domestic violence, dating violence, sexual assault, and stalking in underserved populations. The requirements of the grant programs identified in paragraph (2) shall not apply to this grant program.

"(2) PROGRAMS COVERED.—The programs covered by paragraph (1) are the programs carried out under the following provisions:

"(A) Section 2001 of the Omnibus Crime Control and Safe Streets Act of 1968 (Grants to Combat Violent Crimes Against Women).

"(B) Section 2101 of the Omnibus Crime Control and Safe Streets Act of 1968 (Grants to Encourage Arrest Policies and Enforcement of Protection Orders Program).

"(b) ELIGIBLE ENTITIES.—Eligible entities under this section are—

"(1) population specific organizations that have demonstrated experience and expertise in providing population specific services in the relevant underserved communities, or population specific organizations working in partnership with a victim service provider or domestic violence or sexual assault coalition;

"(2) victim service providers offering population specific services for a specific underserved population; or

"(3) victim service providers working in partnership with a national, State, tribal, or local organization that has demonstrated experience and expertise in providing population specific services in the relevant underserved population.

"(c) PLANNING GRANTS.—The Attorney General may use up to 25 percent of funds available under this section to make one-time planning grants to eligible entities to support the planning and development of specially designed and targeted programs for adult and youth victims in one or more underserved populations, including—

"(1) identifying, building and strengthening partnerships with potential collaborators within underserved populations, Federal, State, tribal, territorial or local government entities, and public and private organizations;

"(2) conducting a needs assessment of the community and the targeted underserved population or populations to determine what the barriers are to service access and what factors contribute to those barriers, using input from the targeted underserved population or populations;

"(3) identifying promising prevention, outreach and intervention strategies for victims from a targeted underserved population or populations; and

"(4) developing a plan, with the input of the targeted underserved population or populations, for implementing prevention, outreach and intervention strategies to address the barriers to accessing services, promoting community engagement in the prevention of domestic violence, dating violence, sexual assault, and stalking within the targeted underserved populations, and evaluating the program.

"(d) IMPLEMENTATION GRANTS.—The Attorney General shall make grants to eligible entities for the purpose of providing or enhancing population specific outreach and services to adult and youth victims in one or more underserved populations, including—

"(1) working with Federal, State, tribal, territorial and local governments, agencies, and organizations to develop or enhance population specific services;

"(2) strengthening the capacity of underserved populations to provide population specific services;

"(3) strengthening the capacity of traditional victim service providers to provide population specific services;

"(4) strengthening the effectiveness of criminal and civil justice interventions by providing training for law enforcement, prosecutors, judges and other court personnel on domestic violence, dating violence, sexual assault, or stalking in underserved populations; or

"(5) working in cooperation with an underserved population to develop and implement outreach, education, prevention, and intervention strategies that highlight available resources and the specific issues faced by victims of domestic violence, dating violence, sexual assault, or stalking from underserved populations.

"(e) APPLICATION.—An eligible entity desiring a grant under this section shall submit an application to the Director of the Office on Violence Against Women at such time, in such form, and in such manner as the Director may prescribe.

"(f) REPORTS.—Each eligible entity receiving a grant under this section shall submit to the Director of the Office on Violence

Against Women a report that describes the activities carried out with grant funds.

"(g) AUTHORIZATION OF APPROPRIATIONS.—In addition to the funds identified in subsection (a)(1), there are authorized to be appropriated to carry out this section $2,000,000 for each of fiscal years 2014 through 2018.

"(h) DEFINITIONS AND GRANT CONDITIONS.—In this section the definitions and grant conditions in section 40002 of the Violence Against Women Act of 1994 (42 U.S.C. 13925) shall apply.".

SEC. 109. CULTURALLY SPECIFIC SERVICES GRANT.

Section 121 of the Violence Against Women and Department of Justice Reauthorization Act of 2005 (42 U.S.C. 14045a) is amended—

(1) in the section heading, by striking "**AND LINGUISTICALLY**";

(2) by striking "and linguistically" each place it appears;

(3) by striking "and linguistic" each place it appears;

(4) by striking subsection (a)(2) and inserting:

"(2) PROGRAMS COVERED.—The programs covered by paragraph (1) are the programs carried out under the following provisions:

"(A) Section 2101 of the Omnibus Crime Control and Safe Streets Act of 1968 (Grants to Encourage Arrest Policies and Enforcement of Protection Orders).

"(B) Section 14201 of division B of the Victims of Trafficking and Violence Protection Act of 2000 (42 U.S.C. 3796gg–6) (Legal Assistance for Victims).

"(C) Section 40295 of the Violence Against Women Act of 1994 (42 U.S.C. 13971) (Rural Domestic Violence, Dating Violence, Sexual Assault, Stalking, and Child Abuse Enforcement Assistance).

"(D) Section 40802 of the Violence Against Women Act of 1994 (42 U.S.C. 14041a) (Enhanced Training and Services to End Violence Against Women Later in Life).

"(E) Section 1402 of division B of the Victims of Trafficking and Violence Protection Act of 2000 (42 U.S.C. 3796gg–7) (Education, Training, and Enhanced Services to End Violence Against and Abuse of Women with Disabilities)."; and

(5) in subsection (g), by striking "linguistic and".

TITLE II—IMPROVING SERVICES FOR VICTIMS OF DOMESTIC VIOLENCE, DATING VIOLENCE, SEXUAL ASSAULT, AND STALKING

SEC. 201. SEXUAL ASSAULT SERVICES PROGRAM.

(a) GRANTS TO STATES AND TERRITORIES.—Section 41601(b) of the Violence Against Women Act of 1994 (42 U.S.C. 14043g(b)) is amended—

(1) in paragraph (1), by striking "other programs" and all that follows and inserting "other nongovernmental or tribal programs and projects to assist individuals who have been

S. 47—28

victimized by sexual assault, without regard to the age of the individual.”;

(2) in paragraph (2)—

(A) in subparagraph (B), by inserting “or tribal programs and activities” after “nongovernmental organizations”; and

(B) in subparagraph (C)(v), by striking “linguistically and”; and

(3) in paragraph (4)—

(A) by inserting “(including the District of Columbia and Puerto Rico)” after “The Attorney General shall allocate to each State”;

(B) by striking “the District of Columbia, Puerto Rico,” after “Guam”;

(C) by striking “0.125 percent” and inserting “0.25 percent”; and

(D) by striking “The District of Columbia shall be treated as a territory for purposes of calculating its allocation under the preceding formula.”.

(b) AUTHORIZATION OF APPROPRIATIONS.—Section 41601(f)(1) of the Violence Against Women Act of 1994 (42 U.S.C. 14043g(f)(1)) is amended by striking “$50,000,000 to remain available until expended for each of the fiscal years 2007 through 2011” and inserting “$40,000,000 to remain available until expended for each of fiscal years 2014 through 2018”.

SEC. 202. RURAL DOMESTIC VIOLENCE, DATING VIOLENCE, SEXUAL ASSAULT, STALKING, AND CHILD ABUSE ENFORCEMENT ASSISTANCE.

Section 40295 of the Violence Against Women Act of 1994 (42 U.S.C. 13971) is amended—

(1) in subsection (a)(1)(H), by inserting “, including sexual assault forensic examiners” before the semicolon;

(2) in subsection (b)—

(A) in paragraph (1)—

(i) by striking “victim advocacy groups” and inserting “victim service providers”; and

(ii) by inserting “, including developing multidisciplinary teams focusing on high risk cases with the goal of preventing domestic and dating violence homicides” before the semicolon;

(B) in paragraph (2)—

(i) by striking “and other long- and short-term assistance” and inserting “legal assistance, and other long-term and short-term victim and population specific services”; and

(ii) by striking “and” at the end;

(C) in paragraph (3), by striking the period at the end and inserting “; and”; and

(D) by adding at the end the following:

“(4) developing, enlarging, or strengthening programs addressing sexual assault, including sexual assault forensic examiner programs, Sexual Assault Response Teams, law enforcement training, and programs addressing rape kit backlogs.

“(5) developing programs and strategies that focus on the specific needs of victims of domestic violence, dating violence, sexual assault, and stalking who reside in remote rural and geographically isolated areas, including addressing the challenges posed by the lack of access to shelters and victims services, and limited law enforcement resources and training, and providing training and resources to Community Health Aides involved in the delivery of Indian Health Service programs."; and

(3) in subsection (e)(1), by striking "$55,000,000 for each of the fiscal years 2007 through 2011" and inserting "$50,000,000 for each of fiscal years 2014 through 2018".

SEC. 203. TRAINING AND SERVICES TO END VIOLENCE AGAINST WOMEN WITH DISABILITIES GRANTS.

Section 1402 of division B of the Victims of Trafficking and Violence Protection Act of 2000 (42 U.S.C. 3796gg–7) is amended—

(1) in subsection (b)—

(A) in paragraph (1), by inserting "(including using evidence-based indicators to assess the risk of domestic and dating violence homicide)" after "risk reduction";

(B) in paragraph (4), by striking "victim service organizations" and inserting "victim service providers"; and

(C) in paragraph (5), by striking "victim services organizations" and inserting "victim service providers";

(2) in subsection (c)(1)(D), by striking "nonprofit and nongovernmental victim services organization, such as a State" and inserting "victim service provider, such as a State or tribal"; and

(3) in subsection (e), by striking "$10,000,000 for each of the fiscal years 2007 through 2011" and inserting "$9,000,000 for each of fiscal years 2014 through 2018".

SEC. 204. ENHANCED TRAINING AND SERVICES TO END ABUSE IN LATER LIFE.

(a) IN GENERAL.—Subtitle H of the Violence Against Women Act of 1994 (42 U.S.C. 14041 et seq.) is amended to read as follows:

"Subtitle H—Enhanced Training and Services To End Abuse Later in Life

"SEC. 40801. ENHANCED TRAINING AND SERVICES TO END ABUSE IN LATER LIFE.

"(a) DEFINITIONS.—In this section—

"(1) the term 'exploitation' has the meaning given the term in section 2011 of the Social Security Act (42 U.S.C. 1397j);

"(2) the term 'later life', relating to an individual, means the individual is 50 years of age or older; and

"(3) the term 'neglect' means the failure of a caregiver or fiduciary to provide the goods or services that are necessary to maintain the health or safety of an individual in later life.

"(b) GRANT PROGRAM.—

"(1) GRANTS AUTHORIZED.—The Attorney General may make grants to eligible entities to carry out the activities described in paragraph (2).

"(2) MANDATORY AND PERMISSIBLE ACTIVITIES.—

S. 47—30

"(A) MANDATORY ACTIVITIES.—An eligible entity receiving a grant under this section shall use the funds received under the grant to—

"(i) provide training programs to assist law enforcement agencies, prosecutors, agencies of States or units of local government, population specific organizations, victim service providers, victim advocates, and relevant officers in Federal, tribal, State, territorial, and local courts in recognizing and addressing instances of elder abuse;

"(ii) provide or enhance services for victims of abuse in later life, including domestic violence, dating violence, sexual assault, stalking, exploitation, and neglect;

"(iii) establish or support multidisciplinary collaborative community responses to victims of abuse in later life, including domestic violence, dating violence, sexual assault, stalking, exploitation, and neglect; and

"(iv) conduct cross-training for law enforcement agencies, prosecutors, agencies of States or units of local government, attorneys, health care providers, population specific organizations, faith-based advocates, victim service providers, and courts to better serve victims of abuse in later life, including domestic violence, dating violence, sexual assault, stalking, exploitation, and neglect.

"(B) PERMISSIBLE ACTIVITIES.—An eligible entity receiving a grant under this section may use the funds received under the grant to—

"(i) provide training programs to assist attorneys, health care providers, faith-based leaders, or other community-based organizations in recognizing and addressing instances of abuse in later life, including domestic violence, dating violence, sexual assault, stalking, exploitation, and neglect; or

"(ii) conduct outreach activities and awareness campaigns to ensure that victims of abuse in later life, including domestic violence, dating violence, sexual assault, stalking, exploitation, and neglect receive appropriate assistance.

"(C) WAIVER.—The Attorney General may waive 1 or more of the activities described in subparagraph (A) upon making a determination that the activity would duplicate services available in the community.

"(D) LIMITATION.—An eligible entity receiving a grant under this section may use not more than 10 percent of the total funds received under the grant for an activity described in subparagraph (B)(ii).

"(3) ELIGIBLE ENTITIES.—An entity shall be eligible to receive a grant under this section if—

"(A) the entity is—

"(i) a State;

"(ii) a unit of local government;

"(iii) a tribal government or tribal organization;

"(iv) a population specific organization with demonstrated experience in assisting individuals over 50 years of age;

"(v) a victim service provider with demonstrated experience in addressing domestic violence, dating violence, sexual assault, and stalking; or

"(vi) a State, tribal, or territorial domestic violence or sexual assault coalition; and

"(B) the entity demonstrates that it is part of a multidisciplinary partnership that includes, at a minimum—

"(i) a law enforcement agency;

"(ii) a prosecutor's office;

"(iii) a victim service provider; and

"(iv) a nonprofit program or government agency with demonstrated experience in assisting individuals in later life;

"(4) UNDERSERVED POPULATIONS.—In making grants under this section, the Attorney General shall give priority to proposals providing services to culturally specific and underserved populations.

"(5) AUTHORIZATION OF APPROPRIATIONS.—There is authorized to be appropriated to carry out this section $9,000,000 for each of fiscal years 2014 through 2018.".

TITLE III—SERVICES, PROTECTION, AND JUSTICE FOR YOUNG VICTIMS OF VIOLENCE

SEC. 301. RAPE PREVENTION AND EDUCATION GRANT.

Section 393A of the Public Health Service Act (42 U.S.C. 280b–1b) is amended—

(1) in subsection (a)—

(A) in the matter preceding paragraph (1), by inserting ", territorial or tribal" after "crisis centers, State"; and

(B) in paragraph (6), by inserting "and alcohol" after "about drugs"; and

(2) in subsection (c)—

(A) in paragraph (1), by striking "$80,000,000 for each of fiscal years 2007 through 2011" and inserting "$50,000,000 for each of fiscal years 2014 through 2018"; and

(B) by adding at the end the following:

"(3) BASELINE FUNDING FOR STATES, THE DISTRICT OF COLUMBIA, AND PUERTO RICO.—A minimum allocation of $150,000 shall be awarded in each fiscal year for each of the States, the District of Columbia, and Puerto Rico. A minimum allocation of $35,000 shall be awarded in each fiscal year for each Territory. Any unused or remaining funds shall be allotted to each State, the District of Columbia, and Puerto Rico on the basis of population.".

SEC. 302. CREATING HOPE THROUGH OUTREACH, OPTIONS, SERVICES, AND EDUCATION FOR CHILDREN AND YOUTH.

Subtitle L of the Violence Against Women Act of 1994 is amended by striking sections 41201 through 41204 (42 U.S.C. 14043c through 14043c–3) and inserting the following:

S. 47—32

"SEC. 41201. CREATING HOPE THROUGH OUTREACH, OPTIONS, SERVICES, AND EDUCATION FOR CHILDREN AND YOUTH ('CHOOSE CHILDREN & YOUTH').

"(a) GRANTS AUTHORIZED.—The Attorney General, working in collaboration with the Secretary of Health and Human Services and the Secretary of Education, shall award grants to enhance the safety of youth and children who are victims of, or exposed to, domestic violence, dating violence, sexual assault, stalking, or sex trafficking and prevent future violence.

"(b) PROGRAM PURPOSES.—Funds provided under this section may be used for the following program purpose areas:

"(1) SERVICES TO ADVOCATE FOR AND RESPOND TO YOUTH.—To develop, expand, and strengthen victim-centered interventions and services that target youth who are victims of domestic violence, dating violence, sexual assault, stalking, and sex trafficking. Services may include victim services, counseling, advocacy, mentoring, educational support, transportation, legal assistance in civil, criminal and administrative matters, such as family law cases, housing cases, child welfare proceedings, campus administrative proceedings, and civil protection order proceedings, population-specific services, and other activities that support youth in finding safety, stability, and justice and in addressing the emotional, cognitive, and physical effects of trauma. Funds may be used to—

"(A) assess and analyze currently available services for youth victims of domestic violence, dating violence, sexual assault, stalking, and sex trafficking, determining relevant barriers to such services in a particular locality, and developing a community protocol to address such problems collaboratively;

"(B) develop and implement policies, practices, and procedures to effectively respond to domestic violence, dating violence, sexual assault, stalking, or sex trafficking against youth; or

"(C) provide technical assistance and training to enhance the ability of school personnel, victim service providers, child protective service workers, staff of law enforcement agencies, prosecutors, court personnel, individuals who work in after school programs, medical personnel, social workers, mental health personnel, and workers in other programs that serve children and youth to improve their ability to appropriately respond to the needs of children and youth who are victims of domestic violence, dating violence, sexual assault, stalking, and sex trafficking, and to properly refer such children, youth, and their families to appropriate services.

"(2) SUPPORTING YOUTH THROUGH EDUCATION AND PROTECTION.—To enable middle schools, high schools, and institutions of higher education to—

"(A) provide training to school personnel, including healthcare providers and security personnel, on the needs of students who are victims of domestic violence, dating violence, sexual assault, stalking, or sex trafficking;

"(B) develop and implement prevention and intervention policies in middle and high schools, including appropriate responses to, and identification and referral procedures for, students who are experiencing or perpetrating domestic violence, dating violence, sexual assault, stalking, or sex trafficking, and procedures for handling the requirements of court protective orders issued to or against students;

"(C) provide support services for student victims of domestic violence, dating violence, sexual assault, stalking, or sex trafficking, such as a resource person who is either on-site or on-call;

"(D) implement developmentally appropriate educational programming for students regarding domestic violence, dating violence, sexual assault, stalking, and sex trafficking and the impact of such violence on youth; or

"(E) develop strategies to increase identification, support, referrals, and prevention programming for youth who are at high risk of domestic violence, dating violence, sexual assault, stalking, or sex trafficking.

"(c) ELIGIBLE APPLICANTS.—

"(1) IN GENERAL.—To be eligible to receive a grant under this section, an entity shall be—

"(A) a victim service provider, tribal nonprofit, or population-specific or community-based organization with a demonstrated history of effective work addressing the needs of youth who are, including runaway or homeless youth affected by, victims of domestic violence, dating violence, sexual assault, stalking, or sex trafficking;

"(B) a victim service provider that is partnered with an entity that has a demonstrated history of effective work addressing the needs of youth; or

"(C) a public, charter, tribal, or nationally accredited private middle or high school, a school administered by the Department of Defense under section 2164 of title 10, United States Code or section 1402 of the Defense Dependents' Education Act of 1978, a group of schools, a school district, or an institution of higher education.

"(2) PARTNERSHIPS.—

"(A) EDUCATION.—To be eligible to receive a grant for the purposes described in subsection (b)(2), an entity described in paragraph (1) shall be partnered with a public, charter, tribal, or nationally accredited private middle or high school, a school administered by the Department of Defense under section 2164 of title 10, United States Code or section 1402 of the Defense Dependents' Education Act of 1978, a group of schools, a school district, or an institution of higher education.

"(B) OTHER PARTNERSHIPS.—All applicants under this section are encouraged to work in partnership with organizations and agencies that work with the relevant population. Such entities may include—

"(i) a State, tribe, unit of local government, or territory;

"(ii) a population specific or community-based organization;

"(iii) batterer intervention programs or sex offender treatment programs with specialized knowledge and experience working with youth offenders; or "(iv) any other agencies or nonprofit, nongovernmental organizations with the capacity to provide effective assistance to the adult, youth, and child victims served by the partnership.

"(d) GRANTEE REQUIREMENTS.—Applicants for grants under this section shall establish and implement policies, practices, and procedures that—

"(1) require and include appropriate referral systems for child and youth victims;

"(2) protect the confidentiality and privacy of child and youth victim information, particularly in the context of parental or third party involvement and consent, mandatory reporting duties, and working with other service providers all with priority on victim safety and autonomy; and

"(3) ensure that all individuals providing intervention or prevention programming to children or youth through a program funded under this section have completed, or will complete, sufficient training in connection with domestic violence, dating violence, sexual assault, stalking, and sex trafficking.

"(e) DEFINITIONS AND GRANT CONDITIONS.—In this section, the definitions and grant conditions provided for in section 40002 shall apply.

"(f) AUTHORIZATION OF APPROPRIATIONS.—There is authorized to be appropriated to carry out this section, $15,000,000 for each of fiscal years 2014 through 2018.

"(g) ALLOTMENT.—

"(1) IN GENERAL.—Not less than 50 percent of the total amount appropriated under this section for each fiscal year shall be used for the purposes described in subsection (b)(1).

"(2) INDIAN TRIBES.—Not less than 10 percent of the total amount appropriated under this section for each fiscal year shall be made available for grants under the program authorized by section 2015 of the Omnibus Crime Control and Safe Streets Act of 1968. The requirements of this section shall not apply to funds allocated under this paragraph.

"(h) PRIORITY.—The Attorney General shall prioritize grant applications under this section that coordinate with prevention programs in the community.".

SEC. 303. GRANTS TO COMBAT VIOLENT CRIMES ON CAMPUSES.

Section 304 of the Violence Against Women and Department of Justice Reauthorization Act of 2005 (42 U.S.C. 14045b) is amended—

(1) in subsection (a)—

(A) in paragraph (1)—

(i) by striking "stalking on campuses, and" and inserting "stalking on campuses,";

(ii) by striking "crimes against women on" and inserting "crimes on"; and

(iii) by inserting ", and to develop and strengthen prevention education and awareness programs" before the period; and

(B) in paragraph (2), by striking "$500,000" and inserting "$300,000";

(2) in subsection (b)—

(A) in paragraph (2)—

(i) by inserting ", strengthen," after "To develop"; and

(ii) by inserting "including the use of technology to commit these crimes," after "sexual assault and stalking,";

(B) in paragraph (4)—

(i) by inserting "and population specific services" after "strengthen victim services programs";

(ii) by striking "entities carrying out" and all that follows through "stalking victim services programs" and inserting "victim service providers"; and

(iii) by inserting ", regardless of whether the services are provided by the institution or in coordination with community victim service providers" before the period at the end; and

(C) by adding at the end the following:

"(9) To develop or adapt and provide developmental, culturally appropriate, and linguistically accessible print or electronic materials to address both prevention and intervention in domestic violence, dating violence, sexual violence, and stalking.

"(10) To develop or adapt population specific strategies and projects for victims of domestic violence, dating violence, sexual assault, and stalking from underserved populations on campus.";

(3) in subsection (c)—

(A) in paragraph (2)—

(i) in subparagraph (B), by striking "any nonprofit" and all that follows through "victim services programs" and inserting "victim service providers";

(ii) by redesignating subparagraphs (D) through (F) as subparagraphs (E) through (G), respectively; and

(iii) by inserting after subparagraph (C), the following:

"(D) describe how underserved populations in the campus community will be adequately served, including the provision of relevant population specific services;"; and

(B) in paragraph (3), by striking "2007 through 2011" and inserting "2014 through 2018";

(4) in subsection (d)—

(A) by redesignating paragraph (3) as paragraph (4); and

(B) by inserting after paragraph (2), the following:

"(3) GRANTEE MINIMUM REQUIREMENTS.—Each grantee shall comply with the following minimum requirements during the grant period:

"(A) The grantee shall create a coordinated community response including both organizations external to the institution and relevant divisions of the institution.

"(B) The grantee shall establish a mandatory prevention and education program on domestic violence, dating violence, sexual assault, and stalking for all incoming students.

"(C) The grantee shall train all campus law enforcement to respond effectively to domestic violence, dating violence, sexual assault, and stalking.

"(D) The grantee shall train all members of campus disciplinary boards to respond effectively to situations involving domestic violence, dating violence, sexual assault, or stalking."; and

(5) in subsection (e), by striking "there are" and all that follows through the period and inserting "there is authorized to be appropriated $12,000,000 for each of fiscal years 2014 through 2018.".

SEC. 304. CAMPUS SEXUAL VIOLENCE, DOMESTIC VIOLENCE, DATING VIOLENCE, AND STALKING EDUCATION AND PREVENTION.

(a) In General.—Section 485(f) of the Higher Education Act of 1965 (20 U.S.C. 1092(f)) is amended—

(1) in paragraph (1)—

(A) in subparagraph (C)(iii), by striking the period at the end and inserting ", when the victim of such crime elects or is unable to make such a report."; and

(B) in subparagraph (F)—

(i) in clause (i)(VIII), by striking "and" after the semicolon;

(ii) in clause (ii)—

(I) by striking "sexual orientation" and inserting " national origin, sexual orientation, gender identity,"; and

(II) by striking the period and inserting "; and"; and

(iii) by adding at the end the following:

"(iii) of domestic violence, dating violence, and stalking incidents that were reported to campus security authorities or local police agencies.";

(2) in paragraph (3), by inserting ", that withholds the names of victims as confidential," after "that is timely";

(3) in paragraph (6)(A)—

(A) by redesignating clauses (i), (ii), and (iii) as clauses (ii), (iii), and (iv), respectively;

(B) by inserting before clause (ii), as redesignated by subparagraph (A), the following:

"(i) The terms 'dating violence', 'domestic violence', and 'stalking' have the meaning given such terms in section 40002(a) of the Violence Against Women Act of 1994 (42 U.S.C. 13925(a))."; and

(C) by inserting after clause (iv), as redesignated by subparagraph (A), the following:

"(v) The term 'sexual assault' means an offense classified as a forcible or nonforcible sex offense under the uniform crime reporting system of the Federal Bureau of Investigation.";

(4) in paragraph (7)—

(A) by striking "paragraph (1)(F)" and inserting "clauses (i) and (ii) of paragraph (1)(F)"; and

(B) by inserting after "Hate Crime Statistics Act." the following: "For the offenses of domestic violence, dating violence, and stalking, such statistics shall be compiled in accordance with the definitions used in section 40002(a) of the Violence Against Women Act of 1994 (42 U.S.C. 13925(a)).";

(5) by striking paragraph (8) and inserting the following:

"(8)(A) Each institution of higher education participating in any program under this title and title IV of the Economic Opportunity Act of 1964, other than a foreign institution of higher education, shall develop and distribute as part of the report described in paragraph (1) a statement of policy regarding—

"(i) such institution's programs to prevent domestic violence, dating violence, sexual assault, and stalking; and

"(ii) the procedures that such institution will follow once an incident of domestic violence, dating violence, sexual assault, or stalking has been reported, including a statement of the standard of evidence that will be used during any institutional conduct proceeding arising from such a report.

"(B) The policy described in subparagraph (A) shall address the following areas:

"(i) Education programs to promote the awareness of rape, acquaintance rape, domestic violence, dating violence, sexual assault, and stalking, which shall include—

"(I) primary prevention and awareness programs for all incoming students and new employees, which shall include—

"(aa) a statement that the institution of higher education prohibits the offenses of domestic violence, dating violence, sexual assault, and stalking;

"(bb) the definition of domestic violence, dating violence, sexual assault, and stalking in the applicable jurisdiction;

"(cc) the definition of consent, in reference to sexual activity, in the applicable jurisdiction;

"(dd) safe and positive options for bystander intervention that may be carried out by an individual to prevent harm or intervene when there is a risk of domestic violence, dating violence, sexual assault, or stalking against a person other than such individual;

"(ee) information on risk reduction to recognize warning signs of abusive behavior and how to avoid potential attacks; and

"(ff) the information described in clauses (ii) through (vii); and

"(II) ongoing prevention and awareness campaigns for students and faculty, including information described in items (aa) through (ff) of subclause (I).

"(ii) Possible sanctions or protective measures that such institution may impose following a final determination of an institutional disciplinary procedure regarding rape, acquaintance rape, domestic violence, dating violence, sexual assault, or stalking.

"(iii) Procedures victims should follow if a sex offense, domestic violence, dating violence, sexual assault, or stalking has occurred, including information in writing about—

"(I) the importance of preserving evidence as may be necessary to the proof of criminal domestic violence, dating violence, sexual assault, or stalking, or in obtaining a protection order;

"(II) to whom the alleged offense should be reported;

"(III) options regarding law enforcement and campus authorities, including notification of the victim's option to—

S. 47—38

"(aa) notify proper law enforcement authorities, including on-campus and local police;

"(bb) be assisted by campus authorities in notifying law enforcement authorities if the victim so chooses; and

"(cc) decline to notify such authorities; and

"(IV) where applicable, the rights of victims and the institution's responsibilities regarding orders of protection, no contact orders, restraining orders, or similar lawful orders issued by a criminal, civil, or tribal court.

"(iv) Procedures for institutional disciplinary action in cases of alleged domestic violence, dating violence, sexual assault, or stalking, which shall include a clear statement that—

"(I) such proceedings shall—

"(aa) provide a prompt, fair, and impartial investigation and resolution; and

"(bb) be conducted by officials who receive annual training on the issues related to domestic violence, dating violence, sexual assault, and stalking and how to conduct an investigation and hearing process that protects the safety of victims and promotes accountability;

"(II) the accuser and the accused are entitled to the same opportunities to have others present during an institutional disciplinary proceeding, including the opportunity to be accompanied to any related meeting or proceeding by an advisor of their choice; and

"(III) both the accuser and the accused shall be simultaneously informed, in writing, of—

"(aa) the outcome of any institutional disciplinary proceeding that arises from an allegation of domestic violence, dating violence, sexual assault, or stalking;

"(bb) the institution's procedures for the accused and the victim to appeal the results of the institutional disciplinary proceeding;

"(cc) of any change to the results that occurs prior to the time that such results become final; and

"(dd) when such results become final.

"(v) Information about how the institution will protect the confidentiality of victims, including how publicly-available recordkeeping will be accomplished without the inclusion of identifying information about the victim, to the extent permissible by law.

"(vi) Written notification of students and employees about existing counseling, health, mental health, victim advocacy, legal assistance, and other services available for victims both on-campus and in the community.

"(vii) Written notification of victims about options for, and available assistance in, changing academic, living, transportation, and working situations, if so requested by the victim and if such accommodations are reasonably available, regardless of whether the victim chooses to report the crime to campus police or local law enforcement.

"(C) A student or employee who reports to an institution of higher education that the student or employee has been a victim of domestic violence, dating violence, sexual assault, or stalking, whether the offense occurred on or off campus, shall be provided with a written explanation of the student or employee's rights and options, as described in clauses (ii) through (vii) of subparagraph (B).";

(6) in paragraph (9), by striking "The Secretary" and inserting "The Secretary, in consultation with the Attorney General of the United States,";

(7) by striking paragraph (16) and inserting the following:

"(16)(A) The Secretary shall seek the advice and counsel of the Attorney General of the United States concerning the development, and dissemination to institutions of higher education, of best practices information about campus safety and emergencies.

"(B) The Secretary shall seek the advice and counsel of the Attorney General of the United States and the Secretary of Health and Human Services concerning the development, and dissemination to institutions of higher education, of best practices information about preventing and responding to incidents of domestic violence, dating violence, sexual assault, and stalking, including elements of institutional policies that have proven successful based on evidence-based outcome measurements."; and

(8) by striking paragraph (17) and inserting the following:

"(17) No officer, employee, or agent of an institution participating in any program under this title shall retaliate, intimidate, threaten, coerce, or otherwise discriminate against any individual for exercising their rights or responsibilities under any provision of this subsection.".

(b) EFFECTIVE DATE.—The amendments made by this section shall take effect with respect to the annual security report under section 485(f)(1) of the Higher Education Act of 1965 (20 U.S.C. 1092(f)(1)) prepared by an institution of higher education 1 calendar year after the date of enactment of this Act, and each subsequent calendar year.

TITLE IV—VIOLENCE REDUCTION PRACTICES

SEC. 401. STUDY CONDUCTED BY THE CENTERS FOR DISEASE CONTROL AND PREVENTION.

Section 402(c) of the Violence Against Women and Department of Justice Reauthorization Act of 2005 (42 U.S.C. 280b–4(c)) is amended by striking "$2,000,000 for each of the fiscal years 2007 through 2011" and inserting "$1,000,000 for each of the fiscal years 2014 through 2018".

SEC. 402. SAVING MONEY AND REDUCING TRAGEDIES THROUGH PREVENTION GRANTS.

(a) SMART PREVENTION.—Section 41303 of the Violence Against Women Act of 1994 (42 U.S.C. 14043d–2) is amended to read as follows:

"SEC. 41303. SAVING MONEY AND REDUCING TRAGEDIES THROUGH PREVENTION (SMART PREVENTION).

"(a) GRANTS AUTHORIZED.—The Attorney General, in consultation with the Secretary of Health and Human Services and the Secretary of Education, is authorized to award grants for the purpose of preventing domestic violence, dating violence, sexual assault, and stalking by taking a comprehensive approach that focuses

S. 47—40

on youth, children exposed to violence, and men as leaders and influencers of social norms.

"(b) USE OF FUNDS.—Funds provided under this section may be used for the following purposes:

"(1) TEEN DATING VIOLENCE AWARENESS AND PREVENTION.—To develop, maintain, or enhance programs that change attitudes and behaviors around the acceptability of domestic violence, dating violence, sexual assault, and stalking and provide education and skills training to young individuals and individuals who influence young individuals. The prevention program may use evidence-based, evidence-informed, or innovative strategies and practices focused on youth. Such a program should include—

"(A) age and developmentally-appropriate education on domestic violence, dating violence, sexual assault, stalking, and sexual coercion, as well as healthy relationship skills, in school, in the community, or in health care settings;

"(B) community-based collaboration and training for those with influence on youth, such as parents, teachers, coaches, healthcare providers, faith-leaders, older teens, and mentors;

"(C) education and outreach to change environmental factors contributing to domestic violence, dating violence, sexual assault, and stalking; and

"(D) policy development targeted to prevention, including school-based policies and protocols.

"(2) CHILDREN EXPOSED TO VIOLENCE AND ABUSE.—To develop, maintain or enhance programs designed to prevent future incidents of domestic violence, dating violence, sexual assault, and stalking by preventing, reducing and responding to children's exposure to violence in the home. Such programs may include—

"(A) providing services for children exposed to domestic violence, dating violence, sexual assault or stalking, including direct counseling or advocacy, and support for the non-abusing parent; and

"(B) training and coordination for educational, afterschool, and childcare programs on how to safely and confidentially identify children and families experiencing domestic violence, dating violence, sexual assault, or stalking and properly refer children exposed and their families to services and violence prevention programs.

"(3) ENGAGING MEN AS LEADERS AND ROLE MODELS.—To develop, maintain or enhance programs that work with men to prevent domestic violence, dating violence, sexual assault, and stalking by helping men to serve as role models and social influencers of other men and youth at the individual, school, community or statewide levels.

"(c) ELIGIBLE ENTITIES.—To be eligible to receive a grant under this section, an entity shall be—

"(1) a victim service provider, community-based organization, tribe or tribal organization, or other non-profit, nongovernmental organization that has a history of effective work preventing domestic violence, dating violence, sexual assault, or stalking and expertise in the specific area for which they are applying for funds; or

"(2) a partnership between a victim service provider, community-based organization, tribe or tribal organization, or other non-profit, nongovernmental organization that has a history of effective work preventing domestic violence, dating violence, sexual assault, or stalking and at least one of the following that has expertise in serving children exposed to domestic violence, dating violence, sexual assault, or stalking, youth domestic violence, dating violence, sexual assault, or stalking prevention, or engaging men to prevent domestic violence, dating violence, sexual assault, or stalking:

"(A) A public, charter, tribal, or nationally accredited private middle or high school, a school administered by the Department of Defense under section 2164 of title 10, United States Code or section 1402 of the Defense Dependents' Education Act of 1978, a group of schools, or a school district.

"(B) A local community-based organization, population-specific organization, or faith-based organization that has established expertise in providing services to youth.

"(C) A community-based organization, population-specific organization, university or health care clinic, faith-based organization, or other non-profit, nongovernmental organization with a demonstrated history of effective work addressing the needs of children exposed to domestic violence, dating violence, sexual assault, or stalking.

"(D) A nonprofit, nongovernmental entity providing services for runaway or homeless youth affected by domestic violence, dating violence, sexual assault, or stalking.

"(E) Healthcare entities eligible for reimbursement under title XVIII of the Social Security Act, including providers that target the special needs of children and youth.

"(F) Any other agencies, population-specific organizations, or nonprofit, nongovernmental organizations with the capacity to provide necessary expertise to meet the goals of the program; or

"(3) a public, charter, tribal, or nationally accredited private middle or high school, a school administered by the Department of Defense under section 2164 of title 10, United States Code or section 1402 of the Defense Dependents' Education Act of 1978, a group of schools, a school district, or an institution of higher education.

"(d) GRANTEE REQUIREMENTS.—

"(1) IN GENERAL.—Applicants for grants under this section shall prepare and submit to the Director an application at such time, in such manner, and containing such information as the Director may require that demonstrates the capacity of the applicant and partnering organizations to undertake the project.

"(2) POLICIES AND PROCEDURES.—Applicants under this section shall establish and implement policies, practices, and procedures that—

"(A) include appropriate referral systems to direct any victim identified during program activities to highly qualified follow-up care;

"(B) protect the confidentiality and privacy of adult and youth victim information, particularly in the context

S. 47—42

of parental or third party involvement and consent, mandatory reporting duties, and working with other service providers;

"(C) ensure that all individuals providing prevention programming through a program funded under this section have completed or will complete sufficient training in connection with domestic violence, dating violence, sexual assault or stalking; and

"(D) document how prevention programs are coordinated with service programs in the community.

"(3) PREFERENCE.—In selecting grant recipients under this section, the Attorney General shall give preference to applicants that—

"(A) include outcome-based evaluation; and

"(B) identify any other community, school, or State-based efforts that are working on domestic violence, dating violence, sexual assault, or stalking prevention and explain how the grantee or partnership will add value, coordinate with other programs, and not duplicate existing efforts.

"(e) DEFINITIONS AND GRANT CONDITIONS.—In this section, the definitions and grant conditions provided for in section 40002 shall apply.

"(f) AUTHORIZATION OF APPROPRIATIONS.—There is authorized to be appropriated to carry out this section, $15,000,000 for each of fiscal years 2014 through 2018. Amounts appropriated under this section may only be used for programs and activities described under this section.

"(g) ALLOTMENT.—

"(1) IN GENERAL.—Not less than 25 percent of the total amounts appropriated under this section in each fiscal year shall be used for each set of purposes described in paragraphs (1), (2), and (3) of subsection (b).

"(2) INDIAN TRIBES.—Not less than 10 percent of the total amounts appropriated under this section in each fiscal year shall be made available for grants to Indian tribes or tribal organizations. If an insufficient number of applications are received from Indian tribes or tribal organizations, such funds shall be allotted to other population-specific programs.".

(b) REPEALS.—The following provisions are repealed:

(1) Sections 41304 and 41305 of the Violence Against Women Act of 1994 (42 U.S.C. 14043d–3 and 14043d–4).

(2) Section 403 of the Violence Against Women and Department of Justice Reauthorization Act of 2005 (42 U.S.C. 14045c).

TITLE V—STRENGTHENING THE HEALTHCARE SYSTEM'S RESPONSE TO DOMESTIC VIOLENCE, DATING VIOLENCE, SEXUAL ASSAULT, AND STALKING

SEC. 501. CONSOLIDATION OF GRANTS TO STRENGTHEN THE HEALTHCARE SYSTEM'S RESPONSE TO DOMESTIC VIOLENCE, DATING VIOLENCE, SEXUAL ASSAULT, AND STALKING.

(a) GRANTS.—Section 399P of the Public Health Service Act (42 U.S.C. 280g–4) is amended to read as follows:

"SEC. 399P. GRANTS TO STRENGTHEN THE HEALTHCARE SYSTEM'S RESPONSE TO DOMESTIC VIOLENCE, DATING VIOLENCE, SEXUAL ASSAULT, AND STALKING.

"(a) IN GENERAL.—The Secretary shall award grants for—

"(1) the development or enhancement and implementation of interdisciplinary training for health professionals, public health staff, and allied health professionals;

"(2) the development or enhancement and implementation of education programs for medical, nursing, dental, and other health profession students and residents to prevent and respond to domestic violence, dating violence, sexual assault, and stalking; and

"(3) the development or enhancement and implementation of comprehensive statewide strategies to improve the response of clinics, public health facilities, hospitals, and other health settings (including behavioral and mental health programs) to domestic violence, dating violence, sexual assault, and stalking.

"(b) USE OF FUNDS.—

"(1) REQUIRED USES.—Amounts provided under a grant under this section shall be used to—

"(A) fund interdisciplinary training and education programs under paragraphs (1) and (2) of subsection (a) that—

"(i) are designed to train medical, psychology, dental, social work, nursing, and other health profession students, interns, residents, fellows, or current health care providers to identify and provide health care services (including mental or behavioral health care services and referrals to appropriate community services) to individuals who are or who have been victims of domestic violence, dating violence, sexual assault, or stalking; and

"(ii) plan and develop culturally competent clinical training components for integration into approved internship, residency, and fellowship training or continuing medical or other health education training that address physical, mental, and behavioral health issues, including protective factors, related to domestic violence, dating violence, sexual assault, stalking, and other forms of violence and abuse, focus on reducing health disparities and preventing violence and abuse,

S. 47—44

and include the primacy of victim safety and confidentiality;

"(B) design and implement comprehensive strategies to improve the response of the health care system to domestic or sexual violence in clinical and public health settings, hospitals, clinics, and other health settings (including behavioral and mental health), under subsection (a)(3) through—

"(i) the implementation, dissemination, and evaluation of policies and procedures to guide health professionals and public health staff in identifying and responding to domestic violence, dating violence, sexual assault, and stalking, including strategies to ensure that health information is maintained in a manner that protects the patient's privacy and safety, and safely uses health information technology to improve documentation, identification, assessment, treatment, and follow-up care;

"(ii) the development of on-site access to services to address the safety, medical, and mental health needs of patients by increasing the capacity of existing health care professionals and public health staff to address domestic violence, dating violence, sexual assault, and stalking, or by contracting with or hiring domestic or sexual assault advocates to provide such services or to model other services appropriate to the geographic and cultural needs of a site;

"(iii) the development of measures and methods for the evaluation of the practice of identification, intervention, and documentation regarding victims of domestic violence, dating violence, sexual assault, and stalking, including the development and testing of quality improvement measurements, in accordance with the multi-stakeholder and quality measurement processes established under paragraphs (7) and (8) of section 1890(b) and section 1890A of the Social Security Act (42 U.S.C. 1395aaa(b)(7) and (8); 42 U.S.C. 1890A); and

"(iv) the provision of training and follow-up technical assistance to health care professionals, and public health staff, and allied health professionals to identify, assess, treat, and refer clients who are victims of domestic violence, dating violence, sexual assault, or stalking, including using tools and training materials already developed.

"(2) PERMISSIBLE USES.—

"(A) CHILD AND ELDER ABUSE.—To the extent consistent with the purpose of this section, a grantee may use amounts received under this section to address, as part of a comprehensive programmatic approach implemented under the grant, issues relating to child or elder abuse.

"(B) RURAL AREAS.—Grants funded under paragraphs (1) and (2) of subsection (a) may be used to offer to rural areas community-based training opportunities, which may include the use of distance learning networks and other available technologies needed to reach isolated rural areas, for medical, nursing, and other health profession students and residents on domestic violence, dating violence, sexual assault, stalking, and, as appropriate, other forms of violence and abuse.

"(C) OTHER USES.—Grants funded under subsection (a)(3) may be used for—

"(i) the development of training modules and policies that address the overlap of child abuse, domestic violence, dating violence, sexual assault, and stalking and elder abuse, as well as childhood exposure to domestic and sexual violence;

"(ii) the development, expansion, and implementation of sexual assault forensic medical examination or sexual assault nurse examiner programs;

"(iii) the inclusion of the health effects of lifetime exposure to violence and abuse as well as related protective factors and behavioral risk factors in health professional training schools including medical, dental, nursing, social work, and mental and behavioral health curricula, and allied health service training courses; or

"(iv) the integration of knowledge of domestic violence, dating violence, sexual assault, and stalking into health care accreditation and professional licensing examinations, such as medical, dental, social work, and nursing boards, and where appropriate, other allied health exams.

"(c) REQUIREMENTS FOR GRANTEES.—

"(1) CONFIDENTIALITY AND SAFETY.—

"(A) IN GENERAL.—Grantees under this section shall ensure that all programs developed with grant funds address issues of confidentiality and patient safety and comply with applicable confidentiality and nondisclosure requirements under section 40002(b)(2) of the Violence Against Women Act of 1994 and the Family Violence Prevention and Services Act, and that faculty and staff associated with delivering educational components are fully trained in procedures that will protect the immediate and ongoing security and confidentiality of the patients, patient records, and staff. Such grantees shall consult entities with demonstrated expertise in the confidentiality and safety needs of victims of domestic violence, dating violence, sexual assault, and stalking on the development and adequacy of confidentially and security procedures, and provide documentation of such consultation.

"(B) ADVANCE NOTICE OF INFORMATION DISCLOSURE.—Grantees under this section shall provide to patients advance notice about any circumstances under which information may be disclosed, such as mandatory reporting laws, and shall give patients the option to receive information and referrals without affirmatively disclosing abuse.

"(2) LIMITATION ON ADMINISTRATIVE EXPENSES.—A grantee shall use not more than 10 percent of the amounts received under a grant under this section for administrative expenses.

"(3) APPLICATION.—

"(A) PREFERENCE.—In selecting grant recipients under this section, the Secretary shall give preference to applicants based on the strength of their evaluation strategies, with priority given to outcome based evaluations.

"(B) SUBSECTION (A)(1) AND (2) GRANTEES.—Applications for grants under paragraphs (1) and (2) of subsection (a) shall include—

"(i) documentation that the applicant represents a team of entities working collaboratively to strengthen the response of the health care system to domestic violence, dating violence, sexual assault, or stalking, and which includes at least one of each of—

"(I) an accredited school of allopathic or osteopathic medicine, psychology, nursing, dentistry, social work, or other health field;

"(II) a health care facility or system; or

"(III) a government or nonprofit entity with a history of effective work in the fields of domestic violence, dating violence, sexual assault, or stalking; and

"(ii) strategies for the dissemination and sharing of curricula and other educational materials developed under the grant, if any, with other interested health professions schools and national resource repositories for materials on domestic violence, dating violence, sexual assault, and stalking.

"(C) SUBSECTION (A)(3) GRANTEES.—An entity desiring a grant under subsection (a)(3) shall submit an application to the Secretary at such time, in such a manner, and containing such information and assurances as the Secretary may require, including—

"(i) documentation that all training, education, screening, assessment, services, treatment, and any other approach to patient care will be informed by an understanding of violence and abuse victimization and trauma-specific approaches that will be integrated into prevention, intervention, and treatment activities;

"(ii) strategies for the development and implementation of policies to prevent and address domestic violence, dating violence, sexual assault, and stalking over the lifespan in health care settings;

"(iii) a plan for consulting with State and tribal domestic violence or sexual assault coalitions, national nonprofit victim advocacy organizations, State or tribal law enforcement task forces (where appropriate), and population specific organizations with demonstrated expertise in domestic violence, dating violence, sexual assault, or stalking;

"(iv) with respect to an application for a grant under which the grantee will have contact with patients, a plan, developed in collaboration with local victim service providers, to respond appropriately to and make correct referrals for individuals who disclose that they are victims of domestic violence, dating violence, sexual assault, stalking, or other types of violence, and documentation provided by the grantee of an ongoing collaborative relationship with a local victim service provider; and "(v) with respect to an application for a grant proposing to fund a program described in subsection (b)(2)(C)(ii), a certification that any sexual assault forensic medical examination and sexual assault nurse examiner programs supported with such grant funds will adhere to the guidelines set forth by the Attorney General.

"(d) ELIGIBLE ENTITIES.—

"(1) IN GENERAL.—To be eligible to receive funding under paragraph (1) or (2) of subsection (a), an entity shall be—

"(A) a nonprofit organization with a history of effective work in the field of training health professionals with an understanding of, and clinical skills pertinent to, domestic violence, dating violence, sexual assault, or stalking, and lifetime exposure to violence and abuse;

"(B) an accredited school of allopathic or osteopathic medicine, psychology, nursing, dentistry, social work, or allied health;

"(C) a health care provider membership or professional organization, or a health care system; or

"(D) a State, tribal, territorial, or local entity.

"(2) SUBSECTION (A)(3) GRANTEES.—To be eligible to receive funding under subsection (a)(3), an entity shall be—

"(A) a State department (or other division) of health, a State, tribal, or territorial domestic violence or sexual assault coalition or victim service provider, or any other nonprofit, nongovernmental organization with a history of effective work in the fields of domestic violence, dating violence, sexual assault, or stalking, and health care, including physical or mental health care; or

"(B) a local victim service provider, a local department (or other division) of health, a local health clinic, hospital, or health system, or any other community-based organization with a history of effective work in the field of domestic violence, dating violence, sexual assault, or stalking and health care, including physical or mental health care.

"(e) TECHNICAL ASSISTANCE.—

"(1) IN GENERAL.—Of the funds made available to carry out this section for any fiscal year, the Secretary may make grants or enter into contracts to provide technical assistance with respect to the planning, development, and operation of any program, activity or service carried out pursuant to this section. Not more than 8 percent of the funds appropriated under this section in each fiscal year may be used to fund technical assistance under this subsection.

"(2) AVAILABILITY OF MATERIALS.—The Secretary shall make publicly available materials developed by grantees under this section, including materials on training, best practices, and research and evaluation.

"(3) REPORTING.—The Secretary shall publish a biennial report on—

"(A) the distribution of funds under this section; and

"(B) the programs and activities supported by such funds.

"(f) RESEARCH AND EVALUATION.—

"(1) IN GENERAL.—Of the funds made available to carry out this section for any fiscal year, the Secretary may use not more than 20 percent to make a grant or enter into a contract for research and evaluation of—

"(A) grants awarded under this section; and

"(B) other training for health professionals and effective interventions in the health care setting that prevent domestic violence, dating violence, and sexual assault across the lifespan, prevent the health effects of such violence, and improve the safety and health of individuals who are currently being victimized.

"(2) RESEARCH.—Research authorized in paragraph (1) may include—

"(A) research on the effects of domestic violence, dating violence, sexual assault, and childhood exposure to domestic, dating or sexual violence on health behaviors, health conditions, and health status of individuals, families, and populations, including underserved populations;

"(B) research to determine effective health care interventions to respond to and prevent domestic violence, dating violence, sexual assault, and stalking;

"(C) research on the impact of domestic, dating and sexual violence, childhood exposure to such violence, and stalking on the health care system, health care utilization, health care costs, and health status; and

"(D) research on the impact of adverse childhood experiences on adult experience with domestic violence, dating violence, sexual assault, stalking, and adult health outcomes, including how to reduce or prevent the impact of adverse childhood experiences through the health care setting.

"(g) AUTHORIZATION OF APPROPRIATIONS.—There is authorized to be appropriated to carry out this section, $10,000,000 for each of fiscal years 2014 through 2018.

"(h) DEFINITIONS.—Except as otherwise provided herein, the definitions provided for in section 40002 of the Violence Against Women Act of 1994 shall apply to this section.".

(b) REPEALS.—The following provisions are repealed:

(1) Section 40297 of the Violence Against Women Act of 1994 (42 U.S.C. 13973).

(2) Section 758 of the Public Health Service Act (42 U.S.C. 294h).

TITLE VI—SAFE HOMES FOR VICTIMS OF DOMESTIC VIOLENCE, DATING VIOLENCE, SEXUAL ASSAULT, AND STALKING

SEC. 601. HOUSING PROTECTIONS FOR VICTIMS OF DOMESTIC VIOLENCE, DATING VIOLENCE, SEXUAL ASSAULT, AND STALKING.

(a) AMENDMENT.—Subtitle N of the Violence Against Women Act of 1994 (42 U.S.C. 14043e et seq.) is amended—

(1) by inserting after the subtitle heading the following:

"CHAPTER 1—GRANT PROGRAMS";

(2) in section 41402 (42 U.S.C. 14043e–1), in the matter preceding paragraph (1), by striking "subtitle" and inserting "chapter";

(3) in section 41403 (42 U.S.C. 14043e–2), in the matter preceding paragraph (1), by striking "subtitle" and inserting "chapter"; and

(4) by adding at the end the following:

"CHAPTER 2—HOUSING RIGHTS

"SEC. 41411. HOUSING PROTECTIONS FOR VICTIMS OF DOMESTIC VIOLENCE, DATING VIOLENCE, SEXUAL ASSAULT, AND STALKING.

"(a) DEFINITIONS.—In this chapter:

"(1) AFFILIATED INDIVIDUAL.—The term 'affiliated individual' means, with respect to an individual—

"(A) a spouse, parent, brother, sister, or child of that individual, or an individual to whom that individual stands in loco parentis; or

"(B) any individual, tenant, or lawful occupant living in the household of that individual.

"(2) APPROPRIATE AGENCY.—The term 'appropriate agency' means, with respect to a covered housing program, the Executive department (as defined in section 101 of title 5, United States Code) that carries out the covered housing program.

"(3) COVERED HOUSING PROGRAM.—The term 'covered housing program' means—

"(A) the program under section 202 of the Housing Act of 1959 (12 U.S.C. 1701q);

"(B) the program under section 811 of the Cranston-Gonzalez National Affordable Housing Act (42 U.S.C. 8013);

"(C) the program under subtitle D of title VIII of the Cranston-Gonzalez National Affordable Housing Act (42 U.S.C. 12901 et seq.);

"(D) the program under subtitle A of title IV of the McKinney-Vento Homeless Assistance Act (42 U.S.C. 11360 et seq.);

"(E) the program under subtitle A of title II of the Cranston-Gonzalez National Affordable Housing Act (42 U.S.C. 12741 et seq.);

"(F) the program under paragraph (3) of section 221(d) of the National Housing Act (12 U.S.C. 1715l(d)) that bears interest at a rate determined under the proviso under paragraph (5) of such section 221(d);

"(G) the program under section 236 of the National Housing Act (12 U.S.C. 1715z–1);

"(H) the programs under sections 6 and 8 of the United States Housing Act of 1937 (42 U.S.C. 1437d and 1437f);

"(I) rural housing assistance provided under sections 514, 515, 516, 533, and 538 of the Housing Act of 1949 (42 U.S.C. 1484, 1485, 1486, 1490m, and 1490p–2); and

"(J) the low income housing tax credit program under section 42 of the Internal Revenue Code of 1986.

"(b) PROHIBITED BASIS FOR DENIAL OR TERMINATION OF ASSISTANCE OR EVICTION.—

S. 47—50

"(1) IN GENERAL.—An applicant for or tenant of housing assisted under a covered housing program may not be denied admission to, denied assistance under, terminated from participation in, or evicted from the housing on the basis that the applicant or tenant is or has been a victim of domestic violence, dating violence, sexual assault, or stalking, if the applicant or tenant otherwise qualifies for admission, assistance, participation, or occupancy.

"(2) CONSTRUCTION OF LEASE TERMS.—An incident of actual or threatened domestic violence, dating violence, sexual assault, or stalking shall not be construed as—

"(A) a serious or repeated violation of a lease for housing assisted under a covered housing program by the victim or threatened victim of such incident; or

"(B) good cause for terminating the assistance, tenancy, or occupancy rights to housing assisted under a covered housing program of the victim or threatened victim of such incident.

"(3) TERMINATION ON THE BASIS OF CRIMINAL ACTIVITY.—

"(A) DENIAL OF ASSISTANCE, TENANCY, AND OCCUPANCY RIGHTS PROHIBITED.—No person may deny assistance, tenancy, or occupancy rights to housing assisted under a covered housing program to a tenant solely on the basis of criminal activity directly relating to domestic violence, dating violence, sexual assault, or stalking that is engaged in by a member of the household of the tenant or any guest or other person under the control of the tenant, if the tenant or an affiliated individual of the tenant is the victim or threatened victim of such domestic violence, dating violence, sexual assault, or stalking.

"(B) BIFURCATION.—

"(i) IN GENERAL.—Notwithstanding subparagraph (A), a public housing agency or owner or manager of housing assisted under a covered housing program may bifurcate a lease for the housing in order to evict, remove, or terminate assistance to any individual who is a tenant or lawful occupant of the housing and who engages in criminal activity directly relating to domestic violence, dating violence, sexual assault, or stalking against an affiliated individual or other individual, without evicting, removing, terminating assistance to, or otherwise penalizing a victim of such criminal activity who is also a tenant or lawful occupant of the housing.

"(ii) EFFECT OF EVICTION ON OTHER TENANTS.—If public housing agency or owner or manager of housing assisted under a covered housing program evicts, removes, or terminates assistance to an individual under clause (i), and the individual is the sole tenant eligible to receive assistance under a covered housing program, the public housing agency or owner or manager of housing assisted under the covered housing program shall provide any remaining tenant an opportunity to establish eligibility for the covered housing program. If a tenant described in the preceding sentence cannot establish eligibility, the public housing agency or owner or manager of the housing shall provide the tenant a reasonable time, as determined by the appropriate agency, to find new housing or to establish eligibility for housing under another covered housing program.

"(C) RULES OF CONSTRUCTION.—Nothing in subparagraph (A) shall be construed—

"(i) to limit the authority of a public housing agency or owner or manager of housing assisted under a covered housing program, when notified of a court order, to comply with a court order with respect to—

"(I) the rights of access to or control of property, including civil protection orders issued to protect a victim of domestic violence, dating violence, sexual assault, or stalking; or

"(II) the distribution or possession of property among members of a household in a case;

"(ii) to limit any otherwise available authority of a public housing agency or owner or manager of housing assisted under a covered housing program to evict or terminate assistance to a tenant for any violation of a lease not premised on the act of violence in question against the tenant or an affiliated person of the tenant, if the public housing agency or owner or manager does not subject an individual who is or has been a victim of domestic violence, dating violence, or stalking to a more demanding standard than other tenants in determining whether to evict or terminate;

"(iii) to limit the authority to terminate assistance to a tenant or evict a tenant from housing assisted under a covered housing program if a public housing agency or owner or manager of the housing can demonstrate that an actual and imminent threat to other tenants or individuals employed at or providing service to the property would be present if the assistance is not terminated or the tenant is not evicted; or

"(iv) to supersede any provision of any Federal, State, or local law that provides greater protection than this section for victims of domestic violence, dating violence, sexual assault, or stalking.

"(c) DOCUMENTATION.—

"(1) REQUEST FOR DOCUMENTATION.—If an applicant for, or tenant of, housing assisted under a covered housing program represents to a public housing agency or owner or manager of the housing that the individual is entitled to protection under subsection (b), the public housing agency or owner or manager may request, in writing, that the applicant or tenant submit to the public housing agency or owner or manager a form of documentation described in paragraph (3).

"(2) FAILURE TO PROVIDE CERTIFICATION.—

"(A) IN GENERAL.—If an applicant or tenant does not provide the documentation requested under paragraph (1) within 14 business days after the tenant receives a request in writing for such certification from a public housing agency or owner or manager of housing assisted under a covered housing program, nothing in this chapter may be construed to limit the authority of the public housing agency or owner or manager to—

"(i) deny admission by the applicant or tenant to the covered program;

"(ii) deny assistance under the covered program to the applicant or tenant;

"(iii) terminate the participation of the applicant or tenant in the covered program; or

"(iv) evict the applicant, the tenant, or a lawful occupant that commits violations of a lease.

"(B) EXTENSION.—A public housing agency or owner or manager of housing may extend the 14-day deadline under subparagraph (A) at its discretion.

"(3) FORM OF DOCUMENTATION.—A form of documentation described in this paragraph is—

"(A) a certification form approved by the appropriate agency that—

"(i) states that an applicant or tenant is a victim of domestic violence, dating violence, sexual assault, or stalking;

"(ii) states that the incident of domestic violence, dating violence, sexual assault, or stalking that is the ground for protection under subsection (b) meets the requirements under subsection (b); and

"(iii) includes the name of the individual who committed the domestic violence, dating violence, sexual assault, or stalking, if the name is known and safe to provide;

"(B) a document that—

"(i) is signed by—

"(I) an employee, agent, or volunteer of a victim service provider, an attorney, a medical professional, or a mental health professional from whom an applicant or tenant has sought assistance relating to domestic violence, dating violence, sexual assault, or stalking, or the effects of the abuse; and

"(II) the applicant or tenant; and

"(ii) states under penalty of perjury that the individual described in clause (i)(I) believes that the incident of domestic violence, dating violence, sexual assault, or stalking that is the ground for protection under subsection (b) meets the requirements under subsection (b);

"(C) a record of a Federal, State, tribal, territorial, or local law enforcement agency, court, or administrative agency; or

"(D) at the discretion of a public housing agency or owner or manager of housing assisted under a covered housing program, a statement or other evidence provided by an applicant or tenant.

"(4) CONFIDENTIALITY.—Any information submitted to a public housing agency or owner or manager under this subsection, including the fact that an individual is a victim of domestic violence, dating violence, sexual assault, or stalking shall be maintained in confidence by the public housing agency or owner or manager and may not be entered into any shared database or disclosed to any other entity or individual, except to the extent that the disclosure is—

"(A) requested or consented to by the individual in writing;

"(B) required for use in an eviction proceeding under subsection (b); or

"(C) otherwise required by applicable law.

"(5) DOCUMENTATION NOT REQUIRED.—Nothing in this subsection shall be construed to require a public housing agency or owner or manager of housing assisted under a covered housing program to request that an individual submit documentation of the status of the individual as a victim of domestic violence, dating violence, sexual assault, or stalking.

"(6) COMPLIANCE NOT SUFFICIENT TO CONSTITUTE EVIDENCE OF UNREASONABLE ACT.—Compliance with subsection (b) by a public housing agency or owner or manager of housing assisted under a covered housing program based on documentation received under this subsection, shall not be sufficient to constitute evidence of an unreasonable act or omission by the public housing agency or owner or manager or an employee or agent of the public housing agency or owner or manager. Nothing in this paragraph shall be construed to limit the liability of a public housing agency or owner or manager of housing assisted under a covered housing program for failure to comply with subsection (b).

"(7) RESPONSE TO CONFLICTING CERTIFICATION.—If a public housing agency or owner or manager of housing assisted under a covered housing program receives documentation under this subsection that contains conflicting information, the public housing agency or owner or manager may require an applicant or tenant to submit third-party documentation, as described in subparagraph (B), (C), or (D) of paragraph (3).

"(8) PREEMPTION.—Nothing in this subsection shall be construed to supersede any provision of any Federal, State, or local law that provides greater protection than this subsection for victims of domestic violence, dating violence, sexual assault, or stalking.

"(d) NOTIFICATION.—

"(1) DEVELOPMENT.—The Secretary of Housing and Urban Development shall develop a notice of the rights of individuals under this section, including the right to confidentiality and the limits thereof.

"(2) PROVISION.—Each public housing agency or owner or manager of housing assisted under a covered housing program shall provide the notice developed under paragraph (1), together with the form described in subsection (c)(3)(A), to an applicant for or tenants of housing assisted under a covered housing program—

"(A) at the time the applicant is denied residency in a dwelling unit assisted under the covered housing program;

"(B) at the time the individual is admitted to a dwelling unit assisted under the covered housing program;

"(C) with any notification of eviction or notification of termination of assistance; and

"(D) in multiple languages, consistent with guidance issued by the Secretary of Housing and Urban Development in accordance with Executive Order 13166 (42 U.S.C. 2000d–1 note; relating to access to services for persons with limited English proficiency).

"(e) EMERGENCY TRANSFERS.—Each appropriate agency shall adopt a model emergency transfer plan for use by public housing agencies and owners or managers of housing assisted under covered housing programs that—

"(1) allows tenants who are victims of domestic violence, dating violence, sexual assault, or stalking to transfer to another available and safe dwelling unit assisted under a covered housing program if—

"(A) the tenant expressly requests the transfer; and

"(B)(i) the tenant reasonably believes that the tenant is threatened with imminent harm from further violence if the tenant remains within the same dwelling unit assisted under a covered housing program; or

"(ii) in the case of a tenant who is a victim of sexual assault, the sexual assault occurred on the premises during the 90 day period preceding the request for transfer; and

"(2) incorporates reasonable confidentiality measures to ensure that the public housing agency or owner or manager does not disclose the location of the dwelling unit of a tenant to a person that commits an act of domestic violence, dating violence, sexual assault, or stalking against the tenant.

"(f) POLICIES AND PROCEDURES FOR EMERGENCY TRANSFER.—The Secretary of Housing and Urban Development shall establish policies and procedures under which a victim requesting an emergency transfer under subsection (e) may receive, subject to the availability of tenant protection vouchers, assistance under section 8(o) of the United States Housing Act of 1937 (42 U.S.C. 1437f(o)).

"(g) IMPLEMENTATION.—The appropriate agency with respect to each covered housing program shall implement this section, as this section applies to the covered housing program.".

(b) CONFORMING AMENDMENTS.—

(1) SECTION 6.—Section 6 of the United States Housing Act of 1937 (42 U.S.C. 1437d) is amended—

(A) in subsection (c)—

(i) by striking paragraph (3); and

(ii) by redesignating paragraphs (4) and (5) as paragraphs (3) and (4), respectively;

(B) in subsection (l)—

(i) in paragraph (5), by striking ", and that an incident or incidents of actual or threatened domestic violence, dating violence, or stalking will not be construed as a serious or repeated violation of the lease by the victim or threatened victim of that violence and will not be good cause for terminating the tenancy or occupancy rights of the victim of such violence"; and

(ii) in paragraph (6), by striking "; except that" and all that follows through "stalking."; and

(C) by striking subsection (u).

(2) SECTION 8.—Section 8 of the United States Housing Act of 1937 (42 U.S.C. 1437f) is amended—

(A) in subsection (c), by striking paragraph (9);

(B) in subsection (d)(1)—

(i) in subparagraph (A), by striking "and that an applicant or participant is or has been a victim of domestic violence, dating violence, or stalking is not an appropriate basis for denial of program assistance or for denial of admission if the applicant otherwise qualifies for assistance or admission"; and

(ii) in subparagraph (B)—

(I) in clause (ii), by striking ", and that an incident or incidents of actual or threatened domestic violence, dating violence, or stalking will not be construed as a serious or repeated violation of the lease by the victim or threatened victim of that violence and will not be good cause for terminating the tenancy or occupancy rights of the victim of such violence"; and

(II) in clause (iii), by striking ", except that:" and all that follows through "stalking.";

(C) in subsection (f)—

(i) in paragraph (6), by adding "and" at the end;

(ii) in paragraph (7), by striking the semicolon at the end and inserting a period; and

(iii) by striking paragraphs (8), (9), (10), and (11);

(D) in subsection (o)—

(i) in paragraph (6)(B), by striking the last sentence;

(ii) in paragraph (7)—

(I) in subparagraph (C), by striking "and that an incident or incidents of actual or threatened domestic violence, dating violence, or stalking shall not be construed as a serious or repeated violation of the lease by the victim or threatened victim of that violence and shall not be good cause for terminating the tenancy or occupancy rights of the victim of such violence"; and

(II) in subparagraph (D), by striking "; except that" and all that follows through "stalking."; and

(iii) by striking paragraph (20); and

(E) by striking subsection (ee).

(3) RULE OF CONSTRUCTION.—Nothing in this Act, or the amendments made by this Act, shall be construed—

(A) to limit the rights or remedies available to any person under section 6 or 8 of the United States Housing Act of 1937 (42 U.S.C. 1437d and 1437f), as in effect on the day before the date of enactment of this Act;

(B) to limit any right, remedy, or procedure otherwise available under any provision of part 5, 91, 880, 882, 883, 884, 886, 891, 903, 960, 966, 982, or 983 of title 24, Code of Federal Regulations, that—

(i) was issued under the Violence Against Women and Department of Justice Reauthorization Act of 2005 (Public Law 109–162; 119 Stat. 2960) or an amendment made by that Act; and

(ii) provides greater protection for victims of domestic violence, dating violence, sexual assault, and stalking than this Act; or

(C) to disqualify an owner, manager, or other individual from participating in or receiving the benefits of the low income housing tax credit program under section 42 of the Internal Revenue Code of 1986 because of noncompliance with the provisions of this Act.

SEC. 602. TRANSITIONAL HOUSING ASSISTANCE GRANTS FOR VICTIMS OF DOMESTIC VIOLENCE, DATING VIOLENCE, SEXUAL ASSAULT, AND STALKING.

Chapter 11 of subtitle B of the Violence Against Women Act of 1994 (42 U.S.C. 13975 et seq.) is amended—

(1) in the chapter heading, by striking "**CHILD VICTIMS OF DOMESTIC VIOLENCE, STALKING, OR SEXUAL ASSAULT**" and inserting "**VICTIMS OF DOMESTIC VIOLENCE, DATING VIOLENCE, SEXUAL ASSAULT, OR STALKING**"; and

(2) in section 40299 (42 U.S.C. 13975)—

(A) in the header, by striking "**CHILD VICTIMS OF DOMESTIC VIOLENCE, STALKING, OR SEXUAL ASSAULT**" and inserting "**VICTIMS OF DOMESTIC VIOLENCE, DATING VIOLENCE, SEXUAL ASSAULT, OR STALKING**";

(B) in subsection (a)(1), by striking "fleeing";

(C) in subsection (b)(3)—

(i) in subparagraph (A), by striking " and" at the end;

(ii) by redesignating subparagraph (B) as subparagraph (C);

(iii) by inserting after subparagraph (A) the following:

"(B) secure employment, including obtaining employment counseling, occupational training, job retention counseling, and counseling concerning re-entry in to the workforce; and"; and

(iv) in subparagraph (C), as redesignated by clause (ii), by striking " employment counseling,"; and

(D) in subsection (g)—

(i) in paragraph (1), by striking "$40,000,000 for each of fiscal years 2007 through 2011" and inserting "$35,000,000 for each of fiscal years 2014 through 2018"; and

(ii) in paragraph (3)—

(I) in subparagraph (A), by striking "eligible" and inserting "qualified"; and

(II) by adding at the end the following:

"(D) QUALIFIED APPLICATION DEFINED.—In this paragraph, the term 'qualified application' means an application that—

"(i) has been submitted by an eligible applicant;

"(ii) does not propose any activities that may compromise victim safety, including—

"(I) background checks of victims; or

"(II) clinical evaluations to determine eligibility for services;

"(iii) reflects an understanding of the dynamics of domestic violence, dating violence, sexual assault, or stalking; and

"(iv) does not propose prohibited activities, including mandatory services for victims.".

SEC. 603. ADDRESSING THE HOUSING NEEDS OF VICTIMS OF DOMESTIC VIOLENCE, DATING VIOLENCE, SEXUAL ASSAULT, AND STALKING.

Subtitle N of the Violence Against Women Act of 1994 (42 U.S.C. 14043e et seq.) is amended—

(1) in section 41404(i) (42 U.S.C. 14043e–3(i)), by striking "$10,000,000 for each of fiscal years 2007 through 2011" and inserting "$4,000,000 for each of fiscal years 2014 through 2018"; and

(2) in section 41405(g) (42 U.S.C. 14043e–4(g)), by striking "$10,000,000 for each of fiscal years 2007 through 2011" and inserting "$4,000,000 for each of fiscal years 2014 through 2018".

TITLE VII—ECONOMIC SECURITY FOR VICTIMS OF VIOLENCE

SEC. 701. NATIONAL RESOURCE CENTER ON WORKPLACE RESPONSES TO ASSIST VICTIMS OF DOMESTIC AND SEXUAL VIOLENCE.

Section 41501(e) of the Violence Against Women Act of 1994 (42 U.S.C. 14043f(e)) is amended by striking "fiscal years 2007 through 2011" and inserting "fiscal years 2014 through 2018".

TITLE VIII—PROTECTION OF BATTERED IMMIGRANTS

SEC. 801. U NONIMMIGRANT DEFINITION.

Section 101(a)(15)(U)(iii) of the Immigration and Nationality Act (8 U.S.C. 1101(a)(15)(U)(iii)) is amended by inserting "stalking;" after "sexual exploitation;".

SEC. 802. ANNUAL REPORT ON IMMIGRATION APPLICATIONS MADE BY VICTIMS OF ABUSE.

Not later than December 1, 2014, and annually thereafter, the Secretary of Homeland Security shall submit to the Committee on the Judiciary of the Senate and the Committee on the Judiciary of the House of Representatives a report that includes the following:

(1) The number of aliens who—

(A) submitted an application for nonimmigrant status under paragraph (15)(T)(i), (15)(U)(i), or (51) of section 101(a) of the Immigration and Nationality Act (8 U.S.C. 1101(a)) during the preceding fiscal year;

(B) were granted such nonimmigrant status during such fiscal year; or

(C) were denied such nonimmigrant status during such fiscal year.

(2) The mean amount of time and median amount of time to adjudicate an application for such nonimmigrant status during such fiscal year.

(3) The mean amount of time and median amount of time between the receipt of an application for such nonimmigrant status and the issuance of work authorization to an eligible applicant during the preceding fiscal year.

S. 47—58

(4) The number of aliens granted continued presence in the United States under section 107(c)(3) of the Trafficking Victims Protection Act of 2000 (22 U.S.C. 7105(c)(3)) during the preceding fiscal year.

(5) A description of any actions being taken to reduce the adjudication and processing time, while ensuring the safe and competent processing, of an application described in paragraph (1) or a request for continued presence referred to in paragraph (4).

SEC. 803. PROTECTION FOR CHILDREN OF VAWA SELF-PETITIONERS.

Section 204(l)(2) of the Immigration and Nationality Act (8 U.S.C. 1154(l)(2)) is amended—

(1) in subparagraph (E), by striking "or" at the end;

(2) by redesignating subparagraph (F) as subparagraph (G); and

(3) by inserting after subparagraph (E) the following:

"(F) a child of an alien who filed a pending or approved petition for classification or application for adjustment of status or other benefit specified in section 101(a)(51) as a VAWA self-petitioner; or".

SEC. 804. PUBLIC CHARGE.

Section 212(a)(4) of the Immigration and Nationality Act (8 U.S.C. 1182(a)(4)) is amended by adding at the end the following:

"(E) SPECIAL RULE FOR QUALIFIED ALIEN VICTIMS.—Subparagraphs (A), (B), and (C) shall not apply to an alien who—

"(i) is a VAWA self-petitioner;

"(ii) is an applicant for, or is granted, nonimmigrant status under section 101(a)(15)(U); or

"(iii) is a qualified alien described in section 431(c) of the Personal Responsibility and Work Opportunity Reconciliation Act of 1996 (8 U.S.C. 1641(c)).".

SEC. 805. REQUIREMENTS APPLICABLE TO U VISAS.

(a) IN GENERAL.—Section 214(p) of the Immigration and Nationality Act (8 U.S.C. 1184(p)) is amended by adding at the end the following:

"(7) AGE DETERMINATIONS.—

"(A) CHILDREN.—An unmarried alien who seeks to accompany, or follow to join, a parent granted status under section 101(a)(15)(U)(i), and who was under 21 years of age on the date on which such parent petitioned for such status, shall continue to be classified as a child for purposes of section 101(a)(15)(U)(ii), if the alien attains 21 years of age after such parent's petition was filed but while it was pending.

"(B) PRINCIPAL ALIENS.—An alien described in clause (i) of section 101(a)(15)(U) shall continue to be treated as an alien described in clause (ii)(I) of such section if the alien attains 21 years of age after the alien's application for status under such clause (i) is filed but while it is pending.".

(b) EFFECTIVE DATE.—The amendment made by subsection (a) shall take effect as if enacted as part of the Victims of Trafficking and Violence Protection Act of 2000 (Public Law 106–386; 114 Stat. 1464).

SEC. 806. HARDSHIP WAIVERS.

(a) IN GENERAL.—Section 216(c)(4) of the Immigration and Nationality Act (8 U.S.C. 1186a(c)(4)) is amended—

(1) in subparagraph (A), by striking the comma at the end and inserting a semicolon;

(2) in subparagraph (B), by striking "(1), or" and inserting "(1); or";

(3) in subparagraph (C), by striking the period at the end and inserting a semicolon and "or"; and

(4) by inserting after subparagraph (C) the following:

"(D) the alien meets the requirements under section 204(a)(1)(A)(iii)(II)(aa)(BB) and following the marriage ceremony was battered by or subject to extreme cruelty perpetrated by the alien's intended spouse and was not at fault in failing to meet the requirements of paragraph (1).".

(b) TECHNICAL CORRECTIONS.—Section 216(c)(4) of the Immigration and Nationality Act (8 U.S.C. 1186a(c)(4)), as amended by subsection (a), is further amended—

(1) in the matter preceding subparagraph (A), by striking "The Attorney General, in the Attorney General's" and inserting "The Secretary of Homeland Security, in the Secretary's"; and

(2) in the undesignated paragraph at the end—

(A) in the first sentence, by striking "Attorney General" and inserting "Secretary of Homeland Security";

(B) in the second sentence, by striking "Attorney General" and inserting "Secretary";

(C) in the third sentence, by striking "Attorney General." and inserting "Secretary."; and

(D) in the fourth sentence, by striking "Attorney General" and inserting "Secretary".

SEC. 807. PROTECTIONS FOR A FIANCÉE OR FIANCÉ OF A CITIZEN.

(a) IN GENERAL.—Section 214 of the Immigration and Nationality Act (8 U.S.C. 1184) is amended—

(1) in subsection (d)—

(A) in paragraph (1), by striking "crime." and inserting "crime described in paragraph (3)(B) and information on any permanent protection or restraining order issued against the petitioner related to any specified crime described in paragraph (3)(B)(i).";

(B) in paragraph (2)(A), in the matter preceding clause (i)—

(i) by striking "a consular officer" and inserting "the Secretary of Homeland Security"; and

(ii) by striking "the officer" and inserting "the Secretary"; and

(C) in paragraph (3)(B)(i), by striking "abuse, and stalking." and inserting "abuse, stalking, or an attempt to commit any such crime."; and

(2) in subsection (r)—

(A) in paragraph (1), by striking "crime." and inserting "crime described in paragraph (5)(B) and information on any permanent protection or restraining order issued against the petitioner related to any specified crime described in subsection (5)(B)(i)."; and

(B) by amending paragraph (4)(B)(ii) to read as follows:

S. 47—60

"(ii) To notify the beneficiary as required by clause (i), the Secretary of Homeland Security shall provide such notice to the Secretary of State for inclusion in the mailing to the beneficiary described in section 833(a)(5)(A)(i) of the International Marriage Broker Regulation Act of 2005 (8 U.S.C. 1375a(a)(5)(A)(i)).''; and

(3) in paragraph (5)(B)(i), by striking "abuse, and stalking." and inserting "abuse, stalking, or an attempt to commit any such crime.".

(b) PROVISION OF INFORMATION TO K NONIMMIGRANTS.—Section 833 of the International Marriage Broker Regulation Act of 2005 (8 U.S.C. 1375a) is amended—

(1) in subsection (a)(5)(A)—

(A) in clause (iii)—

(i) by striking "State any" and inserting "State, for inclusion in the mailing described in clause (i), any"; and

(ii) by striking the last sentence; and

(B) by adding at the end the following:

"(iv) The Secretary of Homeland Security shall conduct a background check of the National Crime Information Center's Protection Order Database on each petitioner for a visa under subsection (d) or (r) of section 214 of the Immigration and Nationality Act (8 U.S.C. 1184). Any appropriate information obtained from such background check—

"(I) shall accompany the criminal background information provided by the Secretary of Homeland Security to the Secretary of State and shared by the Secretary of State with a beneficiary of a petition referred to in clause (iii); and

"(II) shall not be used or disclosed for any other purpose unless expressly authorized by law.

"(v) The Secretary of Homeland Security shall create a cover sheet or other mechanism to accompany the information required to be provided to an applicant for a visa under subsection (d) or (r) of section 214 of the Immigration and Nationality Act (8 U.S.C. 1184) by clauses (i) through (iv) of this paragraph or by clauses (i) and (ii) of subsection (r)(4)(B) of such section 214, that calls to the applicant's attention—

"(I) whether the petitioner disclosed a protection order, a restraining order, or criminal history information on the visa petition;

"(II) the criminal background information and information about any protection order obtained by the Secretary of Homeland Security regarding the petitioner in the course of adjudicating the petition; and

"(III) whether the information the petitioner disclosed on the visa petition regarding any previous petitions filed under subsection (d) or (r) of such section 214 is consistent with the information in the multiple visa tracking database of the Department of Homeland Security, as described in subsection (r)(4)(A) of such section 214."; and

(2) in subsection (b)(1)(A), by striking "or" after "orders" and inserting "and".

SEC. 808. REGULATION OF INTERNATIONAL MARRIAGE BROKERS.

(a) IMPLEMENTATION OF THE INTERNATIONAL MARRIAGE BROKER ACT OF 2005.—

(1) FINDINGS.—Congress finds the following:

(A) The International Marriage Broker Act of 2005 (subtitle D of Public Law 109–162; 119 Stat. 3066) has not been fully implemented with regard to investigating and prosecuting violations of the law, and for other purposes.

(B) Six years after Congress enacted the International Marriage Broker Act of 2005 to regulate the activities of the hundreds of for-profit international marriage brokers operating in the United States, the Attorney General has not determined which component of the Department of Justice will investigate and prosecute violations of such Act.

(2) REPORT.—Not later than 90 days after the date of the enactment of this Act, the Attorney General shall submit to Congress a report that includes the following:

(A) The name of the component of the Department of Justice responsible for investigating and prosecuting violations of the International Marriage Broker Act of 2005 (subtitle D of Public Law 109–162; 119 Stat. 3066) and the amendments made by this Act.

(B) A description of the policies and procedures of the Attorney General for consultation with the Secretary of Homeland Security and the Secretary of State in investigating and prosecuting such violations.

(b) TECHNICAL CORRECTION.—Section 833(a)(2)(H) of the International Marriage Broker Regulation Act of 2005 (8 U.S.C. 1375a(a)(2)(H)) is amended by striking "Federal and State sex offender public registries" and inserting "the National Sex Offender Public Website".

(c) REGULATION OF INTERNATIONAL MARRIAGE BROKERS.—Section 833(d) of the International Marriage Broker Regulation Act of 2005 (8 U.S.C. 1375a(d)) is amended—

(1) by amending paragraph (1) to read as follows:

"(1) PROHIBITION ON MARKETING OF OR TO CHILDREN.—

"(A) IN GENERAL.—An international marriage broker shall not provide any individual or entity with the personal contact information, photograph, or general information about the background or interests of any individual under the age of 18.

"(B) COMPLIANCE.—To comply with the requirements of subparagraph (A), an international marriage broker shall—

"(i) obtain a valid copy of each foreign national client's birth certificate or other proof of age document issued by an appropriate government entity;

"(ii) indicate on such certificate or document the date it was received by the international marriage broker;

"(iii) retain the original of such certificate or document for 7 years after such date of receipt; and

"(iv) produce such certificate or document upon request to an appropriate authority charged with the enforcement of this paragraph.";

S. 47—62

(2) in paragraph (2)—
(A) in subparagraph (A)(i)—
(i) in the heading, by striking "REGISTRIES.—" and inserting "WEBSITE.—"; and
(ii) by striking "Registry or State sex offender public registry," and inserting "Website,"; and
(B) in subparagraph (B)(ii), by striking "or stalking." and inserting "stalking, or an attempt to commit any such crime.";
(3) in paragraph (3)—
(A) in subparagraph (A)—
(i) in clause (i), by striking "Registry, or of the relevant State sex offender public registry for any State not yet participating in the National Sex Offender Public Registry, in which the United States client has resided during the previous 20 years," and inserting "Website"; and
(ii) in clause (iii)(II), by striking "background information collected by the international marriage broker under paragraph (2)(B);" and inserting "signed certification and accompanying documentation or attestation regarding the background information collected under paragraph (2)(B);"; and
(B) by striking subparagraph (C);
(4) in paragraph (5)—
(A) in subparagraph (A)(ii), by striking "A penalty may be imposed under clause (i) by the Attorney General only" and inserting "At the discretion of the Attorney General, a penalty may be imposed under clause (i) either by a Federal judge, or by the Attorney General";
(B) by amending subparagraph (B) to read as follows:
"(B) FEDERAL CRIMINAL PENALTIES.—
"(i) FAILURE OF INTERNATIONAL MARRIAGE BROKERS TO COMPLY WITH OBLIGATIONS.—Except as provided in clause (ii), an international marriage broker that, in circumstances in or affecting interstate or foreign commerce, or within the special maritime and territorial jurisdiction of the United States—
"(I) except as provided in subclause (II), violates (or attempts to violate) paragraph (1), (2), (3), or (4) shall be fined in accordance with title 18, United States Code, or imprisoned for not more than 1 year, or both; or
"(II) knowingly violates or attempts to violate paragraphs (1), (2), (3), or (4) shall be fined in accordance with title 18, United States Code, or imprisoned for not more than 5 years, or both.
"(ii) MISUSE OF INFORMATION.—A person who knowingly discloses, uses, or causes to be used any information obtained by an international marriage broker as a result of a requirement under paragraph (2) or (3) for any purpose other than the disclosures required under paragraph (3) shall be fined in accordance with title 18, United States Code, or imprisoned for not more than 1 year, or both.
"(iii) FRAUDULENT FAILURES OF UNITED STATES CLIENTS TO MAKE REQUIRED SELF-DISCLOSURES.—A person

who knowingly and with intent to defraud another person outside the United States in order to recruit, solicit, entice, or induce that other person into entering a dating or matrimonial relationship, makes false or fraudulent representations regarding the disclosures described in clause (i), (ii), (iii), or (iv) of subsection (d)(2)(B), including by failing to make any such disclosures, shall be fined in accordance with title 18, United States Code, imprisoned for not more than 1 year, or both.

"(iv) RELATIONSHIP TO OTHER PENALTIES.—The penalties provided in clauses (i), (ii), and (iii) are in addition to any other civil or criminal liability under Federal or State law to which a person may be subject for the misuse of information, including misuse to threaten, intimidate, or harass any individual.

"(v) CONSTRUCTION.—Nothing in this paragraph or paragraph (3) or (4) may be construed to prevent the disclosure of information to law enforcement or pursuant to a court order."; and

(C) in subparagraph (C), by striking the period at the end and inserting "including equitable remedies.";

(5) by redesignating paragraphs (6) and (7) as paragraphs (7) and (8), respectively; and

(6) by inserting after paragraph (5) the following:

"(6) ENFORCEMENT.—

"(A) AUTHORITY.—The Attorney General shall be responsible for the enforcement of the provisions of this section, including the prosecution of civil and criminal penalties provided for by this section.

"(B) CONSULTATION.—The Attorney General shall consult with the Director of the Office on Violence Against Women of the Department of Justice to develop policies and public education designed to promote enforcement of this section.".

(d) GAO STUDY AND REPORT.—Section 833(f) of the International Marriage Broker Regulation Act of 2005 (8 U.S.C. 1375a(f)) is amended—

(1) in the subsection heading, by striking "STUDY AND REPORT.—" and inserting "STUDIES AND REPORTS.—"; and

(2) by adding at the end the following:

"(4) CONTINUING IMPACT STUDY AND REPORT.—

"(A) STUDY.—The Comptroller General shall conduct a study on the continuing impact of the implementation of this section and of section of 214 of the Immigration and Nationality Act (8 U.S.C. 1184) on the process for granting K nonimmigrant visas, including specifically a study of the items described in subparagraphs (A) through (E) of paragraph (1).

"(B) REPORT.—Not later than 2 years after the date of the enactment of the Violence Against Women Reauthorization Act of 2013, the Comptroller General shall submit to the Committee on the Judiciary of the Senate and the Committee on the Judiciary of the House of Representatives a report setting forth the results of the study conducted under subparagraph (A).

"(C) DATA COLLECTION.—The Attorney General, the Secretary of Homeland Security, and the Secretary of State shall collect and maintain the data necessary for the Comptroller General to conduct the study required by paragraph (1)(A).".

SEC. 809. ELIGIBILITY OF CRIME AND TRAFFICKING VICTIMS IN THE COMMONWEALTH OF THE NORTHERN MARIANA ISLANDS TO ADJUST STATUS.

Section 705(c) of the Consolidated Natural Resources Act of 2008 (Public Law 110–229; 48 U.S.C. 1806 note), is amended by striking "except that," and all that follows through the end, and inserting the following: "except that—

"(1) for the purpose of determining whether an alien lawfully admitted for permanent residence (as defined in section 101(a)(20) of the Immigration and Nationality Act (8 U.S.C. 1101(a)(20)) has abandoned or lost such status by reason of absence from the United States, such alien's presence in the Commonwealth, before, on or after November 28, 2009, shall be considered to be presence in the United States; and

"(2) for the purpose of determining whether an alien whose application for status under subparagraph (T) or (U) of section 101(a)(15) of the Immigration and Nationality Act (8 U.S.C. 1101(a)(15)) was granted is subsequently eligible for adjustment under subsection (l) or (m) of section 245 of such Act (8 U.S.C. 1255), such alien's physical presence in the Commonwealth before, on, or after November 28, 2009, and subsequent to the grant of the application, shall be considered as equivalent to presence in the United States pursuant to a nonimmigrant admission in such status.".

SEC. 810. DISCLOSURE OF INFORMATION FOR NATIONAL SECURITY PURPOSES.

(a) INFORMATION SHARING.—Section 384(b) of the Illegal Immigration Reform and Immigrant Responsibility Act of 1996 (8 U.S.C. 1367(b)) is amended—

(1) in paragraph (1)—

(A) by inserting "Secretary of Homeland Security or the" before "Attorney General may"; and

(B) by inserting "Secretary's or the" before "Attorney General's discretion";

(2) in paragraph (2)—

(A) by inserting "Secretary of Homeland Security or the" before "Attorney General may";

(B) by inserting "Secretary or the" before "Attorney General for"; and

(C) by inserting "in a manner that protects the confidentiality of such information" after "law enforcement purpose";

(3) in paragraph (5), by striking "Attorney General is" and inserting "Secretary of Homeland Security and the Attorney General are"; and

(4) by adding at the end a new paragraph as follows:

"(8) Notwithstanding subsection (a)(2), the Secretary of Homeland Security, the Secretary of State, or the Attorney General may provide in the discretion of either such Secretary or the Attorney General for the disclosure of information to national security officials to be used solely for a national security purpose in a manner that protects the confidentiality of such information.".

(b) GUIDELINES.—Section 384(d) of the Illegal Immigration Reform and Immigrant Responsibility Act of 1996 (8 U.S.C. 1367(d)) is amended—

(1) by inserting ", Secretary of State," after "The Attorney General";

(2) by inserting ", Department of State," after "Department of Justice"; and

(3) by inserting "and severe forms of trafficking in persons or criminal activity listed in section 101(a)(15)(U) of the Immigration and Nationality Act (8 U.S.C. 1101(a)(15)(u))" after "domestic violence".

(c) IMPLEMENTATION.—Not later than 180 days after the date of the enactment of this Act, the Attorney General, the Secretary of State, and Secretary of Homeland Security shall provide the guidance required by section 384(d) of the Illegal Immigration Reform and Immigrant Responsibility Act of 1996 (8 U.S.C. 1367(d)), consistent with the amendments made by subsections (a) and (b).

(d) CLERICAL AMENDMENT.—Section 384(a)(1) of the Illegal Immigration Reform and Immigrant Responsibility Act of 1986 is amended by striking "241(a)(2)" in the matter following subparagraph (F) and inserting "237(a)(2)".

TITLE IX—SAFETY FOR INDIAN WOMEN

SEC. 901. GRANTS TO INDIAN TRIBAL GOVERNMENTS.

Section 2015(a) of title I of the Omnibus Crime Control and Safe Streets Act of 1968 (42 U.S.C. 3796gg–10(a)) is amended—

(1) in paragraph (2), by inserting "sex trafficking," after "sexual assault,";

(2) in paragraph (4), by inserting "sex trafficking," after "sexual assault,";

(3) in paragraph (5), by striking "and stalking" and all that follows and inserting "sexual assault, sex trafficking, and stalking;";

(4) in paragraph (7)—

(A) by inserting "sex trafficking," after "sexual assault," each place it appears; and

(B) by striking "and" at the end;

(5) in paragraph (8)—

(A) by inserting "sex trafficking," after "stalking,"; and

(B) by striking the period at the end and inserting a semicolon; and

(6) by adding at the end the following:

"(9) provide services to address the needs of youth who are victims of domestic violence, dating violence, sexual assault, sex trafficking, or stalking and the needs of youth and children exposed to domestic violence, dating violence, sexual assault, or stalking, including support for the nonabusing parent or the caretaker of the youth or child; and

"(10) develop and promote legislation and policies that enhance best practices for responding to violent crimes against Indian women, including the crimes of domestic violence, dating violence, sexual assault, sex trafficking, and stalking.".

S. 47—66

SEC. 902. GRANTS TO INDIAN TRIBAL COALITIONS.

Section 2001 of title I of the Omnibus Crime Control and Safe Streets Act of 1968 (42 U.S.C. 3796gg) is amended by striking subsection (d) and inserting the following:

"(d) Tribal Coalition Grants.—

"(1) Purpose.—The Attorney General shall award a grant to tribal coalitions for purposes of—

"(A) increasing awareness of domestic violence and sexual assault against Indian women;

"(B) enhancing the response to violence against Indian women at the Federal, State, and tribal levels;

"(C) identifying and providing technical assistance to coalition membership and tribal communities to enhance access to essential services to Indian women victimized by domestic and sexual violence, including sex trafficking; and

"(D) assisting Indian tribes in developing and promoting State, local, and tribal legislation and policies that enhance best practices for responding to violent crimes against Indian women, including the crimes of domestic violence, dating violence, sexual assault, sex trafficking, and stalking.

"(2) Grants.—The Attorney General shall award grants on an annual basis under paragraph (1) to—

"(A) each tribal coalition that—

"(i) meets the criteria of a tribal coalition under section 40002(a) of the Violence Against Women Act of 1994 (42 U.S.C. 13925(a));

"(ii) is recognized by the Office on Violence Against Women; and

"(iii) provides services to Indian tribes; and

"(B) organizations that propose to incorporate and operate a tribal coalition in areas where Indian tribes are located but no tribal coalition exists.

"(3) Use of amounts.—For each of fiscal years 2014 through 2018, of the amounts appropriated to carry out this subsection—

"(A) not more than 10 percent shall be made available to organizations described in paragraph (2)(B), provided that 1 or more organizations determined by the Attorney General to be qualified apply;

"(B) not less than 90 percent shall be made available to tribal coalitions described in paragraph (2)(A), which amounts shall be distributed equally among each eligible tribal coalition for the applicable fiscal year.

"(4) Eligibility for other grants.—Receipt of an award under this subsection by a tribal coalition shall not preclude the tribal coalition from receiving additional grants under this title to carry out the purposes described in paragraph (1).

"(5) Multiple purpose applications.—Nothing in this subsection prohibits any tribal coalition or organization described in paragraph (2) from applying for funding to address sexual assault or domestic violence needs in the same application.".

SEC. 903. CONSULTATION.

Section 903 of the Violence Against Women and Department of Justice Reauthorization Act of 2005 (42 U.S.C. 14045d) is amended—

(1) in subsection (a)—

(A) by striking "and the Violence Against Women Act of 2000" and inserting ", the Violence Against Women Act of 2000"; and

(B) by inserting ", and the Violence Against Women Reauthorization Act of 2013" before the period at the end;

(2) in subsection (b)—

(A) in the matter preceding paragraph (1), by striking "Secretary of the Department of Health and Human Services" and inserting "Secretary of Health and Human Services, the Secretary of the Interior,"; and

(B) in paragraph (2), by striking "and stalking" and inserting "stalking, and sex trafficking"; and

(3) by adding at the end the following:

"(c) ANNUAL REPORT.—The Attorney General shall submit to Congress an annual report on the annual consultations required under subsection (a) that—

"(1) contains the recommendations made under subsection (b) by Indian tribes during the year covered by the report;

"(2) describes actions taken during the year covered by the report to respond to recommendations made under subsection (b) during the year or a previous year; and

"(3) describes how the Attorney General will work in coordination and collaboration with Indian tribes, the Secretary of Health and Human Services, and the Secretary of the Interior to address the recommendations made under subsection (b).

"(d) NOTICE.—Not later than 120 days before the date of a consultation under subsection (a), the Attorney General shall notify tribal leaders of the date, time, and location of the consultation.".

SEC. 904. TRIBAL JURISDICTION OVER CRIMES OF DOMESTIC VIOLENCE.

Title II of Public Law 90–284 (25 U.S.C. 1301 et seq.) (commonly known as the "Indian Civil Rights Act of 1968") is amended by adding at the end the following:

"SEC. 204. TRIBAL JURISDICTION OVER CRIMES OF DOMESTIC VIOLENCE.

"(a) DEFINITIONS.—In this section:

"(1) DATING VIOLENCE.—The term 'dating violence' means violence committed by a person who is or has been in a social relationship of a romantic or intimate nature with the victim, as determined by the length of the relationship, the type of relationship, and the frequency of interaction between the persons involved in the relationship.

"(2) DOMESTIC VIOLENCE.—The term 'domestic violence' means violence committed by a current or former spouse or intimate partner of the victim, by a person with whom the victim shares a child in common, by a person who is cohabitating with or has cohabitated with the victim as a spouse or intimate partner, or by a person similarly situated to a spouse of the victim under the domestic- or family- violence laws of an Indian tribe that has jurisdiction over the Indian country where the violence occurs.

"(3) INDIAN COUNTRY.—The term 'Indian country' has the meaning given the term in section 1151 of title 18, United States Code.

"(4) PARTICIPATING TRIBE.—The term 'participating tribe' means an Indian tribe that elects to exercise special domestic violence criminal jurisdiction over the Indian country of that Indian tribe.

"(5) PROTECTION ORDER.—The term 'protection order'—

"(A) means any injunction, restraining order, or other order issued by a civil or criminal court for the purpose of preventing violent or threatening acts or harassment against, sexual violence against, contact or communication with, or physical proximity to, another person; and

"(B) includes any temporary or final order issued by a civil or criminal court, whether obtained by filing an independent action or as a pendent lite order in another proceeding, if the civil or criminal order was issued in response to a complaint, petition, or motion filed by or on behalf of a person seeking protection.

"(6) SPECIAL DOMESTIC VIOLENCE CRIMINAL JURISDICTION.—The term 'special domestic violence criminal jurisdiction' means the criminal jurisdiction that a participating tribe may exercise under this section but could not otherwise exercise.

"(7) SPOUSE OR INTIMATE PARTNER.—The term 'spouse or intimate partner' has the meaning given the term in section 2266 of title 18, United States Code.

"(b) NATURE OF THE CRIMINAL JURISDICTION.—

"(1) IN GENERAL.—Notwithstanding any other provision of law, in addition to all powers of self-government recognized and affirmed by sections 201 and 203, the powers of self-government of a participating tribe include the inherent power of that tribe, which is hereby recognized and affirmed, to exercise special domestic violence criminal jurisdiction over all persons.

"(2) CONCURRENT JURISDICTION.—The exercise of special domestic violence criminal jurisdiction by a participating tribe shall be concurrent with the jurisdiction of the United States, of a State, or of both.

"(3) APPLICABILITY.—Nothing in this section—

"(A) creates or eliminates any Federal or State criminal jurisdiction over Indian country; or

"(B) affects the authority of the United States or any State government that has been delegated authority by the United States to investigate and prosecute a criminal violation in Indian country.

"(4) EXCEPTIONS.—

"(A) VICTIM AND DEFENDANT ARE BOTH NON-INDIANS.—

"(i) IN GENERAL.—A participating tribe may not exercise special domestic violence criminal jurisdiction over an alleged offense if neither the defendant nor the alleged victim is an Indian.

"(ii) DEFINITION OF VICTIM.—In this subparagraph and with respect to a criminal proceeding in which a participating tribe exercises special domestic violence criminal jurisdiction based on a violation of a protection order, the term 'victim' means a person specifically protected by a protection order that the defendant allegedly violated.

"(B) DEFENDANT LACKS TIES TO THE INDIAN TRIBE.—A participating tribe may exercise special domestic violence criminal jurisdiction over a defendant only if the defendant—

"(i) resides in the Indian country of the participating tribe;

"(ii) is employed in the Indian country of the participating tribe; or

"(iii) is a spouse, intimate partner, or dating partner of—

"(I) a member of the participating tribe; or

"(II) an Indian who resides in the Indian country of the participating tribe.

"(c) CRIMINAL CONDUCT.—A participating tribe may exercise special domestic violence criminal jurisdiction over a defendant for criminal conduct that falls into one or more of the following categories:

"(1) DOMESTIC VIOLENCE AND DATING VIOLENCE.—An act of domestic violence or dating violence that occurs in the Indian country of the participating tribe.

"(2) VIOLATIONS OF PROTECTION ORDERS.—An act that—

"(A) occurs in the Indian country of the participating tribe; and

"(B) violates the portion of a protection order that—

"(i) prohibits or provides protection against violent or threatening acts or harassment against, sexual violence against, contact or communication with, or physical proximity to, another person;

"(ii) was issued against the defendant;

"(iii) is enforceable by the participating tribe; and

"(iv) is consistent with section 2265(b) of title 18, United States Code.

"(d) RIGHTS OF DEFENDANTS.—In a criminal proceeding in which a participating tribe exercises special domestic violence criminal jurisdiction, the participating tribe shall provide to the defendant—

"(1) all applicable rights under this Act;

"(2) if a term of imprisonment of any length may be imposed, all rights described in section 202(c);

"(3) the right to a trial by an impartial jury that is drawn from sources that—

"(A) reflect a fair cross section of the community; and

"(B) do not systematically exclude any distinctive group in the community, including non-Indians; and

"(4) all other rights whose protection is necessary under the Constitution of the United States in order for Congress to recognize and affirm the inherent power of the participating tribe to exercise special domestic violence criminal jurisdiction over the defendant.

"(e) PETITIONS TO STAY DETENTION.—

"(1) IN GENERAL.—A person who has filed a petition for a writ of habeas corpus in a court of the United States under section 203 may petition that court to stay further detention of that person by the participating tribe.

S. 47—70

"(2) GRANT OF STAY.—A court shall grant a stay described in paragraph (1) if the court—

"(A) finds that there is a substantial likelihood that the habeas corpus petition will be granted; and

"(B) after giving each alleged victim in the matter an opportunity to be heard, finds by clear and convincing evidence that under conditions imposed by the court, the petitioner is not likely to flee or pose a danger to any person or the community if released.

"(3) NOTICE.—An Indian tribe that has ordered the detention of any person has a duty to timely notify such person of his rights and privileges under this subsection and under section 203.

"(f) GRANTS TO TRIBAL GOVERNMENTS.—The Attorney General may award grants to the governments of Indian tribes (or to authorized designees of those governments)—

"(1) to strengthen tribal criminal justice systems to assist Indian tribes in exercising special domestic violence criminal jurisdiction, including—

"(A) law enforcement (including the capacity of law enforcement or court personnel to enter information into and obtain information from national crime information databases);

"(B) prosecution;

"(C) trial and appellate courts;

"(D) probation systems;

"(E) detention and correctional facilities;

"(F) alternative rehabilitation centers;

"(G) culturally appropriate services and assistance for victims and their families; and

"(H) criminal codes and rules of criminal procedure, appellate procedure, and evidence;

"(2) to provide indigent criminal defendants with the effective assistance of licensed defense counsel, at no cost to the defendant, in criminal proceedings in which a participating tribe prosecutes a crime of domestic violence or dating violence or a criminal violation of a protection order;

"(3) to ensure that, in criminal proceedings in which a participating tribe exercises special domestic violence criminal jurisdiction, jurors are summoned, selected, and instructed in a manner consistent with all applicable requirements; and

"(4) to accord victims of domestic violence, dating violence, and violations of protection orders rights that are similar to the rights of a crime victim described in section 3771(a) of title 18, United States Code, consistent with tribal law and custom.

"(g) SUPPLEMENT, NOT SUPPLANT.—Amounts made available under this section shall supplement and not supplant any other Federal, State, tribal, or local government amounts made available to carry out activities described in this section.

"(h) AUTHORIZATION OF APPROPRIATIONS.—There are authorized to be appropriated $5,000,000 for each of fiscal years 2014 through 2018 to carry out subsection (f) and to provide training, technical assistance, data collection, and evaluation of the criminal justice systems of participating tribes.".

SEC. 905. TRIBAL PROTECTION ORDERS.

Section 2265 of title 18, United States Code, is amended by striking subsection (e) and inserting the following:

"(e) TRIBAL COURT JURISDICTION.—For purposes of this section, a court of an Indian tribe shall have full civil jurisdiction to issue and enforce protection orders involving any person, including the authority to enforce any orders through civil contempt proceedings, to exclude violators from Indian land, and to use other appropriate mechanisms, in matters arising anywhere in the Indian country of the Indian tribe (as defined in section 1151) or otherwise within the authority of the Indian tribe.".

SEC. 906. AMENDMENTS TO THE FEDERAL ASSAULT STATUTE.

(a) IN GENERAL.—Section 113 of title 18, United States Code, is amended—

(1) in subsection (a)—

(A) by striking paragraph (1) and inserting the following:

"(1) Assault with intent to commit murder or a violation of section 2241 or 2242, by a fine under this title, imprisonment for not more than 20 years, or both.";

(B) in paragraph (2), by striking "felony under chapter 109A" and inserting "violation of section 2241 or 2242";

(C) in paragraph (3) by striking "and without just cause or excuse,";

(D) in paragraph (4), by striking "six months" and inserting "1 year";

(E) in paragraph (7)—

(i) by striking "substantial bodily injury to an individual who has not attained the age of 16 years" and inserting "substantial bodily injury to a spouse or intimate partner, a dating partner, or an individual who has not attained the age of 16 years"; and

(ii) by striking "fine" and inserting "a fine"; and

(F) by adding at the end the following:

"(8) Assault of a spouse, intimate partner, or dating partner by strangling, suffocating, or attempting to strangle or suffocate, by a fine under this title, imprisonment for not more than 10 years, or both."; and

(2) in subsection (b)—

(A) by striking "(b) As used in this subsection—" and inserting the following:

"(b) DEFINITIONS.—In this section—";

(B) in paragraph (1)(B), by striking "and" at the end;

(C) in paragraph (2), by striking the period at the end and inserting a semicolon; and

(D) by adding at the end the following:

"(3) the terms 'dating partner' and 'spouse or intimate partner' have the meanings given those terms in section 2266;

"(4) the term 'strangling' means intentionally, knowingly, or recklessly impeding the normal breathing or circulation of the blood of a person by applying pressure to the throat or neck, regardless of whether that conduct results in any visible injury or whether there is any intent to kill or protractedly injure the victim; and

"(5) the term 'suffocating' means intentionally, knowingly, or recklessly impeding the normal breathing of a person by covering the mouth of the person, the nose of the person, or both, regardless of whether that conduct results in any visible injury or whether there is any intent to kill or protractedly injure the victim.".

(b) INDIAN MAJOR CRIMES.—Section 1153(a) of title 18, United States Code, is amended by striking "assault with intent to commit murder, assault with a dangerous weapon, assault resulting in serious bodily injury (as defined in section 1365 of this title)" and inserting "a felony assault under section 113".

(c) REPEAT OFFENDERS.—Section 2265A(b)(1)(B) of title 18, United States Code, is amended by inserting "or tribal" after "State".

SEC. 907. ANALYSIS AND RESEARCH ON VIOLENCE AGAINST INDIAN WOMEN.

(a) IN GENERAL.—Section 904(a) of the Violence Against Women and Department of Justice Reauthorization Act of 2005 (42 U.S.C. 3796gg–10 note) is amended—

(1) in paragraph (1)—

(A) by striking "The National" and inserting "Not later than 2 years after the date of enactment of the Violence Against Women Reauthorization Act of 2013, the National"; and

(B) by inserting "and in Native villages (as defined in section 3 of the Alaska Native Claims Settlement Act (43 U.S.C. 1602))" before the period at the end;

(2) in paragraph (2)(A)—

(A) in clause (iv), by striking "and" at the end;

(B) in clause (v), by striking the period at the end and inserting "; and"; and

(C) by adding at the end the following:

"(vi) sex trafficking.";

(3) in paragraph (4), by striking "this Act" and inserting "the Violence Against Women Reauthorization Act of 2013"; and

(4) in paragraph (5), by striking "this section $1,000,000 for each of fiscal years 2007 and 2008" and inserting "this subsection $1,000,000 for each of fiscal years 2014 and 2015".

(b) AUTHORIZATION OF APPROPRIATIONS.—Section 905(b)(2) of the Violence Against Women and Department of Justice Reauthorization Act of 2005 (28 U.S.C. 534 note) is amended by striking "fiscal years 2007 through 2011" and inserting "fiscal years 2014 through 2018".

SEC. 908. EFFECTIVE DATES; PILOT PROJECT.

(a) GENERAL EFFECTIVE DATE.—Except as provided in section 4 and subsection (b) of this section, the amendments made by this title shall take effect on the date of enactment of this Act.

(b) EFFECTIVE DATE FOR SPECIAL DOMESTIC-VIOLENCE CRIMINAL JURISDICTION.—

(1) IN GENERAL.—Except as provided in paragraph (2), subsections (b) through (d) of section 204 of Public Law 90–284 (as added by section 904) shall take effect on the date that is 2 years after the date of enactment of this Act.

(2) PILOT PROJECT.—

(A) IN GENERAL.—At any time during the 2-year period beginning on the date of enactment of this Act, an Indian tribe may ask the Attorney General to designate the tribe as a participating tribe under section 204(a) of Public Law 90–284 on an accelerated basis.

(B) PROCEDURE.—The Attorney General may grant a request under subparagraph (A) after coordinating with the Secretary of the Interior, consulting with affected Indian tribes, and concluding that the criminal justice system of the requesting tribe has adequate safeguards in place to protect defendants' rights, consistent with section 204 of Public Law 90–284.

(C) EFFECTIVE DATES FOR PILOT PROJECTS.—An Indian tribe designated as a participating tribe under this paragraph may commence exercising special domestic violence criminal jurisdiction pursuant to subsections (b) through (d) of section 204 of Public Law 90–284 on a date established by the Attorney General, after consultation with that Indian tribe, but in no event later than the date that is 2 years after the date of enactment of this Act.

SEC. 909. INDIAN LAW AND ORDER COMMISSION; REPORT ON THE ALASKA RURAL JUSTICE AND LAW ENFORCEMENT COMMISSION.

(a) IN GENERAL.—Section 15(f) of the Indian Law Enforcement Reform Act (25 U.S.C. 2812(f)) is amended by striking "2 years" and inserting "3 years".

(b) REPORT.—The Attorney General, in consultation with the Attorney General of the State of Alaska, the Commissioner of Public Safety of the State of Alaska, the Alaska Federation of Natives and Federally recognized Indian tribes in the State of Alaska, shall report to Congress not later than one year after enactment of this Act with respect to whether the Alaska Rural Justice and Law Enforcement Commission established under Section 112(a)(1) of the Consolidated Appropriations Act, 2004 should be continued and appropriations authorized for the continued work of the commission. The report may contain recommendations for legislation with respect to the scope of work and composition of the commission.

SEC. 910. SPECIAL RULE FOR THE STATE OF ALASKA.

(a) EXPANDED JURISDICTION.—In the State of Alaska, the amendments made by sections 904 and 905 shall only apply to the Indian country (as defined in section 1151 of title 18, United States Code) of the Metlakatla Indian Community, Annette Island Reserve.

(b) RETAINED JURISDICTION.—The jurisdiction and authority of each Indian tribe in the State of Alaska under section 2265(e) of title 18, United States Code (as in effect on the day before the date of enactment of this Act)—

(1) shall remain in full force and effect; and

(2) are not limited or diminished by this Act or any amendment made by this Act.

(c) SAVINGS PROVISION.—Nothing in this Act or an amendment made by this Act limits or diminishes the jurisdiction of the State of Alaska, any subdivision of the State of Alaska, or any Indian tribe in the State of Alaska.

S. 47—74

TITLE X—SAFER ACT

SEC. 1001. SHORT TITLE.

This title may be cited as the "Sexual Assault Forensic Evidence Reporting Act of 2013" or the "SAFER Act of 2013".

SEC. 1002. DEBBIE SMITH GRANTS FOR AUDITING SEXUAL ASSAULT EVIDENCE BACKLOGS.

Section 2 of the DNA Analysis Backlog Elimination Act of 2000 (42 U.S.C. 14135) is amended—

(1) in subsection (a), by adding at the end the following new paragraph:

"(7) To conduct an audit consistent with subsection (n) of the samples of sexual assault evidence that are in the possession of the State or unit of local government and are awaiting testing.

"(8) To ensure that the collection and processing of DNA evidence by law enforcement agencies from crimes, including sexual assault and other violent crimes against persons, is carried out in an appropriate and timely manner and in accordance with the protocols and practices developed under subsection (o)(1).";

(2) in subsection (c), by adding at the end the following new paragraph:

"(4) ALLOCATION OF GRANT AWARDS FOR AUDITS.—For each of fiscal years 2014 through 2017, not less than 5 percent, but not more than 7 percent, of the grant amounts distributed under paragraph (1) shall, if sufficient applications to justify such amounts are received by the Attorney General, be awarded for purposes described in subsection (a)(7), provided that none of the funds required to be distributed under this paragraph shall decrease or otherwise limit the availability of funds required to be awarded to States or units of local government under paragraph (3)."; and

(3) by adding at the end the following new subsections:

"(n) USE OF FUNDS FOR AUDITING SEXUAL ASSAULT EVIDENCE BACKLOGS.—

"(1) ELIGIBILITY.—The Attorney General may award a grant under this section to a State or unit of local government for the purpose described in subsection (a)(7) only if the State or unit of local government—

"(A) submits a plan for performing the audit of samples described in such subsection; and

"(B) includes in such plan a good-faith estimate of the number of such samples.

"(2) GRANT CONDITIONS.—A State or unit of local government receiving a grant for the purpose described in subsection (a)(7)—

"(A) may not enter into any contract or agreement with any non-governmental vendor laboratory to conduct an audit described in subsection (a)(7); and

"(B) shall—

"(i) not later than 1 year after receiving the grant, complete the audit referred to in paragraph (1)(A) in accordance with the plan submitted under such paragraph;

"(ii) not later than 60 days after receiving possession of a sample of sexual assault evidence that was not in the possession of the State or unit of local government at the time of the initiation of an audit under paragraph (1)(A), subject to paragraph (4)(F), include in any required reports under clause (v), the information listed under paragraph (4)(B);

"(iii) for each sample of sexual assault evidence that is identified as awaiting testing as part of the audit referred to in paragraph (1)(A)—

"(I) assign a unique numeric or alphanumeric identifier to each sample of sexual assault evidence that is in the possession of the State or unit of local government and is awaiting testing; and

"(II) identify the date or dates after which the State or unit of local government would be barred by any applicable statutes of limitations from prosecuting a perpetrator of the sexual assault to which the sample relates;

"(iv) provide that—

"(I) the chief law enforcement officer of the State or unit of local government, respectively, is the individual responsible for the compliance of the State or unit of local government, respectively, with the reporting requirements described in clause (v); or

"(II) the designee of such officer may fulfill the responsibility described in subclause (I) so long as such designee is an employee of the State or unit of local government, respectively, and is not an employee of any governmental laboratory or non-governmental vendor laboratory; and

"(v) comply with all grantee reporting requirements described in paragraph (4).

"(3) EXTENSION OF INITIAL DEADLINE.—The Attorney General may grant an extension of the deadline under paragraph (2)(B)(i) to a State or unit of local government that demonstrates that more time is required for compliance with such paragraph.

"(4) SEXUAL ASSAULT FORENSIC EVIDENCE REPORTS.—

"(A) IN GENERAL.—For not less than 12 months after the completion of an initial count of sexual assault evidence that is awaiting testing during an audit referred to in paragraph (1)(A), a State or unit of local government that receives a grant award under subsection (a)(7) shall, not less than every 60 days, submit a report to the Department of Justice, on a form prescribed by the Attorney General, which shall contain the information required under subparagraph (B).

"(B) CONTENTS OF REPORTS.—A report under this paragraph shall contain the following information:

"(i) The name of the State or unit of local government filing the report.

"(ii) The period of dates covered by the report.

"(iii) The cumulative total number of samples of sexual assault evidence that, at the end of the reporting period—

"(I) are in the possession of the State or unit of local government at the reporting period;

"(II) are awaiting testing; and

"(III) the State or unit of local government has determined should undergo DNA or other appropriate forensic analyses.

"(iv) The cumulative total number of samples of sexual assault evidence in the possession of the State or unit of local government that, at the end of the reporting period, the State or unit of local government has determined should not undergo DNA or other appropriate forensic analyses, provided that the reporting form shall allow for the State or unit of local government, at its sole discretion, to explain the reasoning for this determination in some or all cases.

"(v) The cumulative total number of samples of sexual assault evidence in a total under clause (iii) that have been submitted to a laboratory for DNA or other appropriate forensic analyses.

"(vi) The cumulative total number of samples of sexual assault evidence identified by an audit referred to in paragraph (1)(A) or under paragraph (2)(B)(ii) for which DNA or other appropriate forensic analysis has been completed at the end of the reporting period.

"(vii) The total number of samples of sexual assault evidence identified by the State or unit of local government under paragraph (2)(B)(ii), since the previous reporting period.

"(viii) The cumulative total number of samples of sexual assault evidence described under clause (iii) for which the State or unit of local government will be barred within 12 months by any applicable statute of limitations from prosecuting a perpetrator of the sexual assault to which the sample relates.

"(C) PUBLICATION OF REPORTS.—Not later than 7 days after the submission of a report under this paragraph by a State or unit of local government, the Attorney General shall, subject to subparagraph (D), publish and disseminate a facsimile of the full contents of such report on an appropriate internet website.

"(D) PERSONALLY IDENTIFIABLE INFORMATION.—The Attorney General shall ensure that any information published and disseminated as part of a report under this paragraph, which reports information under this subsection, does not include personally identifiable information or details about a sexual assault that might lead to the identification of the individuals involved.

"(E) OPTIONAL REPORTING.—The Attorney General shall—

"(i) at the discretion of a State or unit of local government required to file a report under subparagraph (A), allow such State or unit of local government, at their sole discretion, to submit such reports on a more frequent basis; and

"(ii) make available to all States and units of local government the reporting form created pursuant to subparagraph (A), whether or not they are required to submit such reports, and allow such States or units of local government, at their sole discretion, to submit such reports for publication.

"(F) SAMPLES EXEMPT FROM REPORTING REQUIREMENT.—The reporting requirements described in paragraph (2) shall not apply to a sample of sexual assault evidence that—

"(i) is not considered criminal evidence (such as a sample collected anonymously from a victim who is unwilling to make a criminal complaint); or

"(ii) relates to a sexual assault for which the prosecution of each perpetrator is barred by a statute of limitations.

"(5) DEFINITIONS.—In this subsection:

"(A) AWAITING TESTING.—The term 'awaiting testing' means, with respect to a sample of sexual assault evidence, that—

"(i) the sample has been collected and is in the possession of a State or unit of local government;

"(ii) DNA and other appropriate forensic analyses have not been performed on such sample; and

"(iii) the sample is related to a criminal case or investigation in which final disposition has not yet been reached.

"(B) FINAL DISPOSITION.—The term 'final disposition' means, with respect to a criminal case or investigation to which a sample of sexual assault evidence relates—

"(i) the conviction or acquittal of all suspected perpetrators of the crime involved;

"(ii) a determination by the State or unit of local government in possession of the sample that the case is unfounded; or

"(iii) a declaration by the victim of the crime involved that the act constituting the basis of the crime was not committed.

"(C) POSSESSION.—

"(i) IN GENERAL.—The term 'possession', used with respect to possession of a sample of sexual assault evidence by a State or unit of local government, includes possession by an individual who is acting as an agent of the State or unit of local government for the collection of the sample.

"(ii) RULE OF CONSTRUCTION.—Nothing in clause (i) shall be construed to create or amend any Federal rights or privileges for non-governmental vendor laboratories described in regulations promulgated under section 210303 of the DNA Identification Act of 1994 (42 U.S.C. 14131).

"(o) ESTABLISHMENT OF PROTOCOLS, TECHNICAL ASSISTANCE, AND DEFINITIONS.—

"(1) PROTOCOLS AND PRACTICES.—Not later than 18 months after the date of enactment of the SAFER Act of 2013, the Director, in consultation with Federal, State, and local law enforcement agencies and government laboratories, shall develop and publish a description of protocols and practices the Director considers appropriate for the accurate, timely, and effective collection and processing of DNA evidence,

S. 47—78

including protocols and practices specific to sexual assault cases, which shall address appropriate steps in the investigation of cases that might involve DNA evidence, including—

"(A) how to determine—

"(i) which evidence is to be collected by law enforcement personnel and forwarded for testing;

"(ii) the preferred order in which evidence from the same case is to be tested; and

"(iii) what information to take into account when establishing the order in which evidence from different cases is to be tested;

"(B) the establishment of a reasonable period of time in which evidence is to be forwarded by emergency response providers, law enforcement personnel, and prosecutors to a laboratory for testing;

"(C) the establishment of reasonable periods of time in which each stage of analytical laboratory testing is to be completed;

"(D) systems to encourage communication within a State or unit of local government among emergency response providers, law enforcement personnel, prosecutors, courts, defense counsel, crime laboratory personnel, and crime victims regarding the status of crime scene evidence to be tested; and

"(E) standards for conducting the audit of the backlog for DNA case work in sexual assault cases required under subsection (n).

"(2) TECHNICAL ASSISTANCE AND TRAINING.—The Director shall make available technical assistance and training to support States and units of local government in adopting and implementing the protocols and practices developed under paragraph (1) on and after the date on which the protocols and practices are published.

"(3) DEFINITIONS.—In this subsection, the terms 'awaiting testing' and 'possession' have the meanings given those terms in subsection (n).".

SEC. 1003. REPORTS TO CONGRESS.

Not later than 90 days after the end of each fiscal year for which a grant is made for the purpose described in section 2(a)(7) of the DNA Analysis Backlog Elimination Act of 2000, as amended by section 1002, the Attorney General shall submit to Congress a report that—

(1) lists the States and units of local government that have been awarded such grants and the amount of the grant received by each such State or unit of local government;

(2) states the number of extensions granted by the Attorney General under section 2(n)(3) of the DNA Analysis Backlog Elimination Act of 2000, as added by section 1002; and

(3) summarizes the processing status of the samples of sexual assault evidence identified in Sexual Assault Forensic Evidence Reports established under section 2(n)(4) of the DNA Analysis Backlog Elimination Act of 2000, including the number of samples that have not been tested.

SEC. 1004. REDUCING THE RAPE KIT BACKLOG.

Section 2(c)(3) of the DNA Analysis Backlog Elimination Act of 2000 (42 U.S.C. 14135(c)(3)) is amended—

(a) in subparagraph (B), by striking "2014" and inserting "2018"; and

(b) by adding at the end the following:

"(C) For each of fiscal years 2014 through 2018, not less than 75 percent of the total grant amounts shall be awarded for a combination of purposes under paragraphs (1), (2), and (3) of subsection (a).".

SEC. 1005. OVERSIGHT AND ACCOUNTABILITY.

All grants awarded by the Department of Justice that are authorized under this title shall be subject to the following:

(1) AUDIT REQUIREMENT.—Beginning in fiscal year 2013, and each fiscal year thereafter, the Inspector General of the Department of Justice shall conduct audits of recipients of grants under this title to prevent waste, fraud, and abuse of funds by grantees. The Inspector General shall determine the appropriate number of grantees to be audited each year.

(2) MANDATORY EXCLUSION.—A recipient of grant funds under this title that is found to have an unresolved audit finding shall not be eligible to receive grant funds under this title during the 2 fiscal years beginning after the 12-month period described in paragraph (5).

(3) PRIORITY.—In awarding grants under this title, the Attorney General shall give priority to eligible entities that, during the 3 fiscal years before submitting an application for a grant under this title, did not have an unresolved audit finding showing a violation in the terms or conditions of a Department of Justice grant program.

(4) REIMBURSEMENT.—If an entity is awarded grant funds under this Act during the 2-fiscal-year period in which the entity is barred from receiving grants under paragraph (2), the Attorney General shall—

(A) deposit an amount equal to the grant funds that were improperly awarded to the grantee into the General Fund of the Treasury; and

(B) seek to recoup the costs of the repayment to the fund from the grant recipient that was erroneously awarded grant funds.

(5) DEFINED TERM.—In this section, the term "unresolved audit finding" means an audit report finding in the final audit report of the Inspector General of the Department of Justice that the grantee has utilized grant funds for an unauthorized expenditure or otherwise unallowable cost that is not closed or resolved within a 12-month period beginning on the date when the final audit report is issued.

(6) NONPROFIT ORGANIZATION REQUIREMENTS.—

(A) DEFINITION.—For purposes of this section and the grant programs described in this title, the term "'nonprofit organization'" means an organization that is described in section 501(c)(3) of the Internal Revenue Code of 1986 and is exempt from taxation under section 501(a) of such Code.

(B) PROHIBITION.—The Attorney General shall not award a grant under any grant program described in this title to a nonprofit organization that holds money in off-shore accounts for the purpose of avoiding paying the tax described in section 511(a) of the Internal Revenue Code of 1986.

(C) DISCLOSURE.—Each nonprofit organization that is awarded a grant under a grant program described in this title and uses the procedures prescribed in regulations to create a rebuttable presumption of reasonableness for the compensation of its officers, directors, trustees and key employees, shall disclose to the Attorney General, in the application for the grant, the process for determining such compensation, including the independent persons involved in reviewing and approving such compensation, the comparability data used, and contemporaneous substantiation of the deliberation and decision. Upon request, the Attorney General shall make the information disclosed under this subsection available for public inspection.

(7) ADMINISTRATIVE EXPENSES.—Unless otherwise explicitly provided in authorizing legislation, not more than 7.5 percent of the amounts authorized to be appropriated under this title may be used by the Attorney General for salaries and administrative expenses of the Department of Justice.

(8) CONFERENCE EXPENDITURES.—

(A) LIMITATION.—No amounts authorized to be appropriated to the Department of Justice under this title may be used by the Attorney General or by any individual or organization awarded discretionary funds through a cooperative agreement under this Act, to host or support any expenditure for conferences that uses more than $20,000 in Department funds, unless the Deputy Attorney General or the appropriate Assistant Attorney General, Director, or principal deputy as the Deputy Attorney General may designate, provides prior written authorization that the funds may be expended to host a conference.

(B) WRITTEN APPROVAL.—Written approval under subparagraph (A) shall include a written estimate of all costs associated with the conference, including the cost of all food and beverages, audio/visual equipment, honoraria for speakers, and any entertainment.

(C) REPORT.—The Deputy Attorney General shall submit an annual report to the Committee on the Judiciary of the Senate and the Committee on the Judiciary of the House of Representatives on all conference expenditures approved by operation of this paragraph.

(9) PROHIBITION ON LOBBYING ACTIVITY.—

(A) IN GENERAL.—Amounts authorized to be appropriated under this title may not be utilized by any grant recipient to—

(i) lobby any representative of the Department of Justice regarding the award of grant funding; or

(ii) lobby any representative of a Federal, state, local, or tribal government regarding the award of grant funding.

(B) PENALTY.—If the Attorney General determines that any recipient of a grant under this title has violated subparagraph (A), the Attorney General shall—

(i) require the grant recipient to repay the grant in full; and

(ii) prohibit the grant recipient from receiving another grant under this title for not less than 5 years.

SEC. 1006. SUNSET.

Effective on December 31, 2018, subsections (a)(6) and (n) of section 2 of the DNA Analysis Backlog Elimination Act of 2000 (42 U.S.C. 14135(a)(6) and (n)) are repealed.

TITLE XI—OTHER MATTERS

SEC. 1101. SEXUAL ABUSE IN CUSTODIAL SETTINGS.

(a) SUITS BY PRISONERS.—Section 7(e) of the Civil Rights of Institutionalized Persons Act (42 U.S.C. 1997e(e)) is amended by inserting before the period at the end the following: "or the commission of a sexual act (as defined in section 2246 of title 18, United States Code)".

(b) UNITED STATES AS DEFENDANT.—Section 1346(b)(2) of title 28, United States Code, is amended by inserting before the period at the end the following: "or the commission of a sexual act (as defined in section 2246 of title 18)".

(c) ADOPTION AND EFFECT OF NATIONAL STANDARDS.—Section 8 of the Prison Rape Elimination Act of 2003 (42 U.S.C. 15607) is amended—

(1) by redesignating subsection (c) as subsection (e); and

(2) by inserting after subsection (b) the following:

"(c) APPLICABILITY TO DETENTION FACILITIES OPERATED BY THE DEPARTMENT OF HOMELAND SECURITY.—

"(1) IN GENERAL.—Not later than 180 days after the date of enactment of the Violence Against Women Reauthorization Act of 2013, the Secretary of Homeland Security shall publish a final rule adopting national standards for the detection, prevention, reduction, and punishment of rape and sexual assault in facilities that maintain custody of aliens detained for a violation of the immigrations laws of the United States.

"(2) APPLICABILITY.—The standards adopted under paragraph (1) shall apply to detention facilities operated by the Department of Homeland Security and to detention facilities operated under contract with the Department.

"(3) COMPLIANCE.—The Secretary of Homeland Security shall—

"(A) assess compliance with the standards adopted under paragraph (1) on a regular basis; and

"(B) include the results of the assessments in performance evaluations of facilities completed by the Department of Homeland Security.

"(4) CONSIDERATIONS.—In adopting standards under paragraph (1), the Secretary of Homeland Security shall give due consideration to the recommended national standards provided by the Commission under section 7(e).

"(5) DEFINITION.—As used in this section, the term 'detention facilities operated under contract with the Department' includes, but is not limited to contract detention facilities and detention facilities operated through an intergovernmental service agreement with the Department of Homeland Security.

"(d) APPLICABILITY TO CUSTODIAL FACILITIES OPERATED BY THE DEPARTMENT OF HEALTH AND HUMAN SERVICES.—

S. 47—82

"(1) IN GENERAL.—Not later than 180 days after the date of enactment of the Violence Against Women Reauthorization Act of 2013, the Secretary of Health and Human Services shall publish a final rule adopting national standards for the detection, prevention, reduction, and punishment of rape and sexual assault in facilities that maintain custody of unaccompanied alien children (as defined in section 462(g) of the Homeland Security Act of 2002 (6 U.S.C. 279(g))).

"(2) APPLICABILITY.—The standards adopted under paragraph (1) shall apply to facilities operated by the Department of Health and Human Services and to facilities operated under contract with the Department.

"(3) COMPLIANCE.—The Secretary of Health and Human Services shall—

"(A) assess compliance with the standards adopted under paragraph (1) on a regular basis; and

"(B) include the results of the assessments in performance evaluations of facilities completed by the Department of Health and Human Services.

"(4) CONSIDERATIONS.—In adopting standards under paragraph (1), the Secretary of Health and Human Services shall give due consideration to the recommended national standards provided by the Commission under section 7(e).".

SEC. 1102. ANONYMOUS ONLINE HARASSMENT.

Section 223(a)(1) of the Communications Act of 1934 (47 U.S.C. 223(a)(1)) is amended—

(1) in subparagraph (A), in the undesignated matter following clause (ii), by striking "annoy,";

(2) in subparagraph (C)—

(A) by striking "annoy,"; and

(B) by striking "harass any person at the called number or who receives the communication" and inserting "harass any specific person"; and

(3) in subparagraph (E), by striking "harass any person at the called number or who receives the communication" and inserting "harass any specific person".

SEC. 1103. STALKER DATABASE.

Section 40603 of the Violence Against Women Act of 1994 (42 U.S.C. 14032) is amended by striking "$3,000,000" and all that follows and inserting "$3,000,000 for fiscal years 2014 through 2018.".

SEC. 1104. FEDERAL VICTIM ASSISTANTS REAUTHORIZATION.

Section 40114 of the Violence Against Women Act of 1994 (Public Law 103–322; 108 Stat. 1910) is amended by striking "fiscal years 2007 through 2011" and inserting "fiscal years 2014 through 2018".

SEC. 1105. CHILD ABUSE TRAINING PROGRAMS FOR JUDICIAL PERSONNEL AND PRACTITIONERS REAUTHORIZATION.

Subtitle C of the Victims of Child Abuse Act of 1990 (42 U.S.C. 13024) is amended in subsection (a) by striking "$2,300,000" and all that follows and inserting "$2,300,000 for each of fiscal years 2014 through 2018.".

TITLE XII—TRAFFICKING VICTIMS PROTECTION

Subtitle A—Combating International Trafficking in Persons

SEC. 1201. REGIONAL STRATEGIES FOR COMBATING TRAFFICKING IN PERSONS.

Section 105 of the Trafficking Victims Protection Act of 2000 (22 U.S.C. 7103) is amended—

(1) in subsection (d)(7)(J), by striking "section 105(f) of this division" and inserting "subsection (g)";

(2) in subsection (e)(2)—

(A) by striking "(2) COORDINATION OF CERTAIN ACTIVITIES.—" and all that follows through "exploitation.";

(B) by redesignating subparagraph (B) as paragraph (2), and moving such paragraph, as so redesignated, 2 ems to the left; and

(C) by redesignating clauses (i) and (ii) as subparagraphs (A) and (B), respectively, and moving such subparagraphs, as so redesignated, 2 ems to the left;

(3) by redesignating subsection (f) as subsection (g); and

(4) by inserting after subsection (e) the following:

"(f) REGIONAL STRATEGIES FOR COMBATING TRAFFICKING IN PERSONS.—Each regional bureau in the Department of State shall contribute to the realization of the anti-trafficking goals and objectives of the Secretary of State. Each year, in cooperation with the Office to Monitor and Combat Trafficking in Persons, each regional bureau shall submit a list of anti-trafficking goals and objectives to the Secretary of State for each country in the geographic area of responsibilities of the regional bureau. Host governments shall be informed of the goals and objectives for their particular country and, to the extent possible, host government officials should be consulted regarding the goals and objectives.".

SEC. 1202. PARTNERSHIPS AGAINST SIGNIFICANT TRAFFICKING IN PERSONS.

The Trafficking Victims Protection Act of 2000 is amended by inserting after section 105 (22 U.S.C. 7103) the following:

"SEC. 105A. CREATING, BUILDING, AND STRENGTHENING PARTNERSHIPS AGAINST SIGNIFICANT TRAFFICKING IN PERSONS.

"(a) DECLARATION OF PURPOSE.—The purpose of this section is to promote collaboration and cooperation—

"(1) between the United States Government and governments listed on the annual Trafficking in Persons Report;

"(2) between foreign governments and civil society actors; and

"(3) between the United States Government and private sector entities.

"(b) PARTNERSHIPS.—The Director of the office established pursuant to section 105(e)(1) of this Act, in coordination and cooperation with other officials at the Department of State, officials at the Department of Labor, and other relevant officials of the

United States Government, shall promote, build, and sustain partnerships between the United States Government and private entities, including foundations, universities, corporations, community-based organizations, and other nongovernmental organizations, to ensure that—

"(1) United States citizens do not use any item, product, or material produced or extracted with the use and labor from victims of severe forms of trafficking; and

"(2) such entities do not contribute to trafficking in persons involving sexual exploitation.

"(c) PROGRAM TO ADDRESS EMERGENCY SITUATIONS.—The Secretary of State, acting through the Director established pursuant to section 105(e)(1) of this Act, is authorized to establish a fund to assist foreign governments in meeting unexpected, urgent needs in prevention of trafficking in persons, protection of victims, and prosecution of trafficking offenders.

"(d) CHILD PROTECTION COMPACTS.—

"(1) IN GENERAL.—The Secretary of State, in consultation with the Administrator of the United States Agency for International Development, the Secretary of Labor, and the heads of other relevant agencies, is authorized to provide assistance under this section for each country that enters into a child protection compact with the United States to support policies and programs that—

"(A) prevent and respond to violence, exploitation, and abuse against children; and

"(B) measurably reduce the trafficking of minors by building sustainable and effective systems of justice, prevention, and protection.

"(2) ELEMENTS.—A child protection compact under this subsection shall establish a multi-year plan for achieving shared objectives in furtherance of the purposes of this Act. The compact should take into account, if applicable, the national child protection strategies and national action plans for human trafficking of a country, and shall describe—

"(A) the specific objectives the foreign government and the United States Government expect to achieve during the term of the compact;

"(B) the responsibilities of the foreign government and the United States Government in the achievement of such objectives;

"(C) the particular programs or initiatives to be undertaken in the achievement of such objectives and the amount of funding to be allocated to each program or initiative by both countries;

"(D) regular outcome indicators to monitor and measure progress toward achieving such objectives;

"(E) a multi-year financial plan, including the estimated amount of contributions by the United States Government and the foreign government, and proposed mechanisms to implement the plan and provide oversight;

"(F) how a country strategy will be developed to sustain progress made toward achieving such objectives after expiration of the compact; and

"(G) how child protection data will be collected, tracked, and managed to provide strengthened case management and policy planning.

"(3) FORM OF ASSISTANCE.—Assistance under this subsection may be provided in the form of grants, cooperative agreements, or contracts to or with national governments, regional or local governmental units, or non-governmental organizations or private entities with expertise in the protection of victims of severe forms of trafficking in persons.

"(4) ELIGIBLE COUNTRIES.—The Secretary of State, in consultation with the agencies set forth in paragraph (1) and relevant officers of the Department of Justice, shall select countries with which to enter into child protection compacts. The selection of countries under this paragraph shall be based on—

"(A) the selection criteria set forth in paragraph (5); and

"(B) objective, documented, and quantifiable indicators, to the maximum extent possible.

"(5) SELECTION CRITERIA.—A country shall be selected under paragraph (4) on the basis of criteria developed by the Secretary of State in consultation with the Administrator of the United States Agency for International Development and the Secretary of Labor. Such criteria shall include—

"(A) a documented high prevalence of trafficking in persons within the country; and

"(B) demonstrated political motivation and sustained commitment by the government of such country to undertake meaningful measures to address severe forms of trafficking in persons, including prevention, protection of victims, and the enactment and enforcement of anti-trafficking laws against perpetrators.

"(6) SUSPENSION AND TERMINATION OF ASSISTANCE.—

"(A) IN GENERAL.—The Secretary may suspend or terminate assistance provided under this subsection in whole or in part for a country or entity if the Secretary determines that—

"(i) the country or entity is engaged in activities that are contrary to the national security interests of the United States;

"(ii) the country or entity has engaged in a pattern of actions inconsistent with the criteria used to determine the eligibility of the country or entity, as the case may be; or

"(iii) the country or entity has failed to adhere to its responsibilities under the Compact.

"(B) REINSTATEMENT.—The Secretary may reinstate assistance for a country or entity suspended or terminated under this paragraph only if the Secretary determines that the country or entity has demonstrated a commitment to correcting each condition for which assistance was suspended or terminated under subparagraph (A).".

SEC. 1203. PROTECTION AND ASSISTANCE FOR VICTIMS OF TRAFFICKING.

(a) TASK FORCE ACTIVITIES.—Section 105(d)(6) of the Trafficking Victims Protection Act of 2000 (22 U.S.C. 7103(d)(6)) is amended by inserting ", and make reasonable efforts to distribute information to enable all relevant Federal Government agencies to publicize the National Human Trafficking Resource Center Hotline on their websites, in all headquarters offices, and in all field offices throughout the United States" before the period at the end.

(b) CONGRESSIONAL BRIEFING.—Section 107(a)(2) of the Trafficking Victims Protection Act of 2000 (22 U.S.C. 7105(a)(2)) is amended by inserting "and shall brief Congress annually on such efforts" before the period at the end.

SEC. 1204. MINIMUM STANDARDS FOR THE ELIMINATION OF TRAFFICKING.

Section 108(b) of the Trafficking Victims Protection Act of 2000 (22 U.S.C. 7106(b)) is amended—

(1) in paragraph (3)—

(A) by striking "peacekeeping" and inserting "diplomatic, peacekeeping,";

(B) by striking ", and measures" and inserting ", a transparent system for remediating or punishing such public officials as a deterrent, measures"; and

(C) by inserting ", effective bilateral, multilateral, or regional information sharing and cooperation arrangements with other countries, and effective policies or laws regulating foreign labor recruiters and holding them civilly and criminally liable for fraudulent recruiting" before the period at the end;

(2) in paragraph (4), by inserting "and has entered into bilateral, multilateral, or regional law enforcement cooperation and coordination arrangements with other countries" before the period at the end;

(3) in paragraph (7)—

(A) by inserting ", including diplomats and soldiers," after "public officials";

(B) by striking "peacekeeping" and inserting "diplomatic, peacekeeping,"; and

(C) by inserting "A government's failure to appropriately address public allegations against such public officials, especially once such officials have returned to their home countries, shall be considered inaction under these criteria." after "such trafficking.";

(4) by redesignating paragraphs (9) through (11) as paragraphs (10) through (12), respectively; and

(5) by inserting after paragraph (8) the following:

"(9) Whether the government has entered into effective, transparent partnerships, cooperative arrangements, or agreements that have resulted in concrete and measurable outcomes with—

"(A) domestic civil society organizations, private sector entities, or international nongovernmental organizations, or into multilateral or regional arrangements or agreements, to assist the government's efforts to prevent trafficking, protect victims, and punish traffickers; or

"(B) the United States toward agreed goals and objectives in the collective fight against trafficking.".

SEC. 1205. BEST PRACTICES IN TRAFFICKING IN PERSONS ERADICATION.

Section 110(b) of the Trafficking Victims Protection Act of 2000 (22 U.S.C. 7107(b)) is amended—

(1) in paragraph (1)—

(A) by striking "with respect to the status of severe forms of trafficking in persons that shall include—" and inserting "describing the anti-trafficking efforts of the United States and foreign governments according to the minimum standards and criteria enumerated in section 108, and the nature and scope of trafficking in persons in each country and analysis of the trend lines for individual governmental efforts. The report should include— ";

(B) in subparagraph (E), by striking "; and" and inserting a semicolon;

(C) in subparagraph (F), by striking the period at the end and inserting "; and"; and

(D) by inserting at the end the following:

"(G) a section entitled 'Promising Practices in the Eradication of Trafficking in Persons' to highlight effective practices and use of innovation and technology in prevention, protection, prosecution, and partnerships, including by foreign governments, the private sector, and domestic civil society actors.";

(2) by striking paragraph (2);

(3) by redesignating paragraphs (3) and (4) as paragraphs (2) and (3), respectively; and

(4) in paragraph (2), as redesignated, by adding at the end the following:

"(E) PUBLIC NOTICE.—Not later than 30 days after notifying Congress of each country determined to have met the requirements under subclauses (I) through (III) of subparagraph (D)(ii), the Secretary of State shall provide a detailed description of the credible evidence supporting such determination on a publicly available website maintained by the Department of State.".

SEC. 1206. PROTECTIONS FOR DOMESTIC WORKERS AND OTHER NONIMMIGRANTS.

Section 202 of the William Wilberforce Trafficking Victims Protection Reauthorization Act of 2008 (8 U.S.C. 1375b) is amended—

(1) in subsection (a)—

(A) in the subsection heading, by inserting "AND VIDEO FOR CONSULAR WAITING ROOMS" after "INFORMATION PAMPHLET"; and

(B) in paragraph (1)—

(i) by inserting "and video" after "information pamphlet"; and

(ii) by adding at the end the following: "The video shall be distributed and shown in consular waiting rooms in embassies and consulates appropriate to the circumstances that are determined to have the greatest concentration of employment or education-based nonimmigrant visa applicants, and where sufficient video facilities exist in waiting or other rooms where applicants wait or convene. The Secretary of State is authorized to augment video facilities in such consulates or embassies in order to fulfill the purposes of this section.";

S. 47—88

(2) in subsection (b), by inserting "and video" after "information pamphlet";

(3) in subsection (c)—

(A) in paragraph (1), by inserting "and produce or dub the video" after "information pamphlet"; and

(B) in paragraph (2), by inserting "and the video produced or dubbed" after "translated"; and

(4) in subsection (d)—

(A) in paragraph (1), by inserting "and video" after "information pamphlet";

(B) in paragraph (2), by inserting "and video" after "information pamphlet"; and

(C) by adding at the end the following:

"(4) DEADLINE FOR VIDEO DEVELOPMENT AND DISTRIBUTION.—Not later than 1 year after the date of the enactment of the Violence Against Women Reauthorization Act of 2013, the Secretary of State shall make available the video developed under subsection (a) produced or dubbed in all the languages referred to in subsection (c).".

SEC. 1207. PREVENTION OF CHILD MARRIAGE.

(a) IN GENERAL.—Section 106 of the Trafficking Victims Protection Act of 2000 (22 U.S.C. 7104) is amended by adding at the end the following:

"(j) PREVENTION OF CHILD TRAFFICKING THROUGH CHILD MARRIAGE.—The Secretary of State shall establish and implement a multi-year, multi-sectoral strategy—

"(1) to prevent child marriage;

"(2) to promote the empowerment of girls at risk of child marriage in developing countries;

"(3) that should address the unique needs, vulnerabilities, and potential of girls younger than 18 years of age in developing countries;

"(4) that targets areas in developing countries with high prevalence of child marriage; and

"(5) that includes diplomatic and programmatic initiatives.".

(b) INCLUSION OF CHILD MARRIAGE STATUS IN REPORTS.—The Foreign Assistance Act of 1961 (22 U.S.C. 2151 et seq.) is amended—

(1) in section 116 (22 U.S.C. 2151n), by adding at the end the following:

"(g) CHILD MARRIAGE STATUS.—

"(1) IN GENERAL.—The report required under subsection (d) shall include, for each country in which child marriage is prevalent, a description of the status of the practice of child marriage in such country.

"(2) DEFINED TERM.—In this subsection, the term 'child marriage' means the marriage of a girl or boy who is—

"(A) younger than the minimum age for marriage under the laws of the country in which such girl or boy is a resident; or

"(B) younger than 18 years of age, if no such law exists."; and

(2) in section 502B (22 U.S.C. 2304), by adding at the end the following:

"(i) CHILD MARRIAGE STATUS.—

"(1) IN GENERAL.—The report required under subsection (b) shall include, for each country in which child marriage is prevalent, a description of the status of the practice of child marriage in such country.

"(2) DEFINED TERM.—In this subsection, the term 'child marriage' means the marriage of a girl or boy who is—

"(A) younger than the minimum age for marriage under the laws of the country in which such girl or boy is a resident; or

"(B) younger than 18 years of age, if no such law exists.".

SEC. 1208. CHILD SOLDIERS.

Section 404 of the William Wilberforce Trafficking Victims Protection Reauthorization Act of 2008 (22 U.S.C. 2370c–1) is amended—

(1) in subsection (a), by striking "(b), (c), and (d), the authorities contained in section 516 or 541 of the Foreign Assistance Act of 1961 (22 U.S.C. 2321j or 2347)" and inserting "(b) through (f), the authorities contained in sections 516, 541, and 551 of the Foreign Assistance Act of 1961 (22 U.S.C. 2321j, 2347, and 2348)"; and

(2) by adding at the end the following:

"(f) EXCEPTION FOR PEACEKEEPING OPERATIONS.—The limitation set forth in subsection (a) that relates to section 551 of the Foreign Assistance Act of 1961 shall not apply to programs that support military professionalization, security sector reform, heightened respect for human rights, peacekeeping preparation, or the demobilization and reintegration of child soldiers.".

Subtitle B—Combating Trafficking in Persons in the United States

PART I—PENALTIES AGAINST TRAFFICKERS AND OTHER CRIMES

SEC. 1211. CRIMINAL TRAFFICKING OFFENSES.

(a) RICO AMENDMENT.—Section 1961(1)(B) of title 18, United States Code, is amended by inserting "section 1351 (relating to fraud in foreign labor contracting)," before "section 1425".

(b) ENGAGING IN ILLICIT SEXUAL CONDUCT IN FOREIGN PLACES.—Section 2423(c) of title 18, United States Code, is amended by inserting "or resides, either temporarily or permanently, in a foreign country" after "commerce".

(c) UNLAWFUL CONDUCT WITH RESPECT TO DOCUMENTS.—

(1) IN GENERAL.—Chapter 77 of title 18, United States Code, is amended by adding at the end the following:

"§ 1597. Unlawful conduct with respect to immigration documents

"(a) DESTRUCTION, CONCEALMENT, REMOVAL, CONFISCATION, OR POSSESSION OF IMMIGRATION DOCUMENTS.—It shall be unlawful for any person to knowingly destroy, conceal, remove, confiscate, or possess, an actual or purported passport or other immigration document of another individual —

S. 47—90

"(1) in the course of violating section 1351 of this title or section 274 of the Immigration and Nationality Act (8 U.S.C. 1324);

"(2) with intent to violate section 1351 of this title or section 274 of the Immigration and Nationality Act (8 U.S.C. 1324); or

"(3) in order to, without lawful authority, maintain, prevent, or restrict the labor of services of the individual.

"(b) PENALTY.—Any person who violates subsection (a) shall be fined under this title, imprisoned for not more than 1 year, or both.

"(c) OBSTRUCTION.—Any person who knowingly obstructs, attempts to obstruct, or in any way interferes with or prevents the enforcement of this section, shall be subject to the penalties described in subsection (b).".

(2) TECHNICAL AND CONFORMING AMENDMENT.—The table of sections for chapter 77 of title 18, United States Code, is amended by adding at the end the following:

"1597. Unlawful conduct with respect to immigration documents.".

SEC. 1212. CIVIL REMEDIES; CLARIFYING DEFINITION.

(a) CIVIL REMEDY FOR PERSONAL INJURIES.—Section 2255 of title 18, United States Code, is amended—

(1) in subsection (a), by striking "section 2241(c)" and inserting "section 1589, 1590, 1591, 2241(c)"; and

(2) in subsection (b), by striking "six years" and inserting "10 years".

(b) DEFINITION.—

(1) IN GENERAL.—Section 103 of the Trafficking Victims Protection Act of 2000 (22 U.S.C. 7102) is amended—

(A) by redesignating paragraphs (1) through (14) as paragraphs (2) through (15), respectively;

(B) by inserting before paragraph (2), as redesignated, the following:

"(1) ABUSE OR THREATENED ABUSE OF LAW OR LEGAL PROCESS.—The term 'abuse or threatened abuse of the legal process' means the use or threatened use of a law or legal process, whether administrative, civil, or criminal, in any manner or for any purpose for which the law was not designed, in order to exert pressure on another person to cause that person to take some action or refrain from taking some action.";

(C) in paragraph (14), as redesignated, by striking "paragraph (8)" and inserting "paragraph (9)"; and

(D) in paragraph (15), as redesignated, by striking "paragraph (8) or (9)" and inserting "paragraph (9) or (10)".

(2) TECHNICAL AND CONFORMING AMENDMENTS.—

(A) TRAFFICKING VICTIMS PROTECTION ACT OF 2000.—The Trafficking Victims Protection Act of 2000 (22 U.S.C. 7101 et eq.) is amended—

(i) in section 110(e) (22 U.S.C. 7107(e))—

(I) by striking "section 103(7)(A)" and inserting "section 103(8)(A)"; and

(II) by striking "section 103(7)(B)" and inserting "section 103(8)(B)"; and

(ii) in section 113(g)(2) (22 U.S.C. 7110(g)(2)), by striking "section 103(8)(A)" and inserting "section 103(9)(A)".

(B) NORTH KOREAN HUMAN RIGHTS ACT OF 2004.—Section 203(b)(2) of the North Korean Human Rights Act of 2004 (22 U.S.C. 7833(b)(2)) is amended by striking "section 103(14)" and inserting "section 103(15)".

(C) TRAFFICKING VICTIMS PROTECTION REAUTHORIZATION ACT OF 2005.—Section 207 of the Trafficking Victims Protection Reauthorization Act of 2005 (42 U.S.C. 14044e) is amended—

(i) in paragraph (1), by striking "section 103(8)" and inserting "section 103(9)";

(ii) in paragraph (2), by striking "section 103(9)" and inserting "section 103(10)"; and

(iii) in paragraph (3), by striking "section 103(3)" and inserting "section 103(4)".

(D) VIOLENCE AGAINST WOMEN AND DEPARTMENT OF JUSTICE REAUTHORIZATION ACT OF 2005.—Section 111(a)(1) of the Violence Against Women and Department of Justice Reauthorization Act of 2005 (42 U.S.C. 14044f(a)(1)) is amended by striking "paragraph (8)" and inserting "paragraph (9)".

PART II—ENSURING AVAILABILITY OF POSSIBLE WITNESSES AND INFORMANTS

SEC. 1221. PROTECTIONS FOR TRAFFICKING VICTIMS WHO COOPERATE WITH LAW ENFORCEMENT.

Section 101(a)(15)(T)(ii)(III) of the Immigration and Nationality Act (8 U.S.C. 1101(a)(15)(T)(ii)(III) is amended by inserting ", or any adult or minor children of a derivative beneficiary of the alien, as" after "age".

SEC. 1222. PROTECTION AGAINST FRAUD IN FOREIGN LABOR CONTRACTING.

Section 101(a)(15)(U)(iii) of the Immigration and Nationality Act (8 U.S.C. 1101(a)(15)(U)(iii)) is amended by inserting "fraud in foreign labor contracting (as defined in section 1351 of title 18, United States Code);" after "perjury;".

PART III—ENSURING INTERAGENCY COORDINATION AND EXPANDED REPORTING

SEC. 1231. REPORTING REQUIREMENTS FOR THE ATTORNEY GENERAL.

Section 105(d)(7) of the Trafficking Victims Protection Act of 2000 (22 U.S.C. 7103(d)(7)) is amended—

(1) by redesignating subparagraphs (D) through (J) as subparagraphs (I) through (O);

(2) by striking subparagraphs (B) and (C) and inserting the following:

"(B) the number of persons who have been granted continued presence in the United States under section 107(c)(3) during the preceding fiscal year and the mean and median time taken to adjudicate applications submitted under such section, including the time from the receipt of an application by law enforcement to the issuance of continued presence, and a description of any efforts being taken to reduce the adjudication and processing time while ensuring the safe and competent processing of the applications;

"(C) the number of persons who have applied for, been granted, or been denied a visa or otherwise provided status under subparagraph (T)(i) or (U)(i) of section 101(a)(15) of the Immigration and Nationality Act (8 U.S.C. 1101(a)(15)) during the preceding fiscal year;

"(D) the number of persons who have applied for, been granted, or been denied a visa or status under clause (ii) of section 101(a)(15)(T) of the Immigration and Nationality Act (8 U.S.C. 1101(a)(15)(T)) during the preceding fiscal year, broken down by the number of such persons described in subclauses (I), (II), and (III) of such clause (ii);

"(E) the amount of Federal funds expended in direct benefits paid to individuals described in subparagraph (D) in conjunction with T visa status;

"(F) the number of persons who have applied for, been granted, or been denied a visa or status under section 101(a)(15)(U)(i) of the Immigration and Nationality Act (8 U.S.C. 1101(a)(15)(U)(i)) during the preceding fiscal year;

"(G) the mean and median time in which it takes to adjudicate applications submitted under the provisions of law set forth in subparagraph (C), including the time between the receipt of an application and the issuance of a visa and work authorization;

"(H) any efforts being taken to reduce the adjudication and processing time, while ensuring the safe and competent processing of the applications;";

(3) in subparagraph (N)(iii), as redesignated, by striking "and" at the end;

(4) in subparagraph (O), as redesignated, by striking the period at the end and inserting "; and"; and

(5) by adding at the end the following:

"(P) the activities undertaken by Federal agencies to train appropriate State, tribal, and local government and law enforcement officials to identify victims of severe forms of trafficking, including both sex and labor trafficking;

"(Q) the activities undertaken by Federal agencies in cooperation with State, tribal, and local law enforcement officials to identify, investigate, and prosecute offenses under sections 1581, 1583, 1584, 1589, 1590, 1592, and 1594 of title 18, United States Code, or equivalent State offenses, including, in each fiscal year—

"(i) the number, age, gender, country of origin, and citizenship status of victims identified for each offense;

"(ii) the number of individuals charged, and the number of individuals convicted, under each offense;

"(iii) the number of individuals referred for prosecution for State offenses, including offenses relating to the purchasing of commercial sex acts;

"(iv) the number of victims granted continued presence in the United States under section 107(c)(3); and

"(v) the number of victims granted a visa or otherwise provided status under subparagraph (T)(i) or

(U)(i) of section 101(a)(15) of the Immigration and Nationality Act (8 U.S.C. 1101(a)(15)); and

"(R) the activities undertaken by the Department of Justice and the Department of Health and Human Services to meet the specific needs of minor victims of domestic trafficking, including actions taken pursuant to subsection (f) and section 202(a) of the Trafficking Victims Protection Reauthorization Act of 2005 (42 U.S.C. 14044(a)), and the steps taken to increase cooperation among Federal agencies to ensure the effective and efficient use of programs for which the victims are eligible.".

SEC. 1232. REPORTING REQUIREMENTS FOR THE SECRETARY OF LABOR.

Section 105(b) of the Trafficking Victims Protection Act of 2005 (22 U.S.C. 7112(b)) is amended by adding at the end the following:

"(3) SUBMISSION TO CONGRESS.—Not later than December 1, 2014, and every 2 years thereafter, the Secretary of Labor shall submit the list developed under paragraph (2)(C) to Congress.".

SEC. 1233. INFORMATION SHARING TO COMBAT CHILD LABOR AND SLAVE LABOR.

Section 105(a) of the Trafficking Victims Protection Act of 2005 (22 U.S.C. 7112(a)) is amended by adding at the end the following:

"(3) INFORMATION SHARING.—The Secretary of State shall, on a regular basis, provide information relating to child labor and forced labor in the production of goods in violation of international standards to the Department of Labor to be used in developing the list described in subsection (b)(2)(C).".

SEC. 1234. GOVERNMENT TRAINING EFFORTS TO INCLUDE THE DEPARTMENT OF LABOR.

Section 107(c)(4) of the Trafficking Victims Protection Act of 2000 (22 U.S.C. 7105(c)(4)) is amended—

(1) in the first sentence, by inserting "the Department of Labor, the Equal Employment Opportunity Commission," before "and the Department"; and

(2) in the second sentence, by inserting ", in consultation with the Secretary of Labor," before "shall provide".

SEC. 1235. GAO REPORT ON THE USE OF FOREIGN LABOR CONTRACTORS.

(a) IN GENERAL.—Not later than 2 years after the date of the enactment of this Act, the Comptroller General of the United States shall submit a report on the use of foreign labor contractors to—

(1) the Committee on the Judiciary of the Senate;

(2) the Committee on Health, Education, Labor, and Pensions of the Senate;

(3) the Committee on the Judiciary of the House of Representatives; and

(4) the Committee on Education and the Workforce of the House of Representatives.

(b) CONTENTS.—The report under subsection (a) should, to the extent possible—

(1) address the role and practices of United States employers in—

(A) the use of labor recruiters or brokers; or

(B) directly recruiting foreign workers;

(2) analyze the laws that protect such workers, both overseas and domestically;

(3) describe the oversight and enforcement mechanisms in Federal departments and agencies for such laws; and

(4) identify any gaps that may exist in these protections; and

(5) recommend possible actions for Federal departments and agencies to combat any abuses.

(c) REQUIREMENTS.—The report under subsection (a) shall—

(1) describe the role of labor recruiters or brokers working in countries that are sending workers and receiving funds, including any identified involvement in labor abuses;

(2) describe the role and practices of employers in the United States that commission labor recruiters or brokers or directly recruit foreign workers;

(3) describe the role of Federal departments and agencies in overseeing and regulating the foreign labor recruitment process, including certifying and enforcing under existing regulations;

(4) describe the type of jobs and the numbers of positions in the United States that have been filled through foreign workers during each of the last 8 years, including positions within the Federal Government;

(5) describe any efforts or programs undertaken by Federal, State and local government entities to encourage employers, directly or indirectly, to use foreign workers or to reward employers for using foreign workers; and

(6) based on the information required under paragraphs (1) through (3), identify any common abuses of foreign workers and the employment system, including the use of fees and debts, and recommendations of actions that could be taken by Federal departments and agencies to combat any identified abuses.

SEC. 1236. ACCOUNTABILITY.

All grants awarded by the Attorney General under this title or an Act amended by this title shall be subject to the following accountability provisions:

(1) AUDIT REQUIREMENT.—

(A) DEFINITION.—In this paragraph, the term “unresolved audit finding” means an audit report finding in the final audit report of the Inspector General of the Department of Justice that the grantee has used grant funds for an unauthorized expenditure or otherwise unallowable cost that is not closed or resolved during the 12-month period beginning on the date on which the final audit report is issued

(B) REQUIREMENT.—Beginning in the first fiscal year beginning after the date of enactment of this Act, and in each fiscal year thereafter, the Inspector General of the Department of Justice shall conduct audits of recipients of grants under this title or an Act amended by this title to prevent waste, fraud, and abuse of funds by grantees. The Inspector General shall determine the appropriate number of grantees to be audited each year.

S. 47—95

(C) MANDATORY EXCLUSION.—A recipient of grant funds under this title or an Act amended by this title that is found to have an unresolved audit finding shall not be eligible to receive grant funds under this title or an Act amended by this title during the first 2 fiscal years beginning after the end of the 12-month period described in subparagraph (A).

(D) PRIORITY.—In awarding grants under this title or an Act amended by this title, the Attorney General shall give priority to eligible applicants that did not have an unresolved audit finding during the 3 fiscal years before submitting an application for a grant under this title or an Act amended by this title.

(E) REIMBURSEMENT.—If an entity is awarded grant funds under this title or an Act amended by this title during the 2-fiscal-year period during which the entity is barred from receiving grants under subparagraph (C), the Attorney General shall—

(i) deposit an amount equal to the amount of the grant funds that were improperly awarded to the grantee into the General Fund of the Treasury; and

(ii) seek to recoup the costs of the repayment to the fund from the grant recipient that was erroneously awarded grant funds.

(2) NONPROFIT ORGANIZATION REQUIREMENTS.—

(A) DEFINITION.—For purposes of this paragraph and the grant programs under this title or an Act amended by this title, the term "nonprofit organization" means an organization that is described in section 501(c)(3) of the Internal Revenue Code of 1986 and is exempt from taxation under section 501(a) of such Code.

(B) PROHIBITION.—The Attorney General may not award a grant under this title or an Act amended by this title to a nonprofit organization that holds money in offshore accounts for the purpose of avoiding paying the tax described in section 511(a) of the Internal Revenue Code of 1986.

(C) DISCLOSURE.—Each nonprofit organization that is awarded a grant under this title or an Act amended by this title and uses the procedures prescribed in regulations to create a rebuttable presumption of reasonableness for the compensation of its officers, directors, trustees and key employees, shall disclose to the Attorney General, in the application for the grant, the process for determining such compensation, including the independent persons involved in reviewing and approving such compensation, the comparability data used, and contemporaneous substantiation of the deliberation and decision. Upon request, the Attorney General shall make the information disclosed under this subparagraph available for public inspection.

(3) CONFERENCE EXPENDITURES.—

(A) LIMITATION.—No amounts authorized to be appropriated to the Department of Justice under this title or an Act amended by this title may be used by the Attorney General, or by any individual or entity awarded discretionary funds through a cooperative agreement under this title or an Act amended by this title, to host or support any expenditure for conferences that uses more than $20,000 in funds made available to the Department of Justice, unless the Deputy Attorney General or the appropriate Assistant Attorney General, Director, or principal deputy (as designated by the Deputy Attorney General) provides prior written authorization that the funds may be expended to host the conference.

(B) WRITTEN APPROVAL.—Written approval under subparagraph (A) shall include a written estimate of all costs associated with the conference, including the cost of all food, beverages, audio-visual equipment, honoraria for speakers, and entertainment.

(C) REPORT.—The Deputy Attorney General shall submit an annual report to the Committee on the Judiciary of the Senate and the Committee on the Judiciary of the House of Representatives on all conference expenditures approved under this paragraph.

(4) ANNUAL CERTIFICATION.—Beginning in the first fiscal year beginning after the date of enactment of this Act, the Attorney General shall submit, to the Committee on the Judiciary and the Committee on Appropriations of the Senate and the Committee on the Judiciary and the Committee on Appropriations of the House of Representatives, an annual certification indicating whether—

(A) all audits issued by the Office of the Inspector General under paragraph (1) have been completed and reviewed by the appropriate Assistant Attorney General or Director;

(B) all mandatory exclusions required under paragraph (1)(C) have been issued;

(C) all reimbursements required under paragraph (1)(E) have been made; and

(D) includes a list of any grant recipients excluded under paragraph (1) from the previous year.

PART IV—ENHANCING STATE AND LOCAL EFFORTS TO COMBAT TRAFFICKING IN PERSONS

SEC. 1241. ASSISTANCE FOR DOMESTIC MINOR SEX TRAFFICKING VICTIMS.

(a) IN GENERAL.—Section 202 of the Trafficking Victims Protection Reauthorization Act of 2005 (42 U.S.C. 14044a) is amended to read as follows:

"SEC. 202. ESTABLISHMENT OF A GRANT PROGRAM TO DEVELOP, EXPAND, AND STRENGTHEN ASSISTANCE PROGRAMS FOR CERTAIN PERSONS SUBJECT TO TRAFFICKING.

"(a) DEFINITIONS.—In this section:

"(1) ASSISTANT SECRETARY.—The term 'Assistant Secretary' means the Assistant Secretary for Children and Families of the Department of Health and Human Services.

"(2) ASSISTANT ATTORNEY GENERAL.—The term 'Assistant Attorney General' means the Assistant Attorney General for the Office of Justice Programs of the Department of Justice.

"(3) ELIGIBLE ENTITY.—The term 'eligible entity' means a State or unit of local government that—

"(A) has significant criminal activity involving sex trafficking of minors;

"(B) has demonstrated cooperation between Federal, State, local, and, where applicable, tribal law enforcement agencies, prosecutors, and social service providers in addressing sex trafficking of minors;

"(C) has developed a workable, multi-disciplinary plan to combat sex trafficking of minors, including—

"(i) building or establishing a residential care facility for minor victims of sex trafficking;

"(ii) the provision of rehabilitative care to minor victims of sex trafficking;

"(iii) the provision of specialized training for law enforcement officers and social service providers for all forms of sex trafficking, with a focus on sex trafficking of minors;

"(iv) prevention, deterrence, and prosecution of offenses involving sex trafficking of minors;

"(v) cooperation or referral agreements with organizations providing outreach or other related services to runaway and homeless youth; and

"(vi) law enforcement protocols or procedures to screen all individuals arrested for prostitution, whether adult or minor, for victimization by sex trafficking and by other crimes, such as sexual assault and domestic violence; and

"(D) provides assurance that a minor victim of sex trafficking shall not be required to collaborate with law enforcement to have access to residential care or services provided with a grant under this section.

"(4) MINOR VICTIM OF SEX TRAFFICKING.—The term 'minor victim of sex trafficking' means an individual who—

"(A) is younger than 18 years of age, and is a victim of an offense described in section 1591(a) of title 18, United States Code, or a comparable State law; or

"(B)(i) is not younger than 18 years of age nor older than 20 years of age;

"(ii) before the individual reached 18 years of age, was described in subparagraph (A); and

"(iii) was receiving shelter or services as a minor victim of sex trafficking.

"(5) QUALIFIED NONGOVERNMENTAL ORGANIZATION.—The term 'qualified nongovernmental organization' means an organization that—

"(A) is not a State or unit of local government, or an agency of a State or unit of local government;

"(B) has demonstrated experience providing services to victims of sex trafficking or related populations (such as runaway and homeless youth), or employs staff specialized in the treatment of sex trafficking victims; and

"(C) demonstrates a plan to sustain the provision of services beyond the period of a grant awarded under this section.

"(6) SEX TRAFFICKING OF A MINOR.—The term 'sex trafficking of a minor' means an offense described in section 1591(a)

of title 18, United States Code, or a comparable State law, against a minor.

"(b) SEX TRAFFICKING BLOCK GRANTS.—

"(1) GRANTS AUTHORIZED.—

"(A) IN GENERAL.—The Assistant Attorney General, in consultation with the Assistant Secretary, may make block grants to 4 eligible entities located in different regions of the United States to combat sex trafficking of minors.

"(B) REQUIREMENT.—Not fewer than 1 of the block grants made under subparagraph (A) shall be awarded to an eligible entity with a State population of less than 5,000,000.

"(C) GRANT AMOUNT.—Subject to the availability of appropriations under subsection (g) to carry out this section, each grant made under this section shall be for an amount not less than $1,500,000 and not greater than $2,000,000.

"(D) DURATION.—

"(i) IN GENERAL.—A grant made under this section shall be for a period of 1 year.

"(ii) RENEWAL.—

"(I) IN GENERAL.—The Assistant Attorney General may renew a grant under this section for up to 3 1-year periods.

"(II) PRIORITY.—In making grants in any fiscal year after the first fiscal year in which grants are made under this section, the Assistant Attorney General shall give priority to an eligible entity that received a grant in the preceding fiscal year and is eligible for renewal under this subparagraph, taking into account any evaluation of the eligible entity conducted under paragraph (4), if available.

"(E) CONSULTATION.—In carrying out this section, the Assistant Attorney General shall consult with the Assistant Secretary with respect to—

"(i) evaluations of grant recipients under paragraph (4);

"(ii) avoiding unintentional duplication of grants; and

"(iii) any other areas of shared concern.

"(2) USE OF FUNDS.—

"(A) ALLOCATION.—Not less than 67 percent of each grant made under paragraph (1) shall be used by the eligible entity to provide residential care and services (as described in clauses (i) through (iv) of subparagraph (B)) to minor victims of sex trafficking through qualified nongovernmental organizations.

"(B) AUTHORIZED ACTIVITIES.—Grants awarded pursuant to paragraph (2) may be used for—

"(i) providing residential care to minor victims of sex trafficking, including temporary or long-term placement as appropriate;

"(ii) providing 24-hour emergency social services response for minor victims of sex trafficking;

"(iii) providing minor victims of sex trafficking with clothing and other daily necessities needed to keep such victims from returning to living on the street;

"(iv) case management services for minor victims of sex trafficking;

"(v) mental health counseling for minor victims of sex trafficking, including specialized counseling and substance abuse treatment;

"(vi) legal services for minor victims of sex trafficking;

"(vii) specialized training for social service providers, public sector personnel, and private sector personnel likely to encounter sex trafficking victims on issues related to the sex trafficking of minors and severe forms of trafficking in persons;

"(viii) outreach and education programs to provide information about deterrence and prevention of sex trafficking of minors;

"(ix) programs to provide treatment to individuals charged or cited with purchasing or attempting to purchase sex acts in cases where—

"(I) a treatment program can be mandated as a condition of a sentence, fine, suspended sentence, or probation, or is an appropriate alternative to criminal prosecution; and

"(II) the individual was not charged with purchasing or attempting to purchase sex acts with a minor; and

"(x) screening and referral of minor victims of severe forms of trafficking in persons.

"(3) APPLICATION.—

"(A) IN GENERAL.—Each eligible entity desiring a grant under this section shall submit an application to the Assistant Attorney General at such time, in such manner, and accompanied by such information as the Assistant Attorney General may reasonably require.

"(B) CONTENTS.—Each application submitted pursuant to subparagraph (A) shall—

"(i) describe the activities for which assistance under this section is sought; and

"(ii) provide such additional assurances as the Assistant Attorney General determines to be essential to ensure compliance with the requirements of this section.

"(4) EVALUATION.—The Assistant Attorney General shall enter into a contract with an academic or non-profit organization that has experience in issues related to sex trafficking of minors and evaluation of grant programs to conduct an annual evaluation of each grant made under this section to determine the impact and effectiveness of programs funded with the grant.

"(c) MANDATORY EXCLUSION.—An eligible entity that receives a grant under this section that is found to have utilized grant funds for any unauthorized expenditure or otherwise unallowable cost shall not be eligible for any grant funds awarded under the grant for 2 fiscal years following the year in which the unauthorized expenditure or unallowable cost is reported.

"(d) COMPLIANCE REQUIREMENT.—An eligible entity shall not be eligible to receive a grant under this section if, during the 5 fiscal years before the eligible entity submits an application for the grant, the eligible entity has been found to have violated the terms or conditions of a Government grant program by utilizing grant funds for unauthorized expenditures or otherwise unallowable costs.

"(e) ADMINISTRATIVE CAP.—The cost of administering the grants authorized by this section shall not exceed 3 percent of the total amount appropriated to carry out this section.

"(f) AUDIT REQUIREMENT.—For fiscal years 2016 and 2017, the Inspector General of the Department of Justice shall conduct an audit of all 4 eligible entities that receive block grants under this section.

"(g) MATCH REQUIREMENT.—An eligible entity that receives a grant under this section shall provide a non-Federal match in an amount equal to not less than—

"(1) 15 percent of the grant during the first year;

"(2) 25 percent of the grant during the first renewal period;

"(3) 40 percent of the grant during the second renewal period; and

"(4) 50 percent of the grant during the third renewal period.

"(h) NO LIMITATION ON SECTION 204 GRANTS.—An entity that applies for a grant under section 204 is not prohibited from also applying for a grant under this section.

"(i) AUTHORIZATION OF APPROPRIATIONS.—There are authorized to be appropriated $8,000,000 to the Attorney General for each of the fiscal years 2014 through 2017 to carry out this section.

"(j) GAO EVALUATION.—Not later than 30 months after the date of the enactment of this Act, the Comptroller General of the United States shall submit a report to Congress that contains—

"(1) an evaluation of the impact of this section in aiding minor victims of sex trafficking in the jurisdiction of the entity receiving the grant; and

"(2) recommendations, if any, regarding any legislative or administrative action the Comptroller General determines appropriate.".

(b) SUNSET PROVISION.—The amendment made by subsection (a) shall be effective during the 4-year period beginning on the date of the enactment of this Act.

SEC. 1242. EXPANDING LOCAL LAW ENFORCEMENT GRANTS FOR INVESTIGATIONS AND PROSECUTIONS OF TRAFFICKING.

Section 204 of the Trafficking Victims Protection Reauthorization Act of 2005 (42 U.S.C. 14044c) is amended—

(1) in subsection (a)(1)—

(A) in subparagraph (A), by striking ", which involve United States citizens, or aliens admitted for permanent residence, and";

(B) by redesignating subparagraphs (B), (C), and (D) as subparagraphs (C), (D), and (E), respectively; and

(C) by inserting after subparagraph (A) the following:

"(B) to train law enforcement personnel how to identify victims of severe forms of trafficking in persons and related offenses;"; and

(D) in subparagraph (C), as redesignated, by inserting "and prioritize the investigations and prosecutions of those cases involving minor victims" after "sex acts";

(2) by redesignating subsection (d) as subsection (e);

(3) by inserting after subsection (c) the following:

"(d) NO LIMITATION ON SECTION 202 GRANT APPLICATIONS.—An entity that applies for a grant under section 202 is not prohibited from also applying for a grant under this section.";

(4) in subsection (e), as redesignated, by striking "$20,000,000 for each of the fiscal years 2008 through 2011" and inserting "$10,000,000 for each of the fiscal years 2014 through 2017"; and

(5) by adding at the end the following:

"(f) GAO EVALUATION AND REPORT.—Not later than 30 months after the date of enactment of this Act, the Comptroller General of the United States shall conduct a study of and submit to Congress a report evaluating the impact of this section on—

"(1) the ability of law enforcement personnel to identify victims of severe forms of trafficking in persons and investigate and prosecute cases against offenders, including offenders who engage in the purchasing of commercial sex acts with a minor; and

"(2) recommendations, if any, regarding any legislative or administrative action the Comptroller General determines appropriate to improve the ability described in paragraph (1).".

SEC. 1243. MODEL STATE CRIMINAL LAW PROTECTION FOR CHILD TRAFFICKING VICTIMS AND SURVIVORS.

Section 225(b) of the Trafficking Victims Reauthorization Act of 2008 (22 U.S.C. 7101 note) is amended—

(1) in paragraph (1), by striking "and" at the end;

(2) by redesignating paragraph (2) as paragraph (3); and

(3) by inserting after paragraph (1) the following:

"(2) protects children exploited through prostitution by including safe harbor provisions that—

"(A) treat an individual under 18 years of age who has been arrested for engaging in, or attempting to engage in, a sexual act with another person in exchange for monetary compensation as a victim of a severe form of trafficking in persons;

"(B) prohibit the charging or prosecution of an individual described in subparagraph (A) for a prostitution offense;

"(C) require the referral of an individual described in subparagraph (A) to appropriate service providers, including comprehensive service or community-based programs that provide assistance to child victims of commercial sexual exploitation; and

"(D) provide that an individual described in subparagraph (A) shall not be required to prove fraud, force, or coercion in order to receive the protections described under this paragraph;".

Subtitle C—Authorization of Appropriations

SEC. 1251. ADJUSTMENT OF AUTHORIZATION LEVELS FOR THE TRAFFICKING VICTIMS PROTECTION ACT OF 2000.

The Trafficking Victims Protection Act of 2000 (22 U.S.C. 7101 et seq.) is amended—

(1) in section 112A(b)(4) (22 U.S.C. 7109a(b)(4))—

(A) by striking "$2,000,000" and inserting "$1,000,000"; and

(B) by striking "2008 through 2011" and inserting "2014 through 2017"; and

(2) in section 113 (22 U.S.C. 7110)—

(A) subsection (a)—

(i) by striking "$5,500,000 for each of the fiscal years 2008 through 2011" each place it appears and inserting "$2,000,000 for each of the fiscal years 2014 through 2017";

(ii) by inserting ", including regional trafficking in persons officers," after "for additional personnel,"; and

(iii) by striking ", and $3,000 for official reception and representation expenses";

(B) in subsection (b)—

(i) in paragraph (1), by striking "$12,500,000 for each of the fiscal years 2008 through 2011" and inserting "$14,500,000 for each of the fiscal years 2014 through 2017"; and

(ii) in paragraph (2), by striking "to the Secretary of Health and Human Services" and all that follows and inserting "$8,000,000 to the Secretary of Health and Human Services for each of the fiscal years 2014 through 2017.";

(C) in subsection (c)(1)—

(i) in subparagraph (A), by striking "2008 through 2011" each place it appears and inserting "2014 through 2017";

(ii) in subparagraph (B)—

(I) by striking "$15,000,000 for fiscal year 2003 and $10,000,000 for each of the fiscal years 2008 through 2011" and inserting "$10,000,000 for each of the fiscal years 2014 through 2017"; and

(II) by striking "2008 through 2011" and inserting "2014 through 2017"; and

(iii) in subparagraph (C), by striking "2008 through 2011" and inserting "2014 through 2017";

(D) in subsection (d)—

(i) by redesignating subparagraphs (A) through (C) as paragraphs (1) through (3), respectively, and moving such paragraphs 2 ems to the left;

(ii) in the paragraph (1), as redesignated, by striking "$10,000,000 for each of the fiscal years 2008 through 2011" and inserting "$11,000,000 for each of the fiscal years 2014 through 2017"; and

(iii) in paragraph (3), as redesignated, by striking "to the Attorney General" and all that follows and inserting "$11,000,000 to the Attorney General for each of the fiscal years 2014 through 2017.";

(E) in subsection (e)—

(i) in paragraph (1), by striking "$15,000,000 for each of the fiscal years 2008 through 2011" and inserting "$7,500,000 for each of the fiscal years 2014 through 2017"; and

(ii) in paragraph (2), by striking "$15,000,000 for each of the fiscal years 2008 through 2011" and inserting "$7,500,000 for each of the fiscal years 2014 through 2017";

(F) in subsection (f), by striking "$10,000,000 for each of the fiscal years 2008 through 2011" and inserting "$5,000,000 for each of the fiscal years 2014 through 2017"; and

(G) in subsection (i), by striking "$18,000,000 for each of the fiscal years 2008 through 2011" and inserting "$10,000,000 for each of the fiscal years 2014 through 2017".

SEC. 1252. ADJUSTMENT OF AUTHORIZATION LEVELS FOR THE TRAFFICKING VICTIMS PROTECTION REAUTHORIZATION ACT OF 2005.

The Trafficking Victims Protection Reauthorization Act of 2005 (Public Law 109–164) is amended—

(1) by striking section 102(b)(7); and

(2) in section 201(c)(2), by striking "$1,000,000 for each of the fiscal years 2008 through 2011" and inserting "$250,000 for each of the fiscal years 2014 through 2017".

Subtitle D—Unaccompanied Alien Children

SEC. 1261. APPROPRIATE CUSTODIAL SETTINGS FOR UNACCOMPANIED MINORS WHO REACH THE AGE OF MAJORITY WHILE IN FEDERAL CUSTODY.

Section 235(c)(2) of the William Wilberforce Trafficking Victims Protection Reauthorization Act of 2008 (8 U.S.C. 1232(c)(2)) is amended—

(1) by striking "Subject to" and inserting the following:

"(A) MINORS IN DEPARTMENT OF HEALTH AND HUMAN SERVICES CUSTODY.—Subject to"; and

(2) by adding at the end the following:

"(B) ALIENS TRANSFERRED FROM DEPARTMENT OF HEALTH AND HUMAN SERVICES TO DEPARTMENT OF HOMELAND SECURITY CUSTODY.—If a minor described in subparagraph (A) reaches 18 years of age and is transferred to the custody of the Secretary of Homeland Security, the Secretary shall consider placement in the least restrictive setting available after taking into account the alien's danger to self, danger to the community, and risk of flight. Such aliens shall be eligible to participate in alternative to detention programs, utilizing a continuum of alternatives based on the alien's need for supervision, which may include placement of the alien with an individual or an organizational sponsor, or in a supervised group home.".

S. 47—104

SEC. 1262. APPOINTMENT OF CHILD ADVOCATES FOR UNACCOMPANIED MINORS.

Section 235(c)(6) of the William Wilberforce Trafficking Victims Protection Reauthorization Act of 2008 (8 U.S.C. 1232(c)(6)) is amended—

(1) by striking "The Secretary" and inserting the following:

"(A) IN GENERAL.—The Secretary"; and

(2) by striking "and criminal"; and

(3) by adding at the end the following:

"(B) APPOINTMENT OF CHILD ADVOCATES.—

"(i) INITIAL SITES.—Not later than 2 years after the date of the enactment of the Violence Against Women Reauthorization Act of 2013, the Secretary of Health and Human Services shall appoint child advocates at 3 new immigration detention sites to provide independent child advocates for trafficking victims and vulnerable unaccompanied alien children.

"(ii) ADDITIONAL SITES.—Not later than 3 years after the date of the enactment of the Violence Against Women Reauthorization Act of 2013, the Secretary shall appoint child advocates at not more than 3 additional immigration detention sites.

"(iii) SELECTION OF SITES.—Sites at which child advocate programs will be established under this subparagraph shall be located at immigration detention sites at which more than 50 children are held in immigration custody, and shall be selected sequentially, with priority given to locations with—

"(I) the largest number of unaccompanied alien children; and

"(II) the most vulnerable populations of unaccompanied children.

"(C) RESTRICTIONS.—

"(i) ADMINISTRATIVE EXPENSES.—A child advocate program may not use more that 10 percent of the Federal funds received under this section for administrative expenses.

"(ii) NONEXCLUSIVITY.—Nothing in this section may be construed to restrict the ability of a child advocate program under this section to apply for or obtain funding from any other source to carry out the programs described in this section.

"(iii) CONTRIBUTION OF FUNDS.—A child advocate program selected under this section shall contribute non-Federal funds, either directly or through in-kind contributions, to the costs of the child advocate program in an amount that is not less than 25 percent of the total amount of Federal funds received by the child advocate program under this section. In-kind contributions may not exceed 40 percent of the matching requirement under this clause.

"(D) ANNUAL REPORT TO CONGRESS.—Not later than 1 year after the date of the enactment of the Violence Against Women Reauthorization Act of 2013, and annually thereafter, the Secretary of Health and Human Services shall submit a report describing the activities undertaken by the Secretary to authorize the appointment of independent Child Advocates for trafficking victims and vulnerable unaccompanied alien children to the Committee on the Judiciary of the Senate and the Committee on the Judiciary of the House of Representatives.

"(E) ASSESSMENT OF CHILD ADVOCATE PROGRAM.—

"(i) IN GENERAL.—As soon as practicable after the date of the enactment of the Violence Against Women Reauthorization Act of 2013, the Comptroller General of the United States shall conduct a study regarding the effectiveness of the Child Advocate Program operated by the Secretary of Health and Human Services.

"(ii) MATTERS TO BE STUDIED.—In the study required under clause (i), the Comptroller General shall— collect information and analyze the following:

"(I) analyze the effectiveness of existing child advocate programs in improving outcomes for trafficking victims and other vulnerable unaccompanied alien children;

"(II) evaluate the implementation of child advocate programs in new sites pursuant to subparagraph (B);

"(III) evaluate the extent to which eligible trafficking victims and other vulnerable unaccompanied children are receiving child advocate services and assess the possible budgetary implications of increased participation in the program;

"(IV) evaluate the barriers to improving outcomes for trafficking victims and other vulnerable unaccompanied children; and

"(V) make recommendations on statutory changes to improve the Child Advocate Program in relation to the matters analyzed under subclauses (I) through (IV).

"(iii) GAO REPORT.—Not later than 3 years after the date of the enactment of this Act, the Comptroller General of the United States shall submit the results of the study required under this subparagraph to—

"(I) the Committee on the Judiciary of the Senate;

"(II) the Committee on Health, Education, Labor, and Pensions of the Senate;

"(III) the Committee on the Judiciary of the House of Representatives; and

"(IV) the Committee on Education and the Workforce of the House of Representatives.

"(F) AUTHORIZATION OF APPROPRIATIONS.—There are authorized to be appropriated to the Secretary and Human Services to carry out this subsection—

"(i) $1,000,000 for each of the fiscal years 2014 and 2015; and

"(ii) $2,000,000 for each of the fiscal years 2016 and 2017.".

SEC. 1263. ACCESS TO FEDERAL FOSTER CARE AND UNACCOMPANIED REFUGEE MINOR PROTECTIONS FOR CERTAIN U VISA RECIPIENTS.

Section 235(d)(4) of the William Wilberforce Trafficking Victims Protection Reauthorization Act of 2008 (8 U.S.C. 1232(d)(4)) is amended—

(1) in subparagraph (A),

(A) by striking "either";

(B) by striking "or who" and inserting a comma; and

(C) by inserting ", or has been granted status under section 101(a)(15)(U) of the Immigration and Nationality Act (8 U.S.C. 1101(a)(15)(U))," before ", shall be eligible"; and

(2) in subparagraph (B), by inserting ", or status under section 101(a)(15)(U) of the Immigration and Nationality Act (8 U.S.C. 1101(a)(15)(U))," after "(8 U.S.C. 1101(a)(27)(J))".

SEC. 1264. GAO STUDY OF THE EFFECTIVENESS OF BORDER SCREENINGS.

(a) STUDY.—

(1) IN GENERAL.—The Comptroller General of the United States shall conduct a study examining the effectiveness of screenings conducted by Department of Homeland Security personnel in carrying out section 235(a)(4) of the William Wilberforce Trafficking Victims Protection Reauthorization Act of 2008 (8 U.S.C. 1232(a)(4)).

(2) STUDY.—In carrying out paragraph (1), the Comptroller General shall take into account—

(A) the degree to which Department of Homeland Security personnel are adequately ensuring that—

(i) all children are being screened to determine whether they are described in section 235(a)(2)(A) of the William Wilberforce Trafficking Victims Protection Reauthorization Act;

(ii) appropriate and reliable determinations are being made about whether children are described in section 235(a)(2)(A) of such Act, including determinations of the age of such children;

(iii) children are repatriated in an appropriate manner, consistent with clauses (i) through (iii) of section 235(a)(2)(C) of such Act;

(iv) children are appropriately being permitted to withdraw their applications for admission, in accordance with section 235(a)(2)(B)(i) of such Act;

(v) children are being properly cared for while they are in the custody of the Department of Homeland Security and awaiting repatriation or transfer to the custody of the Secretary of Health and Human Services; and

(vi) children are being transferred to the custody of the Secretary of Health and Human Services in a manner that is consistent with such Act; and

(B) the number of such children that have been transferred to the custody of the Department of Health and Human Services, the Federal funds expended to maintain custody of such children, and the Federal benefits available to such children, if any.

(3) ACCESS TO DEPARTMENT OF HOMELAND SECURITY OPERATIONS.—

(A) IN GENERAL.—Except as provided in subparagraph (B), for the purposes of conducting the study described in subsection (a), the Secretary shall provide the Comptroller General with unrestricted access to all stages of screenings and other interactions between Department of Homeland Security personnel and children encountered by the Comptroller General.

(B) EXCEPTIONS.—The Secretary shall not permit unrestricted access under subparagraph (A) if the Secretary determines that the security of a particular interaction would be threatened by such access.

(b) REPORT TO CONGRESS.—Not later than 2 years after the date of the commencement of the study described in subsection (a), the Comptroller General of the United States shall submit a report to the Committee on the Judiciary of the Senate and the Committee on the Judiciary of the House of Representatives that contains the Commission's findings and recommendations.

Speaker of the House of Representatives.

Vice President of the United States and
President of the Senate.

Table of Cases

A

B

C

K

L

M

N

O

P

R

S

T

U

V

W

Index

D

E

P

R